*Real Leaders,
Real Schools*

Real Leaders, Real Schools

Stories of Success Against Enormous Odds

Gerald C. Leader

with
Amy F. Stern

Harvard Education Press
Cambridge, Massachusetts

Library of Congress Control Number 2008928880

Paperback ISBN 978-1-891792-96-0
Library Edition ISBN 978-1-891792-97-7

Published by Harvard Education Press,
an imprint of the Harvard Education Publishing Group

Harvard Education Press
8 Story Street
Cambridge, MA 02138

Cover Design: Perry Lubin

The typefaces used in this book are Adobe Garamond Pro and Optima.

Contents

Acknowledgments

This book grew from the real stories of Kathleen Flannery, Michael Fung, Muriel Leonard, Kim Marshall, and Casel Walker. These leaders courageously opened their daily lives as public school principals for inspection and critique, allowing others to read about and learn from both their victories and their mistakes. For the trust they placed in me, I am deeply appreciative.

Amy Stern, my research and writing collaborator, brought the acute observational skills and narrative traction that gave life and nuance to the book.

Without question, a visionary grant from the General Electric Foundation made researching and writing this book possible. They supported my efforts to bring the Graduate Schools of Management and Education at Boston University together for the purpose of advancing leadership in education.

I owe a debt of gratitude to a group of professional colleagues who helped lay the foundation for this book. Helen Long, my associate in administering the GE Foundation grant, was my intellectual provocateur, helping me formulate ideas that found their place in this book. Susan Markowitz helped initiate the school research and case writing for the Kathleen Flannery chapter. Janelle Heineke assisted in the book's conceptualization and in researching the Kim Marshall chapter. Sonia Caus Gleason was a mentor and collaborator, guiding me in my early understanding of standards-based school reform.

I have benefited enormously from the generous administrative support of Boston University students: Peter Baird, Kathryn Brown, David Chow, Bonnie Guan, Rebecca Jarrett, Merry Kang, Fei Rong, Olivia Sahnas, and especially Jeremy Rothstein and Rishab Jaju, who gave the final push to the manuscript.

I thank Joanna Craig for her masterful final copy editing assistance.

Any capacity—indeed, audacity—I might have to deliver real stories to a professional readership is a gift from my mentor, Jay O'Callahan, weaver of tales par excellence. I am grateful for the support and encouragement from the "Creative Monsters," who have assembled to learn the craft of storytelling twice yearly for the past thirteen years under Jay's guidance.

I honor Douglas Clayton, director of the Harvard Education Publishing Group, for his belief in the value of this book of authentic stories and his decision to publish it.

My wife and life partner, Lucy Aptekar, has relentless belief in me and my ability to produce this book, even when I questioned its feasibility. For this, I will be forever grateful.

Introduction

This book tells real stories, with actual names, of five principals in urban public schools who recognized that they had the potential to raise every student's performance to grade-level proficiency and above. These are stories of successful leadership against enormous odds. With few precedents to follow, the five leaders crafted innovative structures within their schools and empowered their faculty to collaborate to improve student learning. These principals, operating in the Boston Public Schools (BPS), instituted many new practices that today are regarded as "musts" in meeting the requirements of 2002 No Child Left Behind (NCLB) legislation. Their remarkable accomplishments provide leadership lessons beneficial to anyone interested in public school reform.

Principals Accountable for Student Performance

The stories of the five principals portrayed here have special relevance for educators. These leaders were chosen because of their success in creating schools that graduated students with high levels of achievement under some of the most trying and problematic conditions. Success in the challenging environments they inherited frequently yielded leadership lessons not found under more supportive conditions. Their tenures as principals extended over an average of ten years, ensuring that their records were not chance events. Most significantly, these principals were on the vanguard, confronting not only the requirements of the NCLB legislation but also a law with similar impacts and consequences that arrived in Massachusetts four years earlier, in 1998. The Massachusetts legislature passed a far-reaching Education Reform Act in 1993 that anticipated and exceeded many of the requirements of the NCLB legislation. It mandated the creation of a grade-level performance test for all fourth, eighth, and tenth graders, the Massachusetts Comprehensive Assessment System (MCAS). By 2003, a passing score on the state's high-stakes student performance test became a requirement to graduate from high school with a diploma recognized by the state. MCAS scores received widespread news media attention,

1

putting pressure on educators, especially principals, as comparisons were drawn between schools with similar demographic profiles.

Four of the leaders began their principalships in the 1990s and the fifth in 1987, all prior to the first administration of the MCAS. It turned out that unlike most of their colleagues statewide, however, these five principals were ready for the MCAS. In 1998, the five principals had already begun to reshape their schools to focus more on raising their students' academic performance, the outcome demanded by MCAS and the subsequent goal of the 2002 NCLB legislation. Kim Marshall, whose story is described in detail in chapter 2, wholeheartedly welcomed the test because it finally gave him a standard to work toward in aligning his teachers' instructional efforts.

The administration of the MCAS test, which Massachusetts would use as its performance measure on 2002 NCLB legislative requirements, sent a wake-up call to all principals in the state. They, not the teachers in their schools, were now ultimately accountable for the academic achievement of their school's students; there was now a measure calibrating the success of each leader's performance. Now, the school as a whole, not the sum of each teacher's instructional efforts, was thought to make the difference in student learning. The principal's job was given increased significance.

Principals had always held some accountability for student achievement, but it had been indirect and, at best, ambiguous. For high schools, the percentage of graduates accepted into higher education and the status of the university, college, or junior college was of some importance. But these results were rarely calculated and even more infrequently used to confront poor principal performance. SAT scores were often the boast of high-achieving students and the embarrassment of low performers. But these scores were seen as reflections of individual student performance, not the product of a particular school.

Prior to the MCAS and NCLB requirements, there were no agreed-upon measures of middle and grade school performance. If a school appeared to be graduating less-than-adequately prepared students, this could be conveniently attributed to poor teaching. Schools were implicitly viewed as, and most frequently were, assemblages of classrooms linked by corridors. Principals had no direct role in mediating student achievement. The MCAS and NCLB legislation, for better or worse, changed all that. A school's performance would still be a function of good or poor teaching, but now the effect of each grade level on the next and all successive grade levels could be measured. The whole could be greater or less than the sum of the parts, and that outcome could be attributed to the leadership of the principal.

Can Schools Make a Difference?

Early on in their long tenures, the five principals embraced the concept of a total school making a difference in student achievement. Conventional wisdom, however, attributed these effects to student background—with some influence from individual teachers in their separate classrooms—taking credit and responsibility away from the schools themselves.

Some thirty years earlier, in the context of the Civil Rights Act of 1964, the United States Congress commissioned James Coleman, of the University of Chicago, to research and report back to Congress and the president on "the lack of available opportunities for individuals by reason of race, color, religion, or national origin in public institutions."[1] The report's well-publicized findings asserted that schools accounted for only about 10 percent of the variance in student achievement; the characteristics of student background were purported to account for the other 90 percent. Madaus et al. explained that the Coleman Report had two primary effects on perceptions about schooling in America. First, it cast schools as an ineffective agent in equalizing the disparity in students' academic achievement due to environmental factors. Second, it suggested that differences between schools had little, if any, relationship to student achievement.[2]

The five principals presented in this book were unconvinced of Coleman's claims, and they were not alone in questioning family background as the sole determinant of student performance. While a collection of studies, loosely labeled the School Effectiveness Movement and championed by Ronald R. Edmonds, provided counterevidence to Coleman, these findings were not well publicized except in academic circles.[3]

In the 1990s, with the help of large sample size and statistical meta-analysis, Robert J. Marzano published a major synthesis of other research: *What Works in Schools: Translating Research into Action*. This work provided convincing evidence that schools, properly organized and led, could have a powerful influence on student achievement and pointed to those elements of schools that made a difference.[4] By the time this affirming statistical work was published, the five principals were already deeply engaged in their change efforts.

The Local Context

The five principals worked within the Boston Public Schools, a district that was, until the arrival of a new superintendent in 1996, largely dysfunctional. The district regularly graduated inadequately prepared students and, according to the results of the Metropolitan Achievement Test (MAT), a norm referenced test that allowed Boston to compare its student achievement to that of the national population, students performed well below average.

Despite the well-intentioned change efforts of the four superintendents over the preceding twenty years, the Boston school system was effectively paralyzed. Traumatized by a radically altered student population and economically abandoned by paltry city budgets, BPS was neither recruiting new teacher talent nor shoring up veterans. The administration at both the school and district levels lacked the leadership necessary to chart the course for a new education plan in Boston.

In 1974, court-ordered busing to address segregated schools caused "white flight" and an exodus of middle-class blacks and Hispanics from the system. This migration severed the community bonds fostered by local schools. Over the next two decades, newly arrived immigrants from Asia and Central and South America filled the void left by the fleeing population and radically shifted student demographics. When veteran teachers began their work in Boston, most students entering school spoke English as their first language, and their parents were able to provide them with assistance when they were struggling. Many students walked to school on their own or with their parents. By the mid-1990s, however, few students and families matched this description. The majority of students were black or Hispanic, and many came from families where no English was spoken in the home. Parents whose children were systematically bused out of their communities no longer had the same opportunities to be actively involved in their children's schooling.

Some innovative teachers worked hard to change their practices and ensure that they were still reaching their students. Many teachers continued to rely on methods that had served them well in the past, but those methods were inadequate to meet present challenges. Isolated in their classrooms, most Boston teachers did not know how to change their practice to effectively educate the students sitting before them. Racism and socioeconomic discrimination became a covert norm in many Boston schools. The district in the early 1990s simply could not tap into student potential.

Who's in Charge?

Even in the mid-1990s, Boston's schools were predominantly run by the teachers. Principals by and large stayed out of classrooms, and teachers chose their curriculum with little more than a nod toward district prescriptions, subjectively determining which of their students would pass. Teachers resided in one building but taught in their classrooms without communicating with each other. They were the monarchs of their classrooms, and there they reigned supreme. The five principals featured in this book did not question whether great teachers existed, but they were also confident that *schools* could make an impact on student learning for all children. They believed that schools, not just individual teachers, could be the driving entity of educational reform.

At the time, principals were seen not as instructional leaders but as managers nominally in charge. They managed outside the classrooms: safety in the lunchroom and on the playground, bus scheduling, issues of health and welfare, and discipline for bad behavior. They had very little to do with what happened *inside* the classrooms—even who was teaching. The teacher's union, in its agreement with the district, had designed a process by which time-consuming observations and elaborate documentation protected all but the most egregious performers from dismissal. Aware of the tremendous obstacles to dismissing a tenured teacher, many principals gave up on attempting to rid their schools of poor educators. When vacancies did arise through retirement, transfer, or rare dismissal, principals were severely limited in the hiring choices available to them. All hiring was done centrally, and the pool of tenured faculty who did not have a guaranteed position for the coming year had to be exhausted before a new hire could be considered. Boston Public Schools' principals had little formal organizational power to control the destiny of their schools.

Resources for Change

Budgets were thin, and Boston had not yet awakened to the fact that its schools were intellectually bankrupt. The meager funding available to schools from local businesses was piecemeal and not necessarily connected to improving instructional practice. Scattered and unfocused funding spread across 130 schools did not make a sustainable impact anywhere.

Successful principals depended on their own entrepreneurial skills to generate extra resources for their schools. Foundations and local businesses that embraced a social mission could be convinced to offer funds to principals who were adept at casting their schools as the ugly duckling: "With just a little help from a generous benefactor, we could grow into a swan that you could feel proud of having nurtured."

October 1996 proved to be a crucial turning point in public education in Boston. Dr. Thomas Payzant, an experienced urban reformer and a recent senior official in President Clinton's Department of Education, became superintendent of the Boston Public Schools.[5] He quickly realized that in order to radically improve student achievement, major foundation support was needed to supplement the city's education budget. Consolidating previously pledged funding with a grant from the Annenberg Foundation, Payzant created a professional development plan for the school system. The Boston Plan for Excellence (BPE) was explicitly commissioned to assist schools that were ready to participate in whole-school change. To be included, a school's faculty had to agree by a 75 percent affirmative vote that they were ready to accept and implement the mandated change structures. Three of the principals discussed here encouraged their faculties to apply and were accepted to BPE's whole-school change network. The partnership provided teachers with much-needed subject-area expertise to ratchet up instruction in their schools and guide them through standards-based reform efforts. A fourth principal sought extra funding on his own from the private business sector.

Exemplars for School Transformation

The five principals we selected for inclusion in this study demonstrated leadership toward improving student achievement in their schools and exhibited a diversity of leadership styles in changing their schools. In making the selections, preference was given to principals who evidenced success in providing a viable platform for instructional improvement in the first two or three years of their principalships and who built on that success in subsequent years to order to achieve higher student performance.

The narratives, written as self-contained lessons in school reform, trace the leadership trajectories of the five principals. The cases are based on interviews we conducted with both the principals and staff members who worked under their leadership. The Glossary of Terms explains specific terminology used in these case studies. All principals reviewed their narrative chapters and allowed their names and the names of their schools to be used to highlight the accuracy of the account as well as to leave a personal legacy for future school leaders. Names of teachers and administrators in the five schools have been changed except that of Karen Loughran, a teacher and informal teacher leader at Charlestown High School (chapter 4).

Each of these five leaders developed and honed strategies and philosophies that would set a high bar for other principals in meeting the performance standards of NCLB legislation. All chose to draw on their gifts and talents to push through the various challenges the schools presented. In chapter 1, Casel Walker's moral authority, quiet determination, acute listening abilities, and capacity to speak the truth galvanize a sleepy, urban/suburban school into a self-sustaining, high-performing system. In chapter 2, Kim Marshall, educational innovator, designs and doggedly implements one of the first complete instructional systems to continuously improve student performance. In chapter 3, Muriel Leonard's powerful "tough love" challenges teachers and students, demanding them to give and be their best. Inheriting a chaotic situation, she builds a highly functioning school in under five years. In chapter 4, Michael Fung, a political strategist and power broker, succeeds in markedly improving the performance of his ninth and tenth graders by sidestepping union rules and hiring a new cadre of young, inexperienced teachers, placing them in an autonomous instructional unit where they flourish as an instructional team. In chapter 5, Kathleen Flannery brokers her extraordinary talent for listening and embracing the ideas of others to build a school community where teachers and parents genuinely feel accountable for student learning. Chapter 6 synthesizes the "Leadership Lessons" from the five narratives and places them in the context of relevant research and best practices.

Chapter 1

Casel Walker
and Joseph P. Manning
Elementary School
1994–2006

It was June 21, 1999, and Casel Walker sat in the auditorium of Boston's Joseph P. Manning Elementary. The school was holding its annual fifth grade graduation ceremony. Sitting on the sidelines, Casel, the Manning's principal, was overcome with pride. She was proud of the fifth graders, as she was of all her students and their accomplishments. But today her feelings extended beyond the students to the entire Manning community. There were people in the auditorium who had reached defining moments in their professional careers, realizing tremendous accomplishments over the past year. Given time to reflect, she might have understood that she was one of them.

Casel was not a participant in the graduation proceedings that year, merely a member of the audience. Until graduation day, in fact, she had not even set foot in the building since the middle of March. Ordinarily an interim principal would have been placed at a school to cover a principal's extended absence, but that had not happened at the Manning that spring. In a virtually unprecedented move, the teachers of the Manning had come together and self-managed the building on their own for three and a half months.

The Handoff

In February 1999, the back pain that Casel had been experiencing for a year and a half was getting worse. She had initially assumed it was due to her weight, but lately the pain had intensified, and she and her husband were growing concerned. One night during February vacation, on their way to the movies, Casel's husband insisted that they stop at Beth Israel

Hospital to be examined by a friend of a friend. Casel did not expect to get any answers, but she did.

Told that she had a tumor in her spinal cord, she left the hospital that evening in a full body cast—what she later learned to call her "Wonder Woman suit." The cast was needed because the tumor was eating away at the bones in her spine. The doctors told her that her back could collapse at any moment. Thankfully, the tumor was benign, but Casel was told she needed eleven hours of surgery to remove it and to insert a metal plate into her back. She would be temporarily paralyzed after the surgery.

Casel spoke to the staff after the February vacation, before her scheduled surgery. She worked part-time during that interval, trying to get things in order before her leave. She planned to ask a graduate student from Harvard, who had been working as an intern at the Manning, to take over for the remainder of the school year. But before plans could be put into place, two of her teachers approached her with the idea of the staff taking on the leadership of the school, with Yvonne, the third grade teacher, as the teacher-in-charge. Collectively, they felt that not only was Yvonne capable of taking on the extra responsibilities, but they were capable of letting her. Casel, in tremendous pain, worried about her health and her life, readily agreed.

Casel's last day of school before surgery was March 17, 1999. It was a school holiday, but the teachers had come in of their own volition to begin work on a grant the Manning was seeking. The Annenberg Foundation grant application was extensive, but it seemed worth the effort: Annenberg Schools would receive $150,000 over three years. Casel had not given much thought to whether the teachers would move forward on Annenberg without her, but here they were on their day off, downstairs in the Manning, huddled in little teams over the application. Casel remembers standing in the doorway, "watching and crying my eyes out because I wasn't a part of it and because I couldn't be a part of it. That's when I knew they would be okay."

The Annenberg application was due in the spring, and the Manning teachers rose to the challenge. This was something they had decided to go for, and they gave it all they had. They respectfully emailed various components of the application to Casel for her to review on her home computer. But she was on powerful medication during her recovery and couldn't even read.

In her absence, the teachers were awarded the Annenberg grant, making the Manning an Annenberg School. Casel couldn't help but feel that it made it that much sweeter for the teachers that she had nothing to do with the writing of it (someone had even signed her name). The grant was truly theirs.

Also that year, the Manning had to prepare for the district-mandated In-Depth Review (IDR). The district conducted the review to determine how effectively schools were addressing each of the "Six Essentials": 1) schoolwide instructional focus; 2) student work and data; 3) professional development; 4) use of best teaching practices; 5) alignment of resources with instructional focus; and 6) involvement of parents and community. The review was to be the first in what was intended as an accountability process that would be repeated every four years. Therefore, it was imperative that the initial process provide a blueprint for future improvements. The experience gave schools (with the district looking closely over their shoulders) an opportunity to evaluate their work, identifying areas in which they excelled and determining areas that needed further attention. Each school was asked to clearly articulate its direction for the future. The process of preparing for the review itself, which consisted of multiple, comprehensive visits to the school, was a major concern for most BPS schools. The review involved a tremendous effort to gather evidence and compile reports. It asked a lot of principals, and most found it to be a challenging experience. The Manning staff prepared for the IDR without Casel.

Back at School

By the June 1999 graduation, Casel had just learned to walk again. "God is good," she told herself as she sat on the sidelines. She was relieved to see that the Manning had gone forward without her. The work they had all started together had not only continued but progressed. Of course, there was a part of her that felt sad, wondering how it could be that she seemed not to be needed at her own school. But the overwhelming emotion was relief. What a relief it was to see that it had worked! They had been *able* to go on without her. In five years, she had managed to foster a self-sustaining community of teachers who, in her absence, had taken on her values and priorities as their own.

By September, Casel returned—for good—to find that the Manning was a somewhat different school than she had left the previous spring. What the staff, under Yvonne's leadership, had accomplished in Casel's absence was monumental—especially considering that they had just three and a half months to do it. Privately, Casel took a quick moment for self-congratulation. It was just a short pause; she wasn't given to heaping praise on herself. But the teachers' accomplishments in her absence marked a milestone in her own development as a leader. She had worked hard at the Manning to revise a style of leadership that had not served her well in her previous assignment.

Lessons from the Blackstone

Casel Walker had spent her entire professional career inside the Boston Public Schools. Before coming to the Manning, her most recent position had been at the Blackstone Elementary School. The Blackstone had 1,000 students and three assistant principals (AP), of which Casel was one. She was responsible for approximately 300 students in a section of the building called Project Beacon. As an AP, Casel could be as creative as she wanted. She worked under people who trusted her, and because of that she had a lot of leeway. She ran her own program and worked with a group of very creative people, many of whom eventually followed her to the Manning.

After several years at the Blackstone, Casel took an all-too-brief maternity leave to have her second son. Soon after her return, she noticed something of a resentful air among the teachers, and it dawned on her that her staff felt hurt and angry that she had left them to have a baby. In retrospect, it was this realization that triggered a shift in her philosophy regarding her role as a leader. She began to understand that her style of leadership had cultivated an unhealthy dynamic between her and her staff. They had become dependent on her, and it was interfering with their ability to grow as professionals.

At the Blackstone, Casel had come to realize that things were successful because of *her*. There was very little ownership of responsibilities by the staff. With her warm, easygoing personality, her propensity to laugh, and her open and honest demeanor, Casel had had no trouble fostering a strong sense of community at the Blackstone. She did not understand then what it meant to empower people. At that time, she thought it was her job to listen to the good ideas that the staff suggested and transform those ideas into reality. Because she felt personally responsible for making things happen, she worked extremely hard and made sure that things *did* happen. But when she left the Blackstone, it all fell apart. From her new position at the Manning, she watched all of her work crumble within a year of her departure. Witnessing the demise of the incredible program built under her leadership was extremely painful.

She understood that she made a big mistake in not encouraging ownership among her staff. It had not been intentional—she didn't realize she wasn't sharing responsibility with the staff, and they didn't realize they weren't taking any. But because Casel perceived her role as one in which she was supposed to "make things happen" and tell people not to worry about it, they didn't. She was in control; she made all the decisions. Everybody liked and respected her so they went along with her ideas—but there was no buy-in. She had not taken the time to make sure they understood the reasons behind some of the decisions she made.

So when she got to the Manning, she went out of her way to ensure that she did not let herself get too personally involved with the staff. "Becoming an administrator is very lonely, if you're doing it well," she told reflects. "You can't be friends and then tell someone, 'You're teaching horribly,' or even 'You're doing a great job, but it can be better.' You can't evaluate your friends." She was careful not to build another relationship of dependence where much of the work accomplished was carried out only because of the personal relationships she had fostered. She wanted the culture she built at the Manning to be one where the desire for progress was intrinsic.

Her new perspective did not preclude her from forming good, solid relationships with her staff, but now she better understood her role as supervisor. She appreciated how important it was to make people feel empowered. Casel began to build a different kind of relationship with her staff. She made it a point to find their strengths and work with them to cultivate and realize the potential of those strengths. She was especially interested in discovering what talents people had for leadership and team building.

Casel participated in a cooperative discipline course that stressed how crucial it was for students to feel capable, that they were contributing something, and that they were connected to what they were doing. She realized that adults need this reinforcement, too. Everyone wants to feel that what they are doing makes a difference. She began having one-on-one conversations with her staff, telling each one, in distinctive ways, "You don't know how important you are."

No Place to Hide

Casel grew up in a lower-middle-class, black community in New York City. She had the same teacher in first, second, and third grades. Mrs. Brown never hesitated to show up at the Walker home at dinnertime if Casel had not brought her homework to school that day. Casel remembers the doorbell ringing and then thinking, "Oh, God—it's Mrs. Brown! I *know* it's her, 'cause I didn't do . . . ." Mrs. Brown would come in, and Mrs. Walker would offer her a chair and sit and listen to what she had come to say.

It had made such a difference that Mrs. Brown had known her students so well. She knew Casel's birthday; she knew her brother. Casel wanted to do well because she knew it would please her teacher. It was important. As a principal, Casel found that intimacy appealing. She, too, wanted to know her kids well, to know their families, to know each and every student by name. Relationships had always been important to her, and she knew firsthand how important good relationships could be to academic success, especially for urban students. One of her favorite "tricks" was to say something to a student, pertaining to him, that he didn't know she knew, anticipating the look of surprise that crossed the student's face, as if to say, "How did you *know* about that?"

Sharing Leadership

In September 1999, the first month after her return, Casel came to meetings and, quite literally, sat on her hands in an attempt to promote and facilitate a self-sustaining leadership community at the Manning. Her absence had proven to her that she was not as important as she thought she was. It was then that Casel began to think of herself as just a member of the team. Sometimes she was the most important member, but sometimes she was the least important. Sometimes her comments were valued; sometimes nobody would listen to what she had to say. Though she had known it in theory since her first year at the Manning, Casel knew that it probably would have taken her much longer to reach this level of leadership had her absence not accelerated the process. She knew now that they all had to get there together, and she saw herself as a guide, recognizing that sometimes the team needed to "get to the top" first. She realized that she needed to let others make some decisions, make mistakes, and learn from them. She had learned the hard way that it was the only way that teachers would truly be able to grow.

Still, it wasn't easy for Casel to hold back and begin to transfer leadership to the other members of her action teams. She thought back to when the teams were first being implemented in the district and how hard it had been for many principals to give up the autonomy they had previously enjoyed. She, too, had loved sitting in her office deciding what was going to happen. Her immediate impulse was to identify a problem and solve it herself.

Nevertheless, Casel was glad that new principals in the system now had structures in place that nurtured the capacity for teacher ownership. The new teams put in place by the district helped facilitate the ideas of shared leadership that Casel knew were so important. Action teams with various acronyms like ILT (Instructional Leadership Team) and MLT (Math Leadership Team) encouraged teachers to really be a part of the process. These mini-organizations determined where each school was heading in terms of instruction and practice when, historically, teacher control was limited to the classroom.

Casel remembered herself as a teacher. Directives would come down "from above," and teachers would be instructed to throw out their current curriculum and start anew with whatever the "latest and greatest" happened to be. She had "yessed" her principal to death in meetings and then gone back to her classroom, closed the door, and made her own decisions about how she could best teach her kids. She had even trained her kids to switch books when the principal came in the room! But teaching had changed; there was no longer any such thing as going into the classroom and "closing the door" because teaching now was much more collaborative. Yet the attitude still existed among teachers to varying degrees. Casel didn't want that at the Manning. She wanted her teachers to communicate openly with her. She wanted to give her staff an opportunity to prove that their way was better or give them a chance to hear about a new way that might be more effective.

In the past, Casel often felt that if she already had a solution, it was wasteful to sit around waiting for everyone else to slowly arrive at the same conclusion. She liked to jump in, make suggestions, make changes, and make sure her school was getting it right. Casel now saw her role as that of a facilitator who kept great ideas at the forefront of people's minds, helping them implement their initiatives rather than taking them on as her own. "I had the great fortune of working with someone who taught me that you never say 'no' to an idea. When someone brings an idea to you, you smile and say, 'That's a great idea, now how are we going to make this idea work?' I began to try a little bit of that. I tried to really listen to what people wanted to do."

It was not easy putting the new philosophy to work. Not long after Casel had begun implementing her new approach, the fifth grade teacher came to her proposing that the Manning take its fifth graders on a trip to Washington, D.C., for five days. To do this, they would need to raise $300 per student. Casel felt like pulling her hair out. How could they do it? It was impossible! No school in the Boston system would attempt such a thing. Casel went home to her husband and ranted and raved about the lunacy of the idea. To her teacher, however, she said, "Okay, how can we get this to work?" The Manning fifth graders have made the trip every single year since.

Casel's encouragement had built a staff of teachers who were not only knowledgeable in the classroom but also confident about their ability to make broader decisions on a schoolwide scale. She realized that "these were teachers who really wanted to work. They really wanted to be proud of what they were doing. Once I began to pick up on this, my role became finding the resources and the supports for them to allow them to take risks themselves. It was my job to find out what their options were."

Boston's Suburban Urban School

Most of what Casel knew about the Manning prior to accepting the principalship was based on the experiences of the principal she succeeded, a woman she had attended college with and with whom she had recently reconnected. Casel remembered the woman speaking about how intimate things were in her small school, so different from the school Casel was working in at the time. The Blackstone had 1,000 students, the Manning only 175. At the Manning, it was easy enough to know every student by name and to have relationships with many of their families as well. This appealed to Casel for many reasons, not the least of which the memories it rekindled of her own elementary school experience.

Aside from the intimacy a small school can generate, there were other qualities to recommend the Manning. One of them was its location. The Manning was only technically an urban school. Located in the middle of Boston, the Manning was nestled in the picturesque Moss Hill area of Jamaica Plain. The school had the usual playground and basketball courts, but it also had Slocum Brook trickling through its yard, wooded areas on both sides (housing a flock of wild turkeys, among other wildlife), and upscale homes peeking through the trees. So though it was a full-fledged Boston Public School, the Manning had become known as the little "private" school in the woods.

The Manning's reputation had allowed it to withstand the "white flight" so many urban schools experienced. In 1994, when Casel first came to the Manning, about 40 percent of the students were white, a stark contrast to the rest of the Boston Public School system where the white population had dipped to below 25 percent. Indeed, in many Boston schools, minorities made up as much as 85 percent of the student body.

The school might have been 40 percent white, but the vast majority of those white students were enrolled in the primary grades. The K–2 classes were about 75 percent white. In the twenty-five-student kindergarten class, twenty-two were white, and the one black student was the district attorney's child. The only Asian student had a parent on the school committee, and the only Hispanic student was the child of the director of the North Zone Parent Information Center. It was clear that a lot of political maneuvering took place to get children into the Manning School. But when Casel talked to the staff, she discovered that few of these kids were likely to remain there. They would stay for two years, K1 and K2, and then be shipped off by their parents to private or parochial schools.

It seemed that parents of white children, drawn by the small, quiet school, the experienced teaching staff, and the solid reputation, were willing to try the Boston Public Schools—at least this one. They would enroll their children and take advantage of the primary grades. But by third grade, a significant number of these children were either enrolled in independent or parochial schools in Boston or had moved to the suburbs. This meant that a group of kids streaming in did not have the benefit of attending the Manning's early grades, and it was hard to build and sustain progress with students since so few continued for more than a couple of years. By the upper grades, the racial imbalance at the Manning reversed, and the students were almost all minorities.

This pattern of shifting enrollment had a tremendous impact on the school. When the kids from the primary grades left, new students were assigned to the Manning in order to keep the numbers up. And in order to maintain the overall racial balance at the school, most of the students transferred in by the district were minorities. Because BPS cannot simply involuntarily reassign students from one school to another, many of the incoming students were either new to the school system or were subject to a transfer because of problems they were having at their previous school.

Casel knew she needed to take a good, hard look at some of the issues the Manning was struggling with. Though she had a great deal of respect for the outgoing principal, she knew that because she'd been there for a while, she had become blind to the flaws. Casel thought of herself as a new pair of eyes for the school: Because she was seeing it all for the first time, it was easy to understand how it really functioned.

As Casel got to know her new school, she realized that it was not a child-centered place. Everything seemed organized around the adults. Classrooms, scheduling, discipline, and administration all seemed to be responsive to the adults' needs. Casel had set up time to meet with teachers individually about their goals and priorities, but all she heard at these meetings was "me," "my," and "I." Teachers talked about their schedules, how they had to have lunch at a certain time, and so on. They explained why they couldn't greet their students outside in the morning (they had to be in their classrooms preparing for the day). Casel recognized that a school catering to the comfort of adults provided little positive pressure to grow and meet the demands of a continually changing student population.

She also could see that the Manning was too comfortable. Parents were either largely content (in the primary grades) or uninvolved (in the elementary), and those who were involved tended to leave the public schools. The latter group was shrugged off as "the type of people who didn't like to use the public schools anyway." Test scores were fine, with the exception of the troubling tendency to decline in the upper grades. Even then, scores were certainly not low enough to draw attention from the stressed school system. Standardized test scores put the school solidly above the district average, and the Manning had a good track record of sending students on to the city's accelerated programs and exam schools. So there was not much external pressure for change. Casel knew that change would have to come from within. It would have to come from her.

A principal's "honeymoon period" provides a special opportunity for making major, unilateral change. But Casel knew that these kinds of changes were risky: They could successfully pave the way for whole-school transformation, or they could be disastrous and create enemies in the building, even sometimes driving a principal out of a school after just one year. She decided to start slow.

Tackling the Hard Stuff

As her career had progressed, Casel learned about herself as a professional. So by the time she arrived at the Manning for her first principalship, she already had a good idea of what came easily to her and what she had to work harder at. She knew, for example, that she was more of an *instructional* leader than an *operational* person. She was great at creating programs and implementing them, coming up with assemblies for the kids, and generating ideas to embrace learning. But she just did not care as much about things like scheduling, busing, or candy sales. She knew she would have to learn to tackle those "hard" things at the Manning, though. "If you can only do half the job, it all falls apart," she told herself.

For Casel, the most important things were teaching and learning as they related to the culture and climate of her school. But she began to realize that without first addressing the *structures* of the school, she could not move on to *learning*. She was beginning to see how things were connected. Everything was integrated—a clean building, supplies, budget, professional development. If these elements weren't in place, the things that really mattered would never happen.

Casel hated writing staff evaluations. She had to force herself to see the connection between writing the evaluation and the quality of work she was seeing in the classroom, the quality of the relationships that she was building with people, the support she was giving them, and how she was rewarding them. She needed to find a connection between what she liked—improving the quality of her teaching staff and the relationships she had with them—and what she didn't like, the writing of the evaluations themselves.

In her early days at the Manning, Casel had an important realization: How the school day began was often quite indicative of how it continued. A positive opening of the day could prevent chaos. So Casel had immediately insisted that teachers begin their day outside, where they would start their classroom day with students reciting the school pledge: "I am somebody special and smart, with kindness and love in my heart. I pledge to work hard every day, so I may proudly say, 'I am the best at what I do—I can even teach you!'"

There were other things she felt needed to be changed immediately as well, but they seemed harder to approach. "I didn't have a school that someone had to go and fix," she said. "I had just the opposite; I had a school where everyone was relatively comfortable. But they could no longer see the spots on the wall because they had lived with them for so long. I was a new pair of eyes. I could see things that people had lived with and meant to change. I could see how the wonderful 'country club' school was probably the dirtiest building that I had ever seen. I started pointing out the concrete things at first."

She began by taking snapshots of what was going on in the classroom—sometimes literally taking pictures of the room—to help her see how things worked. One day, for example, Casel walked into the kindergarten room, pointed to the color chart, and said, "Do you realize that 'red' is gray and 'blue' is gray?" The teacher looked up. "Oh! I didn't even notice that!" And she also gently challenged teachers by asking such uncomfortable questions as "Why are virtually *all* the kids in the fifth grade advanced reading group girls?" or "Why are *all* the third grade remedial readers black boys?"

The latter question particularly interested Casel. She noticed that when the honor roll came out, few black students were on it, even in the upper grades, where they were the overwhelming majority. Most of the students on the honor role across all the grades were white. Casel knew this was not a simple issue; race and class were often difficult to tease apart. The children who did well in school were generally middle class, and the middle-class students at the Manning were generally white. Still, she winced each time she passed by the bulletin board outside of her office, where the names and photos of the honor roll students were posted. For her, it was a graphic reminder of the school's failure to unlock the potential of all of its kids.

This inequity had been introduced to her on her arrival at the Manning, when she was informed by the Title 1 teacher (a federally funded position that was intended to provide support to low-achieving children in high-poverty schools) that she did not work with low-performing students. Instead, she had arranged with the previous principal to work *only* with gifted and talented Manning students. One day, this teacher invited Casel to a celebration of her students' writing. All fifteen of her students were white, with the exception of a couple "light-skinned" children of color. Casel felt she had to point this out. While she was not trying to accuse the teacher of anything, she felt it was something that needed to be acknowledged.

Casel did not want to launch into a discussion about attitudes or values with any member of her staff. Thankfully, she did not consider the things she was seeing at the Manning to be instances of racial animosity. She put a lot of effort into dealing with what she saw without bringing race to the forefront. She felt it was important for this particular population of teachers—who really considered themselves liberals—that race not be the issue. She could see that her teachers were caring and affectionate toward all of their students.

Instead, she wanted to talk about methods that could help reach those kids who were not performing. In a small school like the Manning, it was possible for her to have one-on-one conversations with her staff about these difficult issues. She felt that when having hard conversations with people, it was important to try to keep the emotions out of it and stick to the facts. She might not be able to change a teacher's mind-set, but she could set clear expectations. Casel developed a way of thinking about her concerns and used this language to talk with her teachers. There were "negotiables," which could be addressed via a discussion and a compromise, and "non-negotiables," which were exactly as they sounded; Casel would stand firm on these issues.

Same Teachers, Different Students

Many of the teachers at the Manning had been there a long time. Some had been teaching in the Boston Public Schools for as long as thirty years, having started when many more of Boston's Public Schools' students were white and middle class. Because they already had a long history of teaching behind them, many members of the staff employed traditional teaching methods and practices that they felt were successful, time-tested, and good for all kids. These teachers were not even aware that their unspoken ideas about what a "model" student should look like did not correspond with current realities. Some of them just did not understand the impact their ideas had on students who didn't fit the mold.

Casel had an encounter with one of her primary teachers, a hard-working, dedicated teacher of long service, which exemplified the problem in all its messy complexity. She had gone into this teacher's classroom to talk about the students' work, but the teacher spoke to her instead about other troubles she was having in her classroom. She complained that some students would not use folders to keep their work organized, and some did not have backpacks, which made it difficult for her to send notices home. The teacher could not understand why her students' families did not seem interested in helping their children to do well in school by making sure that they had the tools they needed to stay organized.

Casel knew that not every child had a family that valued personal organization, but she also knew that every student needed to be successful in school. She felt it was vital to level the playing field so that class differences would be less apparent. If the teacher felt that her students needed backpacks or notebooks or folders to keep organized, Casel resolved that the school would provide them. It would help the students succeed and make it harder for teachers to use these small differences to make excuses.

The New Currency of Exchange: Data

Casel also began to emphasize the importance of looking at data and using it to target improvements. She used data to start building her case for schoolwide improvement. Data showed that scores dropped in the upper grades, creating a self-reinforcing negative cycle. Low scores discouraged parents from having their children continue into the upper grades, yet having these children withdraw generally made low scores all the more likely. Casel shared with her teachers the data that showed increasing numbers of children, particularly middle-class children, leaving in the third and fourth grades. Because there was agreement among the staff that it was desirable to keep middle-class families and maintain some racial and social balance in the school, teachers began to truly understand the need to improve scores, even in those pre–education reform days.

Casel also made it clear to teachers that improvement was a school-wide issue. Raising fifth grade scores was an issue for more than just the fifth grade teacher; the only way to sustain higher scores was to improve instruction across all grade levels. She wanted to push teachers to go farther. "I learned quickly that I can't change everybody's beliefs. So there are times when I don't care what you believe, this is what's going to happen. We're embedded in who we are, and what we believe and what we don't believe and I had to learn that quickly with some people. I can't change your upbringing, whatever it was that brought you to this point. But if you are going to be here, here are the things that you are going to have to do. You're going to have to give me evidence."

An example of this determination came one afternoon when a teacher approached Casel to talk about a student in her class, saying, "You know, he's just not going to get it." Casel replied, "Why? How do you know?" "Well," the teacher explained, "I just know. I've been doing this for twenty years, and my gut feeling tells me that he just can't do this." Casel was firm. "Your gut feeling is worth absolutely nothing in this office. Bring me the evidence that this child cannot do this." Although Casel could not change this teacher's beliefs about this particular little boy, or these "types" of little boys, she did prove to her that if she could bring her the evidence, they could examine it and make plans to implement changes. The teacher came back to Casel and said, "You know, he can do it. I tried this, and actually he can." Casel was thrilled. She had been able to change the teacher's beliefs about the child—not by trying to convince her but by having her gather the evidence herself. Casel was making strides toward the child-centered school she intended to build and foster.

Casel presented data to teachers in many different ways. As part of the literacy program, they worked together to "rank" children, trying to find out which children were below average and then developing safety nets for those students. They started early in October, because a safety net program cannot wait to be developed in January; by then, it's too late. Casel pushed for evidence from each teacher about why they had ranked their children the way they did. At first, she heard a lot of "I just know" responses. But really pushing for evidence made all of them to start looking in-depth at the student data over the years and also forced them to come up with their own assessments. Casel convinced them that this was the right path using a teacher evaluation as an example: "The teacher sits down, and I say, 'You know what, you're an unsatisfactory teacher. I know that because of my gut feeling.'" She paused and watched them think this over. "Are you going to buy that?" Soon the Manning staff was giving scores on a regular basis and engaging in what Casel thought of as "healthy assessing."

They Are All Our Students and Families

There were other cultural aspects that needed changing as well. How to refer students to various classes raised important questions. The Manning had one regular education classroom at every grade level, K1–5, plus three substantially separate special education (SPED) classes: an LD class (Learning Disabilities Program—a class for students with a diagnosed learning disability but average cognitive ability who perform significantly below grade level academically), an SAR class (Supportive Academic Remediation—a class for students with moderate cognitive delays who require educational support in all academic areas), and a LAB class (Learning Adaptive Behavior—a class for students with moderate behavioral problems who require a program with an integral behavior management component). These classes were considerably smaller than the regular education classes.

Casel had spent her early teaching career in Boston's Special Education Department, starting out as a speech therapist, a position she held for six years, before moving into her own substantially separate classroom for students with language disabilities, where she worked for another six years. With twelve years of special education experience behind her, Casel had an important place in her heart for these students. She did not like the way they were categorized and labeled at the Manning. "We had to come up with labels for our children that were acceptable to me. I was not going to allow signs on the classroom doors that indicated, SPED, or LAB class, or Regular Ed. We had to come up with new ways to define the classrooms. That was the first real push and pull." When the teachers asked, "How are we going to know that it's this class and not that class?" Casel told them that the solution was simple: they would start calling everybody by room numbers. "That was a simple solution to a problem that, I think, had underlying assumptions behind it."

Another "separatist" practice taking place at the Manning in the mid-1990s had to do with kindergarten. These classes had an utterly separate life at the Manning. Because families came for K1 and K2, not expecting to attend grade one, they felt that the less they had to do with the rest of the school, the better. Kindergarten students did not have lunch with the rest of the Manning. They used their own bathrooms and had their own separate entrance. It was like a different school.

Kindergarten, Casel determined, could not occupy an isolated space. That was a non-negotiable. The classes would have to use the same door as everyone else to enter the school in the morning, and they would have to come to the auditorium for lunch with everybody else. Casel knew that she risked losing some families with these changes, and she did, but she didn't waver. All the students would have the same "Manning experience."

Casel worked hard to dispel the image of the Manning as a preparation academy for well-off neighborhood families who would eventually send their kids to private and parochial schools. She wanted her school to be a desirable place for all students to attend. A woman of deep conviction, she had entered teaching and school leadership with the firm belief that each school needed to offer the same opportunity for success to every child.

The message that Casel wanted to send to the whole school community was that the school belonged to the children. It existed to meet *their* needs and focus on *their* learning, not to cater to the needs of the parents, teachers, or the school department. She tried to reinforce this message in a variety of ways.

This was Casel's first year, and she knew that she would not have an opportunity to repeat it. She had to let people know who she was and what she stood for. For years a small group of parents and many Manning teachers had carried out their own, separate agendas for the school. Casel knew it was time for her to take charge and let them know *her* agenda.

She made it clear to her staff that she was not going to go along with attempts to move a child out of a classroom or the school. A longstanding practice was to "core out" troublesome children. (The battery of tests administered to determine learning or emotional disabilities is referred to as a "core evaluation."). These students would leave regular education classrooms at the Manning and be placed in Manning LD or LAB classrooms, or be transferred to another school. Her message to the staff was that it would take a really strong argument to convince her that a particular student did not belong in regular education: "Success for all kids means just that—all kids. Not just the ones you chose to keep around. Any child who walks through our doors is one of our children, and this is their school." She brought together her early elementary staff and told them that she would not even consider a core evaluation referral for a child in K2. Children at that age varied immensely in maturation, and five-year-olds were simply too young to judge and too young to be labeled.

Although Casel's policy changes may have caused an upset in the traditional workings of the Manning, her remarks were difficult to challenge. Staff had no choice but to be left thinking, "She cares about the kids and she cares about teaching and learning." Casel stressed that these changes were not intended to isolate the teaching staff or to withhold needed services from children. She told them, "I will work with you in every way that I can. Together, we'll try hard to figure out what is going on with a particular child and what will make this a successful match for both you and the child." Their efforts would determine the success or failure of a child at their school, but the message was clear: We will find a way to work with every child who attends this school.

Casel wanted all parents to feel that they were welcome in the Manning community on equal terms. She wanted to engage a wider variety of parents but knew that meeting schedules were standing in the way of this goal. School Site Council meetings, for example, were held monthly at noon at the home of a neighborhood parent, who served tea and cookies. All those who could attend found it homey and relaxing, community-oriented and welcoming, but the midday meeting time prevented many parents from attending. Casel couldn't let it go on. She told the attendees, "Wow, this time must really make it difficult for working parents to get here! I guess they'd have to choose between going to work and coming to the meeting." The Manning School Site Council changed its meeting schedule in order to accommodate more working parents.

Getting Her Priorities Straight

Another issue that bothered her was the library. All of the teachers talked about how important literacy was, but the Manning library was the smallest room in the building. Even the bathrooms were bigger! Casel wanted to move the library to a larger, more appropriate location, but the only room big enough was the computer room. This was one possibility, but she wasn't sure whether it would really be a good move. If the computer room became the library, where would computer classes take place? Casel talked her thoughts over with a good friend and the two of them agreed that computers were tools, just like chalk, books, or pencils, and that they belonged in the classroom with the other tools, not isolated in a computer lab. That conversation helped Casel make what the staff considered an absurd decision.

Casel told her teachers, "If literacy is really important to us, we need to validate that importance. The only other room we have is the computer room, so we're moving out all of the computers and the computers are going into the classrooms." Everyone looked at her like she had lost her mind. She was getting rid of the computer classes? "We don't need to have one person who's an expert," Casel went on, referring to the full-time computer teacher. "We all need to be experts."

In that first year without the computer lab, the computers sat in the classrooms gathering dust. Some teachers were afraid of technology, or resistant to being asked to learn something new. But Casel provided as much training and support as she could for all of her staff, especially the resistant ones. And several years later, the people who were initially most resistant were writing articles about how to integrate computers into the classroom. Casel was beginning to prove to herself and her staff the benefits of empowering teachers.

The Calculated Risk

By late spring of her first year, Casel was pleased with all the changes she had been able to effect in her short time at the Manning, but she felt that progress was too slow. The incremental changes she was making might eventually add up to a shift in culture and thinking at the Manning, but then again they might not. Some members of her staff were simply too set in their ways to allow for much change in their practices. Casel had several regular education teachers who seemed too stubborn, too comfortable, or too unwilling to work toward making the changes that were needed.

The special education teachers were the worst. Casel felt the existing SPED program was a disaster and should be scrapped altogether. What she had seen in those classrooms since her arrival was very discouraging. The philosophy of the teachers seemed to be that students in these classrooms were only capable of learning life skills, so their days were filled with sewing and coloring rather than reading and math. The SAR teacher prided herself on the fact that her kids could do such lovely craft projects. The LD teacher congratulated herself on the fact that she had no behavior problems and that her kids were never sent to the office. The LAB teacher was assigned only four students because she was considered the worst LAB teacher in the BPS system, and the district was unwilling to subject more children to her supervision and teaching.

Casel longed to implement a change so dramatic within the school that teachers would be compelled to step up and challenge themselves, to look at their students through new eyes, and to rededicate themselves to their profession. If they weren't able to do so, she expected them to choose to move to another school and make room for her to bring in new, energized staff. She racked her brain to think of creative solutions. She knew that, in terms of traditional methods, her hands were tied. District rules and the Boston Teachers Union (BTU) contract stipulated that there were few ways to move staff out of the building.

But, taking a gamble, she decided to speak to Caroline in the district's SPED department, telling her that she felt she had to do something about the program in her school. She was considering eliminating the SPED classes and replacing them with an early childhood inclusion class. Early childhood seemed like a safe option. The ineffectual SPED teachers could be removed from the building, and perhaps without the close proximity of the SPED classes at the Manning, regular education teachers would be more inclined to take responsibility for all of their students. The plan was sound, but, unfortunately, the district did not need another early childhood program. What the district did need was a LAB cluster. Would she be willing to take that?

A Learning Adaptive Behavior cluster differs from a SPED classroom in that students' emotional and behavioral disabilities are more severe. The cluster offers students a multidisciplinary team with a strong behavioral management component. Clusters are generally comprised of several LAB classrooms catering to different grades or age levels. With a shortage of LAB clusters within the system, the district was obligated to educate children who required them *outside* the system, in residential placements that catered to their needs. This was a substantial financial cost to the school system. If BPS could boost its capacity to assign students to LAB clusters *within* the system, it was certainly in their best interest to do so.

Casel needed to make her decision quickly. She was enthusiastic to include the cluster—she had practically leapt at the chance! But first she wanted to get some feedback from her "network," a group including Casel and five other principals who had come together informally to bounce ideas off of one another. The people in Casel's "network" were individuals she respected, whom she felt shared similar beliefs about what their schools should and should not be; these were principals whose actions Casel felt she could learn from. The network members were honest with each other and comfortable speaking out if they thought a colleague was making a wrong move. Casel found it stimulating to surround herself with principals who were bright and smart, who kept her on her toes and made her think about her day-to-day work more deeply. After consulting with her network, Casel made a quick call to the SPED department. "OK," she told them, "I'll take it."

The LAB Cluster as a Strategic Intervention

There were considerable benefits to taking on the cluster, both social and, perhaps more powerfully, economic. The Manning was a small school with a small budget. A LAB cluster would bring in a considerable number of new school staff. The Manning would automatically be entitled to eight staff members (four teachers and four paraprofessionals) for every thirty-two students, significantly preferable to their current ratio of three teachers for every thirty-six kids. Casel knew that even if these positions were primarily for the cluster, the more staff in the school, the better. It was a simple matter of increased resources. The cluster would also bring in a full-time clinical coordinator and a program director—two additional administrators in a school so small that it currently had only one, Casel. Bringing in people with extensive background in clinical intervention and therapy, beyond just SPED training, would be beneficial to the whole school.

Taking on the LAB cluster meant eliminating the Manning's traditional SPED program and the reshuffling of several classroom positions. With this restructuring, she would be able to post new job opportunities and hire a significant number of new teachers and staff, giving her the chance to weed out old staff members unwilling to change. "This is really an unattractive program for many people," Casel reasoned, "so I don't have to worry about people who don't want to work hard applying for the new positions. People who don't want to be a part of it will leave."

In her view, the cluster model was clay for the Manning to mold. It meant that the school would have new staff and significant new resources at its disposal. "And we aren't bound by the BPS design," Casel realized. "*We* can make the decisions about how to use these new resources and shape them to fit our needs." She intended to bring the staff into the discussion of how the new resources could best be utilized and how the school could be shaped to most effectively serve all of its students.

In thinking back, Casel understands that the move to take on the LAB cluster was also the politically correct thing to do. "I wish I could say that at the time I knew that—that, oh yes, I knew what I was doing. Here Boston was struggling with what to do with these kids who just wouldn't behave, who would waltz into the classroom and act disruptively, and everybody just wanted them to go 'someplace.' The timing was absolutely right."

Overall, she was pleased with the strategy. Rather than spending years trying to "evaluate out" unacceptable teachers, this move gave her the opportunity for a quick fix. Taking on the cluster meant that Casel could wipe everything out and start anew. She knew that she would lose some children. One whole program would be gone, after all, and those children with it. But the "great change" would allow her to act quickly. Casel felt a sense of urgency; she imagined that while she sat back and planned for the future, thinking about what would be good in the long run, she would be losing generations of children.

She knew the proposal of bringing a LAB cluster to the Manning would be contentious and divisive. It would be a difficult topic to discuss with both the Manning's teachers and parents. Casel thought well of her staff in many ways, considering them caring, wonderful people, but she saw them as being in their own little bubble. They had already made their excuses and decided that things were "okay," that nothing needed to change. Casel's sense of urgency was so great, however, that she felt she didn't have time to wait for people to "come around" on the matter.

She first brought the idea to the School Site Council. This group of parents, teachers, and community members, headed by the principal, was legally chartered to be only an advisory agency to the principal. The principal had the final say. But the Manning School Site Council, under the previous principal, had taken on the role of a governing agency for the school, voting on rules, policies, and other executive issues affecting how the school was run. The School Site Council put the cluster idea to a vote and voted it down. This was disappointing for Casel and indicative of the uphill battle she faced, but she knew that the school district's SPED department had the power to supersede any vote of the Manning School Site Council. The vote of the council was powerless against the stronger vote of the district.

Nevertheless, Casel recognized how important it was to garner support from her community before moving forward. She decided to hold a series of meetings for Manning parents and community members to explain the nature of the cluster and clarify any misunderstandings they may have had about it. Casel hoped that eventually, given an accurate picture of the cluster and all it could do for the school, parents would vote to bring it in. Again, Casel knew that no matter how parents voted, there *was* going to be LAB cluster at the Manning; she was not asking for permission. However, her need for support was strong, and she wanted the people to stand with her.

Racism: Alive and Well

Data showed that most of the students in LAB clusters were black males. The Manning cluster would be comprised of four classes of eight students each and would, therefore, essentially guarantee that approximately thirty black, male students would "infiltrate" the Manning's 175-student body. At the parent and community meetings Casel organized, it immediately became apparent that it was not just that the community didn't want these kids who had been thrown out of other schools; what they especially did not want were *black* kids who had been thrown out of other schools.

Casel knew that she was lucky and, until that point, had really not come across much racism in her adult life. She had reached a point where, as an adult, she had chosen to surround herself with people who thought like she did. And so she was not prepared to hear things like, "We don't want *those* kids here. You're going to destroy the school." For the most part, it wasn't blatant (only one person used the n-word), but the meetings Casel held that year to discuss the cluster confirmed for her that racism was still very much alive and well.

She found herself reassuring parents that this new group of students would not disrupt the school or prevent their children from receiving an education. She reassured concerned neighbors who worried about vandalism and violence. She made promises to both parents and neighbors that she would not allow the LAB students to get out of control. She even pledged to work hard to make the Manning cluster diverse in terms of gender, class, and race, to fight the stereotype of the LAB cluster consisting entirely of poor, black, male students.

Casel took a group of parents and teachers to visit LAB clusters at other schools. At one school the Manning team visited, the principal showed off a gratelike fence that could be pulled down to block off the hallway where the cluster was housed, in case of emergency. Casel was horrified. But the parents on the tour would point to this as an example of the kind of precautions the Manning did not have the resources to take. "But we don't have what the Jackson has," they would explain to other parents at future meetings to reiterate why the cluster was not a good idea for their school. "They have the grate they can pull down. Our school is so small—we don't have things like that."

The tensions ran high on the day the parents came together to vote. Casel was not sure which way they would go, or how she would proceed if they voted it down as the Council had, which she suspected they would. She anticipated that there would be considerable backlash when the community realized that, regardless of the vote, she planned to move ahead and bring the cluster to the Manning.

As it turned out, Casel was spared that struggle. She did get an affirmative vote that day, but only by a very narrow margin. Even so, many families chose to leave the Manning. Interestingly, the very people who voted for the cluster ended up sending their children to other schools. In Casel's opinion, those that left had always been unsure about staying with the public schools. They were Boston's white middle-class: concerned about the public schools' ability to meet their children's needs yet leaning toward parochial schools anyway. They had wanted to "do the right thing," in terms of the cluster, but they feared their children might "suffer the consequences."

Unfortunately, the exodus of many white, middle-class families disrupted the racial and socioeconomic balance of the Manning. This meant that recruiting new students through the parent-choice system would be even more challenging.

Building a New School

After the dust settled, Casel was finally able to hire new staff members and was delighted with the professionals she was able to bring on. Several of the best people from the Blackstone, where she had been assistant principal, elected to apply for positions. The four she hired had a proven record of accomplishment, and she was confident they were just what she was looking for: energetic, hard working, skilled, and committed to teaching. She also knew that they shared her views about success for all children.

Three SPED teachers from within the Manning applied for the new positions. Casel chose to retain one of the three, a teacher who was so politically connected to the school that Casel could not cast her out without stirring up bad feelings among the remaining staff. She kept her on and complemented her with three dynamite teachers of about the same age who were energetic and passionate about their work. The veteran Manning teacher tried, at first, to close her door and conduct her classroom autonomously, but the other cluster teachers, who believed in collaborative practice, wouldn't let her. The veteran came to Casel's office discouraged: "I don't know if I can do this. I'm not as good as these other people." Casel replied, "You're right. You're not as good as they are—but you could be, if you wanted to be."

Indeed, the veteran rose to the challenge. She began to see what great teaching really meant and all that a good teacher could do for a troubled child. She was given support; the catalysts for her transformation were her colleagues. She soon became just as effective as her peers, eventually going on to receive several awards for her teaching.

Tough Going

When Casel had enthusiastically pursued the LAB cluster, she did not fully realize how tough it was going to be. She had said to Caroline in the district SPED department, "They're just kids. You can change any kid with a good teacher." Caroline had replied, "Casel, this is a little different. . . These are the kids that we're throwing out of the Boston Public Schools."

It didn't take long for Casel to realize that Caroline had been right. These were *tough* kids! Many of them had been out of the system because of their emotional and behavioral problems; some had come from BPS schools where they had been having significant problems. At the Manning, Casel and the staff discovered that some of these students had no trouble picking up and throwing chairs at their teachers or swearing at younger students. Casel came to recognize that she would need to have a sense of humor about her pre-cluster naivete. The first year was going to be chaotic. The Manning staff even found themselves chasing kids down the hallways. The scenes were sometimes overwhelming, sometimes laughable, but the staff came together, sat down, brainstormed, and began to troubleshoot the problems and make contracts with kids. These were teachers who would not give up.

During the transitional period, the Manning lost a lot of families, three classroom teachers, and the computer teacher, but Casel brought on three new teachers, four new paraprofessionals, a clinical coordinator, and a program director. In the end, the cluster ended up making the Manning a better school. It clearly articulated who Casel was and what she stood for, and it sent a clear message to the great majority of the staff that had chosen to stay: They saw that the Manning was a school focused on children. They also saw that Casel was fair and willing to listen to what people had to say—as long as priorities were child-focused.

Casel was happy with her decision to bring the LAB cluster to the Manning. It was the right decision at the right time.

New ideas, new goals, and reinvigorated staff were only the beginning of the change effort at the Manning. Casel knew the hardest work was still ahead of them. The school needed to work on integrating this new program and making the children in the cluster a fundamental part of the Manning community. They needed to reach out to families to make the Manning an attractive option for all children. Most importantly they needed to work classroom by classroom on improving teaching and learning. This meant looking at curriculum, reassessing programs, and introducing new initiatives in reading and math. Teachers needed support, materials, and training in new approaches. The Manning was embarking on a long journey, and whether or not it reached its destination would now depend on Casel's day-to-day leadership and the skill and commitment of the staff. Now they could start to think about real learning.

Diversity as a Core Value

When Casel first arrived at the Manning, the diversity of the student body was one of her most fundamental concerns. She would not tolerate a school that was segregated—with the white students in the primary grades and the black and Hispanic students in the elementary grades. Casel knew that "connected," primarily white families were playing political games to get their children into the Manning, and she wanted this practice to stop.

She contacted the Parent Information Center, the department that controlled school assignment under Boston's School Choice program, and demanded an explanation for why children of color were not being assigned to her school in the early grades. She tried to be both pointed and persuasive. "Look," she said, "you can't tell me that we get eighteen blond-haired, blue-eyed kids out of twenty-four by chance, or that those are the only kids who say they want to come here." Her goal was to ensure that any child that wanted to attend the Manning had the opportunity to do so. "I'd like families to understand that this is a six-year commitment and not just a place to go until grade one and then off to parochial school. This is a place for all children and the diversity in the classrooms should begin in our kindergarten classroom and continue up through all of the grades. Let's get some balance. Let's aim for eight black kids, eight white kids, and eight Hispanic kids, and eight Asian kids—something like that."

Casel told the Center that if outreach was needed, she would be willing to help. It was, and she did. Through her assistance, progress was made to recruit black families to enter the Manning in the early grades. The adoption of the LAB cluster also brought about an abrupt solution, driving many of the white primary students from the school. During the transitional period, the Manning student body in grades K2–5 was almost entirely minority.

After some time, with active recruitment and outreach, the school became more diverse. By the 1999–2000 school year, Casel and the Manning had achieved the near-perfect diversity for which she had hoped: the incoming kindergarten class had eight white children, eight black children, and eight Hispanic children.

Coming Full Circle to Create a Highly Successful School

By 2004–2005, however, that same group of kids, now in grade five, represented the last diverse class in the school; the majority of the forty-one students in the LAB cluster were black, and nearly all the regular education students were white. Children of color once again became the minority; represented by only two or three students in each classroom.

At the beginning of the 2000–2001 school year, just one year after she had achieved her "ideal" diversity goal, Casel held her annual K2 orientation. As always, she sent letters to the homes of incoming students inviting their families to participate. Looking back, she marvels that she didn't notice that all of the addresses had the same zip code.

On the day of the orientation, as families began to trickle in, Casel became aware of differences between these families and the ones who had attended orientation in the past few years. There seemed to be two parents representing nearly every student, a highly unusual occurrence. The Manning generally hosted twenty or so adults at orientation, yet here were nearly fifty—so many that they had to move the event to a larger room. More importantly, there were only two students of color present. The incoming class was almost entirely white. The diversity that Casel had so heartily celebrated the previous year had attracted many white families. She had been too successful in proving to white families that the Manning was an exceptional school, a better place for all students. She had made the Manning a school that white families identified as "the place to be."

The Manning's attractiveness was a product of its student-centered culture and its growing instructional competence. Student performance on the MCAS had demonstrated a pattern of continuous improvement since 2000. The year 2004 was an exception because many top students were withdrawn by their parents due to an unusually large number of behavioral incidents that had taken place earlier in their Manning experience. (See Tables 1.1 and 1.2.)

The Principal Recruits

Casel realized that more white families were moving back to Boston and that the Manning was reaping the benefits of this influx. But she was increasingly concerned about diversity in her school. As she looked around the room at parent meetings, Casel too often found that *she* was the only person of color. If she was to have a diverse school, she had to recruit students of color.

Table 1.1 Grade 4 Manning ELA MCAS Scores Compared to Other Boston Schools

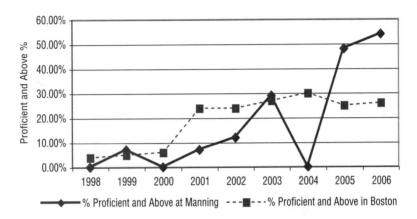

Source: www.doe.mass.edu

Table 1.2 Grade 4 Manning Math MCAS Scores Compared to Other Boston Schools

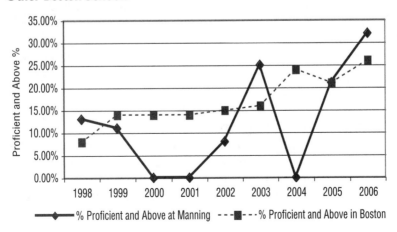

Source: www.doe.mass.edu

She began to do some advertising for the Manning within the communities she was trying to attract. She conducted readings at branch libraries in nearby black neighborhoods, such as Roxbury. Every Saturday she camped out at local Massachusetts Bay Transportation Authority (MBTA) stations. Sundays, she went to black churches, advertising that families could "come meet the principal." She held a huge open house one Saturday at school, trying to attract families of color. But the next year was the same as the one before—the incoming kindergarten class was all white, except for one child of color.

Casel returned to her recruitment plan and thought of all the places she should have gone but had not because she had run out of time. This year, she told herself, she'd hit those places too. But by the end of the year, her family had had enough. "You're going to make us spend another Saturday at the T?" they complained. "Another Sunday dragging us around to some other church?" Even with all of her efforts, the 2003–2004 incoming kindergarten class was entirely white—all twenty-two students—and when Casel looked at her waiting list, she saw that out of the sixty students on it, only four were of color.

Still committed to diversity, in 2004 Casel started going after the families of the students who were entering into Boston's Metropolitan Council for Educational Opportunity (METCO) program, started in 1966 to offer inner-city families of color the opportunity to send their children to schools in the suburbs. Boston Public Schools had improved immeasurably in recent years, and was now, at least at the elementary level, considered a quality district. But despite the fact that Boston has exerted a great deal of effort attracting white families back to its public schools, the city had not begun the conversation about whether or not it was still important to continue sending their black students to the suburbs through the METCO program.

Unfortunately, whether or not it was true, many families, both black and white, still thought that suburbs like Brookline and Lexington would offer their children a higher-quality education than they would be able to receive in Boston. Casel tried to convince these families that the Boston Public Schools were a viable option. She encouraged families that had expressed interest in the Manning but were also considering the METCO option to apply to the Manning; they could always go with METCO if they didn't get in.

A Postscript

One of the side effects of this new, "reversed" problem of diversity at the Manning was that students began to enter kindergarten very well prepared for school. Many kids came with reading skills, some with an understanding of money, and some even with the ability to tell time. Because socioeconomic status at the Manning had improved, families were better educated and equipped to prepare their kids for the structure of school. Although this was a good thing, it was also a situation that the teachers at the Manning had to struggle with.

Urban teachers are trained to teach children who are *not* prepared for school. They expect to have to start from the very beginning—teach basic communication and life skills before teaching math, remediate reading problems before tackling content areas, see huge leaps of progress from the beginning of the year to the end. Casel was faced with dedicated teachers who were saying, "You know, I'm just not needed here. These children don't need the skills that I have. They are already reading, they have all this knowledge. What can I give them?" To these expressions of frustration Casel replied, "You are absolutely needed here. What are you saying about yourself as a teacher? Are you saying that you can't teach children who come into the first grade already reading at a third grade level? You can't challenge these children?"

The faculty members Casel worked with in 2006 were very different from those she had worked with ten years earlier. Their conversations reflected this. In the past, the child who was easier to teach was the academically advanced one. The new staff, however, thought of the needy child as being easier to teach. Casel had to challenge this, too: "Is it far more rewarding to take a child who is just so needy and throw some crumbs [at them] and watch how they blossom?" It was a challenge for Casel, too. She still believed that schools made a difference in every student's life, no matter who walked through the door; yet when a child came to school very "ready," she felt at risk of losing that perspective. "I think it became really easy to take the kid who *couldn't* and measure the jumps and milestones, but to take the kid who *could* and continue pushing was now our harder challenge."

It was true; teachers were not prepared for their student's preparedness. Even the professional development that teachers received was geared toward making progress with low-level learners. The Manning had to seek out a different kind of training and really examine how to teach in-depth, asking themselves during their collaborative professional development sessions, "How do you take a piece of writing that's damn good and make it better?"

Casel felt that she had come full circle, now wondering if she could lead what she had created. What, she wondered, would be the long-term effects of what the Manning had become?

Chapter 2

Kim Marshall
and Mather Elementary School
1987–2002

Kim Marshall felt a sense of relief. His Harvard classmate Jeff Howard, founder of the Efficacy Institute, was working magic at Boston's Mather Elementary, the school to which Kim had recently been appointed acting principal. Jeff Howard spent the morning of October 24, 1987, leading a professional development workshop with the Mather staff while Kim observed from the back of the classroom. Jeff's powerful message seemed convincing to most of the forty-two teachers, especially the ten black teachers. At lunchtime, the faculty lounge buzzed with excitement, and Kim sensed that bringing in such a high-voltage, black speaker at the beginning of his principalship was going to pay off. Most of the staff seemed to be buying into Howard's Efficacy philosophy that students are not born smart but can work hard to get smart.

Unfortunately, the Efficacy message was not sitting well with all of the Mather staff. Unbeknownst to Kim, the Mather's "Gang of Six," as he had privately labeled a group of veteran white teachers, had retreated to a classroom during lunch to gripe about the day's events. He later noted that they were "profoundly uneasy about the Efficacy message and the way the faculty seemed to be slipping out of their control. One of them was overheard saying in the ladies' room, 'If I had a gun, I'd shoot Jeff Howard dead.'"

Kim felt that the "Gang of Six" was leading a campaign to discredit him, the new principal. In part, their outrage could be attributed to Kim's first round of required teacher performance evaluations, in which he had given most Mather teachers a "satisfactory" rating on Boston's three-point scale, believing that he did not know each teacher's skills well enough to rate them as "excellent," the score they were used to receiving from his predecessor. However, Kim's philosophy that "all students can

41

learn" was also perceived by these teachers as an insult to their teaching abilities. Many teachers blamed students' low achievement on family background and poverty and were not optimistic about the school's ability to overcome those demographics. At meetings with faculty and staff, the "Gang of Six," claiming to represent the feelings of the whole staff, insisted that "people are outraged" and "morale has never been worse."

After the lunch break, another Efficacy consultant took over for Jeff Howard, leading the staff through an exercise in which teachers estimated the overall achievement of each of their students from the previous year on a 4-3-2-1 scale, noting their race and gender. The consultant charted on butcher paper the achievement data for the whole school by race and grade. Using this method, it became abundantly clear that after third grade the achievement of black male students nose-dived; by fifth grade nearly all were achieving at the lowest level on the scale. As the afternoon wore on, Kim noticed that

> staff members became increasingly defensive. Was the consultant saying that they were racist? [He hadn't said anything of the kind, but some white staff members heard this implication.] Was he saying that they were bad teachers? [Again, neither he nor Jeff Howard had said this, but they read that implication into the data on the wall.] And what was he suggesting that they ought to be doing? The Efficacy consultant did not have ready answers to any of these questions and struggled to control the emotions in the room. Kim stood at the back, not believing what was happening. It was clear from teachers' body language, the increasingly hostile questions, and the fact that some people actually got up and walked out, that the positive energy from the morning had evaporated.[1]

Kim Marshall

Kim, a thirty-nine-year-old white man, came to the Mather bursting with ideas for how the school could make a difference in the lives of its 600 students. He was eager to take on the challenge of the Mather. Intellectually, he was prepared; as some of the teachers would later note, perhaps he was overprepared.

Educated at a prep school in England and with an undergraduate degree from Harvard, Kim had taught at the Martin Luther King Jr. Middle School in Boston's Dorchester neighborhood for nine years. During that time, he had developed a series of books to teach English, reading, vocabulary, and math. He completed a Masters Degree at Harvard University's Graduate School of Education, where he steeped himself in the Effective Schools research, which identified the key factors that contributed to successful urban schools. In preparation for his new administrative career, Kim worked at Boston Public Schools' central headquarters for six years as assistant to two superintendents. There he guided and coordinated the rewriting of Boston's K–12 curriculum.

The Mather

The Mather was located in a crime-ridden neighborhood that had been suffering from white flight since Boston's 1974 ruling mandating crosstown busing to address issues of desegregation. Eighty-five percent of the Mather's 600 students were eligible for free or reduced-price meals. The student body was 68 percent black, 17 percent white, 10 percent Hispanic, and 4 percent Asian.

When Kim arrived at the Mather in 1987, he brought a wealth of acquired knowledge: how to teach in urban schools, the substance of Boston's K–5 curriculum, and how urban schools and their teaching staffs might be remolded to better educate underprivileged and underserved students. Kim fervently believed that a student's racial and socioeconomic status need not predict his or her academic destiny. According to Kim, *all* children could learn, and the Mather could and should facilitate that process.

Many of the teachers at the Mather neither shared his aspirations for improved student achievement nor thought them realistic. They interpreted the butcher paper data display from the Efficacy retreat as evidence that the vast majority of students was uneducable. In contrast, Kim interpreted the findings to be a "confluence of social, economic, and psychological factors and the absence of a concerted, focused, well-led program in the school to overcome these external forces."

The "Gang of Six" took advantage of the tensions caused by the Efficacy training, going so far as to circulate an anonymous, underground newsletter among the staff. It was obvious to Kim that the six "bristled at the idea of change and at the thought that a new principal might be able to exercise more influence than they over the faculty at large." It was obviously intended to discredit Kim, referring to him as "Peter Pan" and "the boy with the rose-colored glasses." One staff member recalled, "Some of those teachers were evil. They had a voodoo doll of Kim with pins in it up in the teacher's lounge!" The doll sat in the lounge for days. Many of the teachers were afraid to touch it. Eventually, someone had the courage to throw it away. Although the Efficacy training did not have the outcomes Kim had envisioned, his determination to increase the Mather's academic capabilities was made very clear to the staff. Three of the "Gang of Six" left the school the following year.

Kim tried to use Efficacy training to "unfreeze" the Mather and move staff away from the comfortable, self-satisfied culture that permeated the school. Student achievement, as measured by the district's norm-referenced Metropolitan Achievement Test (MAT), had been steadily declining; in 1987 scores were in the mid–twentieth percentile. Although the Mather had one of the lowest showings of any elementary school in Boston, the staff members were not dissatisfied with the student achievement. Significantly, they did not seem to think that the low achievement of Mather students was any reflection on their own teaching. "Fundamentally, they saw themselves as brave soldiers fighting in a hopeless cause. They taught well, but many students did not learn. Mather teachers seemed talented, worked hard, and in many cases spent hundreds of dollars of their own money on classroom supplies. Yet they held fast to the belief that students' poverty and family background prevented the school from doing much better."[2]

Rally Around the 350th

Taken aback by the vehemence of teacher resistance during the Efficacy fiasco, Kim looked to avoid further confrontation by attempting to unite the faculty around some common purpose. He remembered that the minister of the church next to the school, on Boston's historic Meeting House Hill, had mentioned that the Mather's 350th anniversary was coming up in two years, in 1989. The school, the minister informed him, was established in 1639, making it the nation's oldest public elementary school.

The anniversary would fall during Kim's third year as principal, and he realized that it could prove to be a powerful opportunity for him to bring the Mather community together—if they began planning right away. He decided to make a big deal of the event, even going so far as to invite the 1988 presidential candidates, George H. W. Bush and Michael Dukakis. Somehow, Kim managed to weave a $1.5 million physical renovation and an academic overhaul of the school into the context of the event. He generated excitement among staff with statements like "the president's going to be here, and we should have more to show him than just the building."

Though Bush did not end up attending the event, Dukakis and several significant national and local politicians were present, and the event served as a tremendous "morale surge in the school."[3] It provided an opportunity for Kim and the Mather staff to come together in a successful collaboration.

In a rueful moment several years later, Kim wondered if "that might have been time for me to leave. [Others could have said,] 'He turned the school around, fixed it up and moved on.' But I didn't [leave]; I stayed for twelve more years."

Kim Reaches Out to the Staff

In 1990, a year after the 350th, Kim decided to build on the positive mood resulting from the anniversary. He organized a workshop to analyze staff results on the Myers Briggs Type Indicator (MBTI), the most popular personality assessment instrument in U.S. The twenty-minute exercise, during which participants were asked to choose between familiar terms in a number of word pairs, revealed to the test taker a portrait of his or her personality characteristics.

During the workshop, Kim thought to himself, "This is what I should have done in the beginning. Instead of bringing in Jeff Howard, which was so high-risk, I should have brought in the MBTI program and worked with the facilitator and staff in sort of a touchy-feely fashion. I could have said, 'Our kids are failing. What are we going to do, guys? Let's pull together.'"

Kim, as a participant in the program, had his profile displayed in the meeting room along with those of all staff members. The workshop leader skillfully addressed the differences between most of the teachers' personality styles and Kim's. The leader pointed out that their principal was a "driven innovator" and that most of the staff members were predominantly "intuitive" and "feeling." They complemented each other. His message was, "You need him and he needs you."

The workshop, much to Kim's relief, was a great success. He recalled that "people loved it." For years, the staff's MBTI profiles, Kim's included, hung in the teacher's room, providing a constant reminder of how they could use their differences to really work together. Yet Kim did not take much solace from the positive outcome. He had succeeded in demonstrating that he was not an ogre, but he did not aspire to be just one of the gang either. He felt that the MBTI workshop's success was really just a temporary diversion of the staff's energy from confronting the Mather's most serious problem: low student achievement.

During his tenure as a principal, Kim prodded, probed, and challenged the Mather staff to become more educationally informed. Teachers couldn't turn around without being confronted with Kim's word to the wise on how they could do a better job of educating their students; his exhortations were omnipresent, and their cumulative effect was positive.

Kim's first pedagogical salvo after arriving at the Mather was to distribute the *Mather Memo*, a single sheet, double-sided, daily newsletter, to every staff mailbox first thing in the morning. He continued this practice every school day for his fifteen years as principal, save for the day of his father's funeral—2,699 editions in all. The *Mather Memo*, which Kim rose at 5:00 A.M. to compose, was his way of communicating daily with faculty and staff. The front of the newsletter highlighted the recess locations for the day, staff and student birthdays, compliments to staff members, comments on exemplary performance by students, a calendar item documenting an event that happened on this day in history (e.g., Elvis's birthday) with a few facts on the subject, daily reminders of events taking place (e.g., field trips or assemblies), and school concerns ranging from upcoming meetings to candy sales to strange odors on the east side of the building. The Friday edition included a funny cartoon to lighten the tone. On the back, Kim reproduced a relevant article from the professional literature that he felt the staff could benefit from reading. He was committed to the idea that everyone on his staff should be in-the-know both about what was going on at the Mather and what was happening in education nationally.

Mission Clarity

Kim calculated that it would take years to fully implement all the activities he envisioned for a new Mather. But first the school needed a mission statement with a clear purpose to provide direction for students, families, and especially staff. He tried out a variety of slogans over the years—"America's oldest public elementary school," "All children can learn," "A safe and caring community focused on learning," and "We can touch the world"—but, wordsmith that he was, Kim was also aware that words, however meaningful to the author, might be mere abstractions to others.

He greatly valued feedback and religiously surveyed his staff and parents at the end of each school year. In a 1992 questionnaire, 76 percent of the staff said that the Mather had a clear sense of purpose and mission. But, when asked to write the mission, only fifteen out of thirty-nine even tried, and there were fifteen different answers. Kim concluded, "If everyone in school doesn't know the mission—you don't have one!"

Challenged by the staff's failure to internalize the Mather's mission, Kim reasoned that one statement was insufficient for the multiple areas that a school purpose needed to address. Over a period of several years, he and his teachers developed a unified spectrum from the most abstract to the most concrete set of statements that provided the framework for Mather's goals and objectives. Marshall and the Mather teachers wanted their students to be well-educated enough to be successful in middle and high school, move on to college, and lead happy and productive lives. Their final mission statement captured all these elements, "We respect, nurture, and educate all of our students so they can confidently and successfully take the next step in their lives." Subsequently, to provide a clear objective for this overarching statement, the school added that for this to happen, "Mather fifth graders need to graduate on or above grade level in Reading, Writing, Math, and Social Competency."

It was not enough to clarify the school's mission for teachers and parents. *Students* had to internalize the school's purpose. A Mather pledge was the perfect opportunity. Kim believed there was a need for a pledge that had more meaning to students than the Pledge of Allegiance. Though a positive secular ritual, phrases such as "one nation, indivisible" were difficult for children to understand. Kim and a group of teachers wrote a complement to the Pledge that reinforced the Efficacy message. The new Mather School Pledge was led by a student every morning over the public address system, along with the Pledge of Allegiance.

Mather's Vision, Mission, Core Values, and Core Beliefs

The Mather's Vision:

We respect, nurture, and educate all of our students so they can confidently and successfully take the next step in their lives.

The Mather's Mission:

Mather fifth graders need to graduate on or above grade level in Reading, Writing, Math, and Social Competency.

The Mather's Core Values:

The Mather School is a safe, caring community of learners. Relationships within the school, and between home and school, are marked by mutual respect and trust, teamwork and creativity, and a continuous quest for better and better ways to help all students learn and grow. Our philosophy of teaching and learning can be summed up as WHAM!: **W**hole language, **H**ands-on, **A**ctive, cooperative learning with **M**ulticultural content.

The Mather's Core Beliefs:

1. Some say that it is children's economic background, not the quality of schools, that determine life chances. We believe that an effective school using research-based programs makes a huge difference in the future of each student.

2. Some say that children are born "very smart, sorta smart, or kinda dumb" (to use Jeff Howard's ironic terms), and that schools cannot change the genetically-determined pecking order. We believe (as do Asian cultures) that good teachers and effective effort lead to students who did not seem smart, getting smart.

3. Some believe that only a few very talented students can reach high levels of academic achievement. We believe that the fifth-grade curriculum is not rocket science, and that virtually all students (except those with serious cognitive deficits) can be at least on grade level when they leave elementary school.

4. Some believe that good teachers are born, not made. We believe that being an effective teacher requires talent and a caring heart, but is mostly hard work, reaching out to the knowledge base, looking at students' work, analyzing data, and sharing ideas with colleagues.

(continued)

Mather's Vision, Mission, Core Values, and Core Beliefs
(continued)

5. Some believe that teachers are happiest and most effective when they close the doors and work as "self-employed entrepreneurs" (Grant Wiggins). We believe that the true potential of teachers is released when they work in effective grade-level teams, constantly looking at their students' work and sharing best practices—in other words "working smart."
6. Some believe that students do best with teachers who are free to teach what they love best in the way they see fit. We believe that students are best served when teachers discipline themselves and align their classroom curriculum with external standards. This is especially important in Massachusetts, where, in the very near future, 10th graders will not get a high school diploma if they do not pass the very rigorous MCAS test.

The Mather School Pledge

I must work hard today, get smarter in every way,
Helped by my teachers, my family, and my friends.
If I make some mistakes, I have what it takes
To keep trying 'til I really succeed.

Stalking Teaching

Kim was up against two major impediments in making real headway in improving classroom instruction: 1) being constantly overpowered by the day-to-day demands of students, teachers, and parents requiring his attention; and 2) being unable to get close to the educational core of the Mather—the classroom. Teachers saw their classrooms as their sacrosanct domains, and the union contract with the school system required the completion of the full performance evaluation form at any observational visit. This amount of paperwork seriously restricted frequent classroom visits.

Kim felt that for each day he was unable to provide in-depth coaching in a classroom, one more group of students was being educationally short-changed. He believed that "the rich get richer and the poor get poorer. Students who enter school with disadvantages learn very little and fall further and further behind, and the gap between the haves and the have-nots gets wider each year." He was determined to puncture the artificial barrier that kept him from the classroom. He had been a teacher and for nine years had taught some of the most difficult middle school students in the city. He knew what good teaching looked like, and he could coach those who most needed it. Despite the union stipulation, Kim, with a pad of paper in hand, dropped in on classes unannounced, took notes, and produced detailed write-ups for teachers, many of which were overwhelmingly positive and appreciative.

The practice of visiting classrooms unannounced, without a formal appointment, was not the norm in the Boston Public Schools at the time, and lengthy supervisory write-ups were even rarer. Some teachers appreciated his feedback; others did not. Those who did not took advantage of Kim's violation of the precedent of principals staying out of the classroom and formally grieved the visits with the union and won. Kim was told that he could not visit classrooms and write observational summaries unless he used the formal, seven-page BPS evaluation document in its entirety. The union expected the ruling to demoralize Kim, forcing his retreat. It did temporarily, but the maneuver was a vast underestimation of Kim's resolve and determination. The next year, Kim went through a phase of doing quick drop-ins to every classroom every day and did the minimum required in terms of annual (or biannual) performance evaluations using the system's document.

He then tried a new approach, asking teachers to propose times when they wanted to be observed. Never once invited to observe a class, he reluctantly scheduled appointments, and, as predicted, teachers played it safe by preparing careful lessons. Kim continued to feel that he really didn't know what was going on in Mather classrooms on a daily basis. "This really frustrated me. I felt that my failure to connect with teachers via meaningful supervision meant that I was not a genuine instructional leader. I aspired to be the kind of principal who was always in and out of classrooms and who had useful insights to share that would help teachers make an even greater difference in children's lives. Good supervision is central to being a good principal, and I felt blocked from doing that part of my job."[4]

Intent on trying every possible approach, the next year Kim visited each of the Mather's thirty-nine classrooms every single day. He was nearly as frustrated with the superficiality of the short fifteen-second daily visits as the longer yearly ones. He recalled, "I saw no details and had nothing to say to the teachers afterwards."

Beating HSPS

The thirty-nine-visits-a-day pace was representative of Kim's long and hectic workday. It was impossible to keep up, but Kim did achieve a sense of exhilaration from the demanding schedule. He wrote, "I began to find the frenetic pace enjoyable, ego-boosting, and quite addictive. There was something energizing about being in demand, rushing around solving problems, attending to this and that. I was becoming what a friend calls an 'intensity junkie.'"[5]

He named that style of school leadership the Hyperactive Superficial Principal Syndrome (HSPS), and he became known nationally for it after publishing his experience and remediation efforts in the prestigious educational journal, *Phi Delta Kappan.*[6] He realized that there were two extremes to the teaching observation continuum: 1) annual observation and evaluation and 2) brief superficial visits. He asked himself whether middle ground could be found and thought about how long he would have to be in a classroom to form a meaningful impression and have valuable feedback for the teacher. He remembered a research study where the researchers had taken half-minute soundless videotapes of teachers teaching. They found that they could see a great deal in only thirty seconds and that impressions formed during that time correlated highly with longer, in-depth evaluations.

At the end of his sixth year as principal, Kim formulated a plan to begin brief, five-minute classroom visits, frequent enough to provide a real picture of what went on in the classrooms. His visits were unannounced, and he made sure to provide verbal feedback within twenty-four hours of each visit. The feedback took the form of a dialogue with teachers; nothing was written down and no formal evaluation took place. During his visits, he tried to be invisible, finding it useful to look at the kids and the teacher and ask himself, "What's going on here? What are the issues? What's the teaching point?" He circulated, looking at individual children's work and occasionally asking students questions, but he never wrote any notes while in the classroom. Most teachers reacted positively, and Kim felt that he was having productive conversations with teachers each day. More importantly, he felt that he was doing his job as an instructional leader. One teacher said,

> I've been in schools where you get your date and the principal comes in just for 45 minutes, and you hand in your lesson plans in ahead of time. And inevitably you either do wonderfully or bomb. It's usually not a mediocre thing. But [Mr. Marshall] sort of pops in randomly and I like that. I think he gets to see much more of what happens. When I first came here, he used to do longer visits and take process notes. He was very meticulous. I've never seen anybody who can take notes the way he does! Now he gives feedback within the next couple of days. He'll come up to me and say, "I was really impressed with this and that, but I have a question," or something like that. Whether he praises or questions, he's always specific about what he saw. So I believe he really did see something as opposed to a general, "oh that was great."

Kim's pace often allowed him to visit all forty-five Mather teachers once every two weeks. He averaged about 500 visits per year over eight years. According to him, the process of "getting into four or five classrooms a day was always a struggle. Like a recovering addict, I would sometimes lapse back into HSPS and went for several days without visiting a single classroom. It took a lot of self discipline to keep on track." He noted,

> My superiors never bought into the system. Not once did my boss ask me how many classrooms I visited each day, how long I stayed, how I gave feedback to teachers, how I kept track of my visits, how many cycles I aimed to complete in a year, or how my visits were factored into formal evaluations. These are all good questions to ask any principal. With no encouragement or prodding from outside, it was completely up to me how often I visited the classrooms. The only thing that kept me going was the faith that visits were good for teaching and learning.[7]

Jump-Starting Teachers to Better Teaching

Kim's frequent classroom-based conversations with teachers opened the door for him to provide more authentic feedback.

I found that frequent visits were the key to being able to deliver honest criticism to teachers without sending them into a tailspin. The hardest thing for a teacher to handle is getting negative feedback when the administrator hasn't visited in three months and hasn't seen hundreds of successful teaching moments. . . . But if the principal is making a dozen visits a year, and nine of them are followed by generally positive comments, it is a lot easier for a teacher to hear criticism after the other three.[8]

With open access to classrooms and a precedent for giving instructional feedback, Kim had pulled off an educational coup of major proportions, one recognized by a national audience but unappreciated by his own superiors and most of his peers. With his five-minute program, Kim had taken the formulaic teacher evaluation process and turned it into a real device for improving instruction, launching the Mather on a trajectory of continuous instructional improvement. Though insufficient on its own, Kim's method of classroom observations and feedback to teachers, done regularly and systematically, was a necessary component for increasing student achievement.

A Try at Curriculum Coordination

For Kim, the five-minute feedback program was just the tip of the iceberg in instructional improvement. The Mather would never make it as a continually improving instructional system on just his time-limited drop-ins and feedback alone. Kim could coach the teachers on *how* they taught, but he had little influence over *what* they taught. A well-crafted and well-executed third grade unit on writing style and voice might excite students but leave them unprepared for their fourth grade unit on mechanics and punctuation.

From his first day at the Mather, Kim was troubled by the school's helter-skelter curriculum. Many teachers taught what *they* thought important, with only a nod to the BPS curriculum or the curriculum choices of their colleagues. It was very rare for teachers at the same grade level to give a common assessment or to check with the next grade level for what its bottom-line curriculum expectations were.

In a previous position, Kim had worked at BPS central office and had authored the district's K–12 curriculum, which had since been superseded.

He was painfully aware that curriculum at the Mather and other Boston schools had little resemblance to the BPS Master Plan. What troubled Kim was that there was no clear, grade-by-grade learning expectations and no assessments to hold students accountable for learning the material.

Ironically, as principal of the Mather, Kim did not have enough authority to implement the BPS curriculum he had created. He needed more leverage, and he thought he could get it from the Metropolitan Achievement Test (MAT) that was administered annually to all students in grades one through twelve. Kim reasoned that if he could identify the curriculum needed to achieve success in each grade levels' test, the Mather would have a unified curriculum. Although the questions used in the norm-referenced test were kept secret from teachers and students, Kim took a calculated risk and extracted from the MAT the key knowledge and skills required for each grade level. He then wrote an integrated, grades 1–5 set of learning expectations specifically for use at the Mather School. If implemented, teachers would be able to successfully hand off students who were truly prepared for the next grade level.

Unfortunately, the Mather teachers ignored Kim's efforts. He lamented, "Did teachers use my pages and pages of goals? They did not!" He believed that teachers did not care enough about the Mather's pathetic showing on the *Boston Globe*'s list of published school-by-school MAT results. Boston's central office was not giving any indication that they should take notice. Teachers wrote off the low scores: their students were at fault, not they themselves.

Kim blamed himself. He simply had not conveyed the importance of the situation. The reformatted MAT results did not create sufficient urgency for the teachers to suspend their individual agendas and coordinate their teaching efforts to promote students from grade to grade based on proficiency standards at each grade level.

Crisis of Confidence

Six years into Kim's principalship, he inadvertently precipitated a crisis that nearly obliterated all of his hard-won progress in achieving professional rapport with his staff. It began in a classroom where Kim was giving a lesson one Friday afternoon as a part of a course he was teaching to all fifth graders. In Kim's view, the teacher objected to both the lesson and the way he was teaching it and was determined to undermine him by allowing the students to be "extraordinarily disrespectful and disruptive." According to Kim, outraged by the teacher's disrespect, at dismissal time he found her sitting in her open-windowed car. Calmly, perhaps icily, he told her he was unhappy with her "outrageous, unprofessional" behavior in the classroom. He told her they needed to talk first thing Monday morning. Later, Kim received a call from his supervisor, who said the teacher had alleged that he verbally and physically assaulted her. Kim maintained he did not even touch her.

For five months, the Mather suffered as the conflict played itself out behind closed doors. The teacher hired a lawyer. They met with Kim and his supervisors, but no charges were ever filed and no resolution could be reached. Staff morale hit an all-time low, and that spring student achievement, as measured by the MAT, took a precipitous drop. Kim felt that the incident "turned the school completely upside down." The staff felt torn and confused—the accusation didn't seem to fit with what they knew of Kim, yet the accuser, a strong personality in the school, was unequivocal about her story.

By June, Kim and the staff were at an impasse. At a faculty meeting, Kim laid out the possible paths for the future. "Either a), it's time for a new principal; b), just accept that the Mather will always be fractious, always difficult, always contentious, always at each other; or c), seriously solve this problem and move on. You vote me out, and I'm out. I'll accept the results." After a prolonged staff discussion, the staff voted by secret ballot. The results were four votes for option a, no votes for option b, and forty-two votes for option c. The staff appreciated Kim's courage in putting his job on the line and voted to move forward with the agenda to improve student learning.

Rubrics to the Rescue

In 1996, Kim attended a summer workshop run by educational reform guru Grant Wiggins. He came back convinced that crafting student writing scoring rubrics in teacher teams could be the Mather's salvation. Kim would be one of the very first to utilize a protocol for integrating and aligning a school's curriculum. The work of teasing out the specifics of the writing rubrics was a breakthrough. Before it, according to Kim, "Mather staff worked hard and prided themselves on . . . a friendly staff culture. . . . But the staff culture was one of congeniality, not collegiality;

most teachers worked in isolation and there was little discussion of students, curriculum, or classroom practice in the faculty lounge."

Leading a fall Rubrics Retreat, his enthusiasm was contagious, and teachers responded to and absorbed the message. The rubrics, agreed-on written protocols for scoring student work, differentiated four levels of achievement, with 4 being the highest and 1 the lowest. Mather teachers found rubrics appealing; there was something reassuring about the concept of reliable scoring, that they could score a piece of writing and be reasonably sure that another teacher would score it the same way.

Teachers passed around examples of students' written work they had brought with them, a sticky note on the back of each recording the teacher's "gut" 4-3-2-1 score. There was a bit of nervous tension in the room as teachers wondered how their scores would compare with others'. Tension dissipated as teams of teachers from each grade level met to come to consensus about what criteria would define a 4.

Kim, the master of ceremonies for the occasion, stood by an easel, ready to record the grade-level teams' results. "What do you have? What makes these papers a 4?" he asked. The bulleted descriptions of their responses provided the raw material for the first elements of Mather's writing rubrics. They worked methodically through the sample work. What constituted a 3, a 2, or a 1 for each grade level?

After capturing the specifics of their "gut" reactions, a subcommittee of teachers grouped the elements of student writing into three categories that had been decided on previously: Mechanics and Usage, Content and Organization, and Style and Voice. Bit by bit, Mather teachers worked together to complete the rubrics that would become the standards for student performance thereafter.

Now teachers came out of their classrooms and actually enjoyed working together on an instructionally meaningful project. It didn't feel so bad to them after all, and the way the Mather thought of and scored writing was now significantly better aligned.

Unrealized at the time, except by Kim, the Mather had made another big step. Beginning with writing, the school would no longer grade subjectively. They now had a fixed standard of performance with four levels of proficiency that would allow the realization of Kim's mantra and the Efficacy philosophy that "all children can learn." Students now had a clear and measurable goal to shoot for, and most everyone could achieve it. For some it would take longer or involve more effort; but no longer would a subjective grading system ensure failure for some students.

Grade 2 Mather School Expository Writing Rubric, October 1997

Mechanics and Usage

4
Neat printing, well-spaced
Capitals at beginning of sentences, proper names, I
Very neatly laid out on the page
Correct spelling for high-frequency, Dolch list words
Able to hear and write sounds in words (beginning, middle, end)
Thoughts in complete sentences
Correct use of . ? ! , ' "-"
Correct plurals, subject, verb tense agreement most of the time

3
Legible printing, well-spaced
Mostly correct use of capitals
Presentably laid out on the page
Most high-frequency words spelled correctly
Hears and writes most sounds in words
Most sentences are complete
Mostly correct use of . ? ! , ' "-"
A few errors in plurals, subject, verb tense

2
Uneven printing, spacing of words
Several errors in capitalizing
Uneven layout on the page
Several spelling errors of high-frequency words
Several errors in writing sounds
Several incomplete sentences
Several errors in use of . ? ! , ' "-"
Several plural, subject, verb tense errors

1
Writing very difficult to read
Multiple errors with capitalizing
Jumbled layout on the page
High-frequency words misspelled
Multiple errors writing sounds
Most sentences are incomplete
Multiple errors in . ? ! , ' "-"
Multiple grammar, usage errors

Kim Pushes On

Following the rubrics retreat, Kim collected the drafts, took them home, and created a rubric for each grade level, maintaining the three separate criteria for scoring. He synthesized and cleaned up the content and then ran countless drafts back and forth to grade-level teams and the whole staff to capture their suggestions for improvement and refinement.

Rather than using students' everyday written work to evaluate writing proficiency, Kim suggested that the Mather use "cold prompts" to assess student writing four times per year. They were used to focus short, student essays that could be scored more uniformly. For example, one kindergarten assignment asked the students to "write about someone you know." Teachers would now have the capacity to give more systematic feedback to their students about their writing skills. Unbeknownst to the Mather community at the time, the new procedure would actually prepare Mather students to navigate the open-ended questions of the state-mandated MCAS, which would be administered for the first time the very next year. Kim was ahead of his time; he had created an educational infrastructure that would become key to elevating Mather students' performance.

Kim created a Microsoft Excel spreadsheet for each grade-level team that included the assessment period, writing element, and score with the expectation that the teams fill in data for all of their students. For several years, the teams did quite well with the four-times-a-year writing prompts, scoring them together and looking at the results to drive improvement. However, this was a lot to ask of the teacher teams, and their attention to the process dwindled over time. Kim attributed this to his own failure to monitor as well as to poor data displays that did not clarify learning gains and too-infrequent assessments.

Setting Goals

In 1997, the Mather had at least a theoretical system for ratcheting up student writing—but where did it lead? Kim knew that the Mather needed an overall instructional goal. The school had a mission statement, but it didn't go far enough to address what Mather students should know and be able to do by graduation.

The MAT had failed him, and the new superintendent had since substituted another norm-referenced test, the Stanford 9. These test results were scored on a 4-3-2-1 scale that claimed to match the criterion-referenced set of standards. The superintendent made the change for many of the same reasons that Kim had created scoring rubrics: It made it possible to set an unwavering, concrete, and measurable target that wouldn't slip up or down depending on the aptitudes of those taking the test in any one year. This had been the biggest downside of the norm-referenced MAT.

Now the Mather could set a compelling educational goal that could provide it with common purpose and direction. At a retreat in May 1997, with facilitator Jeff Howard, they did just that. Jeff advocated a four-year improvement plan, using the percent of students scoring Proficient and above on the Stanford 9 as the measurable target. Kim thought that by 2001, in four years, 100 percent of Mather's third graders should be able to score at least Proficient (Level 3 on a four-point scale) on the Stanford 9 in the two subject areas (reading and mathematics) and on the writing rubric as well as meet the Mather's unique Social Competency requirement. Jeff and the teachers, however, thought this highly unrealistic. The group compromised and settled on 85 percent. But the teachers still pushed back. "Is this the target for *all* third grade Mather students in 2001?" they asked. "What about the kids who don't come to us until 1998 or 2000? Do we have the same expectations for them?" Jeff's answer was no. The Mather's 85 percent target would be *just* for those third grade students who had been at the Mather since kindergarten, and even this would be a real stretch, because only 10 percent of the students were Proficient in 1997.

Get Smart

Finally, Kim had his long-sought prize: a results-oriented target for the Mather. He had succeeded in getting his staff to appreciate the value of achieving a schoolwide, measurable goal. Meeting the goal, however, would be difficult. Teachers might be on the same page in regard to assessing writing, but there was no consensus when it came to reading and math. Kim needed to figure out what the teachers needed to accomplish with their students for the Mather to achieve its four-year goal.

Students often came to school with limited academic skills, but the Mather now had to ensure that as they wound their way through the curriculum, their ability to meet grade-level standards would increase until finally, in third grade, 85 percent would score at Level 3 (Proficient) or 4 in each of the subject areas. Kim reasoned that each team had to know precisely what its grade level was responsible for, using district and state standards to prepare students for the next grade. Kim liked the idea of starting with a kindergarten cohort and increasing goals for them until they reached the 85 percent Proficient benchmark in third grade, four years later. This demanded precise goals for each grade and subject.

This was the agenda for grade-level teams at the fall 1997 retreat. "Precise" became the operative term, and Kim was ready to provide the tools to make precision happen. Schooled in a professional development workshop the summer before, Kim proselytized that each grade level and subject area needed a concrete goal, a SMART goal: specific, measurable, attainable, results-oriented, and time-bound. Teacher teams responded by developing SMART goals for the end of the 19971998 school year in each subject area: reading, writing, math, and social competency. They were examined by the whole staff before being ratified. These SMART goals were for the first year of the four-year stretch and were redone each year thereafter.

This was new and perilous territory for teachers. Never before had they been asked to put themselves on the line by committing to producing a precise student outcome to be concretely evaluated by a test. It was risky, but somewhat reluctantly the teams gathered momentum and enthusiasm as they proceeded to formulate measurable grade-level and subject-area goals. The kindergarten teachers carried the most immediate burden; they represented the first step in meeting the school's target. If the successive grade-level teachers kept to the same high standard, students would achieve the 85 percent proficiency goal by grade three.

Kim was elated. He took the SMART goals drawn up by teacher teams and framed them in a matrix for each grade level and subject area. (See Table 2.1.) He transferred the data to an Excel spreadsheet to create a Mather scorecard with student performance goals in each cell. The matrix would be revised upward annually as the Mather's 1997 kindergarten cohort advanced through the school.

Table 2.1 1997's Targeted SMART Goals for 2001

Subject Area	Target for 2001
Reading	85% Level 3 or 4 on Stanford 9
Writing	85% Level 3 or 4 on Mather rubrics
Math	85% Level 3 or 4 on BPS Math Final
Social Competency	85% Level 3 or 4 in report card conduct grade

While the teacher teams set their own SMART goals and were apparently comfortable with them, they knew there were no major consequences in failing achievement, so there was no emotional attachment to the results. Something else was needed to propel a major leap forward, and it came from an unexpected source.

No More Lone Ranger

In the spring of 1998, Kim invited Jeff Howard to facilitate another workshop, this time to review the elements of the MCAS test on one of the days it was first administered at the Mather. This simultaneous timing provoked the dramatic events that would follow. Enter Elizabeth, the senior and most well-respected fourth grade teacher at the Mather. She had just finished monitoring the MCAS in her classroom and, in the process, had read portions of the test booklet over students' shoulders. In the midst of the meeting, Elizabeth dropped into a chair and bursts into tears, exclaiming, "No more lone ranger!" She pleaded with her colleagues in kindergarten, first, second, and third grades: "I can't work by myself anymore. I need everybody to work with me. I won't have my students humiliated ever again by that test. They were beat up; they weren't prepared." It was a watershed moment for the school.

High academic standards were on the way to becoming the norm at the Mather. Elizabeth, one of their own, who had far greater credibility with the staff than Kim did, had announced that the Mather needed fixing. Kim was thrilled. Without even knowing the Mather's MCAS scores or how they compared to those of other schools, he already had the teachers' attention in a way that was unprecedented. He had waited for this moment for eleven years. "I had never really been able to get people serious about looking at what they should be teaching and what student outcomes should be. But the MCAS was a big step in that direction," he said. "Having a fourth grade [teacher] saying that all the kids are accountable for a large body of knowledge that, at the Mather, the students clearly didn't know was a major breakthrough."

For Elizabeth's dream of having her students pass the MCAS with flying colors to come true, her fourth graders needed the fundamental building blocks that could only be provided to them in the preceding grades. What were these building blocks? Kim had a ready answer: They had to utilize the Massachusetts Department of Education (DOE) bridge documents that clarified test expectations with sample items. Kim argued that they had to tease back from the results, working backward from the state Grade 4 frameworks to set grade-by-grade objectives so each team could contribute to the readiness of fourth graders. The preparation couldn't and wouldn't all be on the shoulders of the fourth grade teachers.

Elizabeth's cry for help had struck a resonant chord with the Mather teachers. There was palpable enthusiasm at the summer 1998 workshop Kim had organized to plan using from the DOE bridge documents. Three committees, ELA, Math, and Science/Technology, were made up of paid teacher-volunteers, each with outside curriculum consultants paid for by a grant from a business partner Kim had solicited for this very purpose. The state's bridge documents had just been released and were vital to bridging the gap between the MCAS and the standards; they made explicit the narrowing-down decisions that the test's creators had made. The teams used their judgment and knowledge of developmentally appropriate learning for each grade and teased back each standard from kindergarten to fourth and up to fifth. They finished by the end of the summer. The specific, tangible curricular objectives generated excitement for the team-based, schoolwide exercise. Now the new high standards to which they were being held accountable were not abstractions lodged in a long-winded, central office curriculum document. The MCAS questions were real.

Win the Battle but Lose the War

The final grade-by-grade learning expectations were to become the teachers' marching orders. But the physical size and length of each of the K–5 grade-level documents were cumbersome. Their very bulk seemed to dilute their usefulness. Kim summarized, "It was a lot of work, but what came out of the summer's efforts was completely unusable. What we had were thick, thick, daunting documents. They had done a wonderful job, but it wasn't readable at all."

Kim was not going to let his staff off the hook. He wanted clear, end-of-year curricular outcomes for each grade level that stated what the kids should know and be able to do. He called the teachers back for a day-long retreat in the fall of 1998 and passed back the summer's voluminous products. He asked teams to pull out material from all subjects for just their grade and create a user-friendly booklet that could clearly answer any question about what students needed to know and do by the end of the grade and give examples of proficient work.

The documents that they created for each subject made clear what the curriculum would be (the "what") but left the methodology (the "how") up to the teachers. The focus was on outcomes and followed Kim's dictum that "you never talk about curriculum without giving specific examples of what students will be asked to do." It was up to teachers to determine what materials and instructional strategies they would use to implement the curricular expectations.

The teachers cut and pasted, but it was a daunting job and they had no model to work from. They had reached their limit. The final documents varied quite a bit in their quality, and Kim found himself in a dilemma: "Do I override them all so that all grade levels look the same, or do I empower them and allow them to do it differently?" He decided on the former, certain that grade level expectations needed to be aligned. Kim chose a creative strategy, however, to achieve his need for curricular uniformity. The strategy leveraged peer influence rather than reliance on a unilateral directive. It represented a sophisticated influence tactic that identified Kim as one who could learn from his previous mistakes.

Kim found that the second grade's cut-and-pasted curricular summary was the best model to follow. According to him, they had the basic idea: brevity, clarity, examples. "Taking tremendous liberties," he recrafted their submission into a tight curriculum document. He gave it back to them, letting them know that he had tweaked it a bit and asked them what they thought of the revised product. He held his breath, lest they might be offended by the changes he had made. But his doubts were unfounded. "They were thrilled and flattered that I had picked them," he recalls.

Kim polished the second-year grade-level booklet some more, show-ing it to the other teams and the parents as an example of what the oth-er booklets might look like. They were generally pleased, although sev-eral parents on the School Site Council pushed back on some jargon, and the third grade team, a feisty and independent bunch, wanted to do theirs differently. Kim felt strongly that the same format K–5 was needed,

> I personally word processed drafts for each grade level, using the sec-ond grade booklet as a model, so that they all followed the same for-mat and distributed them. I got some pushback comments, most-ly from the third grade team. The rest were just tweaks. By January [1999], we had consensus; or at least consensus by exhaustion. We got strong encouragement from the parent-involved School Site Council, which helped us. Our corporate partners printed them, and we dis-tributed them to the parents and staff. The booklets became the opera-tional guidelines and standards. Everything about this whole process felt right to me; this was a first.

Kim spoke with pride. "From that time on, whenever a new teacher arrived, or a parent wanted to know what the curriculum was," he said, "I reached up to the appropriate pile in my office and voila—there it was in about twelve pages, complete with exemplars of student writing at that grade and the level of reading passage they needed to be able to read by the end of the year."

The Mather's Educational Engine

By the end of the 1998–1999 school year, Kim had put in place an in-novative educational improvement system, predating by at least five years any other national or state standards-based reform effort. Using the MCAS to align grade-by-grade curriculum with state standards was, at the time, a revolutionary idea. It would become standard practice in many schools over the years to come. The Mather system used consen-sually derived SMART goals for direction; demonstrated curricular and instructional alignment, both internally and with district standards; and had the capacity to generate interim assessments of student prog-ress from which grade-level teams could make remedial improvements in their instruction.

Table 2.2 Actual Results in 2001 Based on Targeted SMART Goals for Mather School Set in 1997

	Target for 2001 set in 1997	2001 Actual Results of Students Entering Mather at Kindergarten	2001 Actual Results of Students Entering Mather after Kindergarten
Reading	85% Level 3 or 4 on MCAS Prelim	80%	45%
Writing	85% 3 or 4 on Mather rubrics	80%	45%
Math	85% Level 3 or 4 on BPS Math Final	67%	46%
Social Competency	85% 3 or 4 in report card conduct grades	67%	46%

Kim was invited on two separate occasions to Boston Public Schools central office to present the Mather's model. Many administrators and other principals in the audience strongly advocated wider circulation of the Mather's MCAS-focused curriculum, SMART goals, and the student performance assessment system. The district was reluctant, however, to formally distribute Mather's innovation.

Nevertheless, Kim's highly systematic, goal-directed data feedback system had traction, and the results indicated that it was working. The Mather's MCAS tallies over time provided some evidence of the system's functioning, but the school's internal tracking of student performance lent even more substance to the argument that the school's efforts were paying off. School year 2000–2001 was obviously a critical test. Third graders of that year had started at the Mather when the SMART goal-setting process was first initiated. When the assessments came in June 2001, the school had chalked up some admirable results against demanding standards.

Comparing the achievement of students who were the beneficiaries of Mather's educational system for four years with those who had only spent a portion of that time at the school, the results were rather dramatic (see Table 2.2): 80 percent of the long-term students had achieved the demanding goal of Level 3 or 4 on MCAS Prelim, with comparable results in writing. These percentages were almost double those of students who had transferred to the Mather after kindergarten. Although the outcomes were slightly less dramatic, student achievement in math and social competency confirmed that the Mather had an integrated instructional system in which each grade level was building on the previous one to produce educated students who were able to score at Level 3 or 4.

Kim Looks Back

In February 2002, Kim decided that he had taken the Mather as far as he could. There were resources that had not been leveraged in the school, but, in Kim's opinion, it would take a new leader to capitalize on them. "I have brought the Mather as far as I can with my particular set of skills," he said. "A different principal with different strengths stands a better chance of taking the Mather to the next level with the continuing hard work of a fantastic staff and all of the expertise we've developed over the years."

Under Kim's fifteen-year leadership, the Mather had changed from a school with one of the most dismal academic records in Boston to one with a proven capacity to graduate students with Proficient (or better) academic performance. By 2001, the Mather had made the largest gain in total MCAS scores of any large-sized elementary school in the state. On average, 28 percent of Mather students scored Proficient or higher on the MCAS in ELA and 21 percent scored Proficient or higher in math. (See Tables 2.3 and 2.4.)

There had been deterioration in staff morale since 1997–1998, as captured by Kim's year-end questionnaires to the staff. The staff perceived that Kim's overall performance and his ability to "coalesce the staff as a team" had diminished. The teachers increasing negativity could, in part, be explained by a perceived deterioration in discipline over the same time period, for which they held Kim responsible. The Mather suspensions increased starting in academic year 2000–2001, the product of a few very troubled students.

In large measure, the disciplinary issue was a function of Kim's difficulty in finding a suitable replacement for two assistant principals who, for six years, had worked well with him in establishing and maintaining a well-ordered disciplinary policy. From 1999–2002, four candidates were less effective in maintaining discipline in the 600-plus student body. This frustrated Kim, who relied on his assistant principals to maintain the school's disciplinary policy while he worked to improve the school's instructional system.

Table 2.3   Grade 4 Mather ELA MCAS Scores Compared to Other Boston Schools

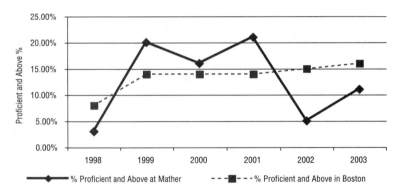

Source: www.doe.mass.edu

Table 2.4   Grade 4 Mather Math MCAS Scores Compared to Other Boston Schools

Source: www.doe.mass.edu

From Kim's view, the Mather had made substantial progress, and he was proud of the school's instructional system. He was deeply frustrated in his efforts, however, after having tried every possible option to make it work as he had envisioned. He lamented, "The highly-sophisticated, state-of-the-art, ready-to-fly 747 hadn't taken off." This, more than anything, prompted his decision to resign his principalship. He had tried his damnedest. Now it was someone else's turn to guide the Mather to takeoff.

He believed that the results were not better because the interim assessments were being used only in writing, not in the other content areas, and that even in writing they weren't being used frequently enough. Teachers were also not using the assessments to track their progress toward meeting their SMART goals.

He held himself responsible for the missed opportunity.

I didn't get the teams invested in looking at and caring about the data. I was the data guy, not them, and it simply wasn't first and foremost on their radar screens as they met. Each year I was so overwhelmed at the end of the year that I didn't crunch the numbers until the middle of the summer, so teams left in June without knowing whether they had hit their SMART goal. Not good! In writing, the one area in which we were using interim assessments and were looking at formative data in teams, we did a lousy job of presenting the interim data graphically. Our Excel spreadsheets were far too complex, took far too long to produce, and they didn't clearly show teachers, immediately after the assessment, the progress that had been made and the specific areas teachers needed to focus on.

Kim, in the end, could take pride in the enormous progress the Mather had made under his leadership, but he always strove for perfection, and thus his success was tinged with regret.

"I know we were ahead of our time and have a lot to be proud of, but I'm seriously frustrated that we didn't put it all together. I'm especially unhappy with my leadership style, not getting the teacher teams more invested in their data and the interim results. I did too much for them, and didn't push them hard enough."

Chapter 3

Muriel Leonard
and Robert Gould Shaw
Middle School
1994–1999

Can't Get Out Fast Enough

On the first day of school in September 1994, Muriel Leonard, the newly appointed principal of the Robert Gould Shaw Middle School, looked out her window at 1:50 P.M. onto a deserted parking lot. Confused, she turned to her secretary. "The teacher's parking lot is empty!" she exclaimed. "What's going on?" The secretary, unperturbed, glanced up at the clock. "Well, it's 1:50," she shrugged. "School's over at 1:35. The union contract says that teachers only have to stay fifteen minutes past closing."

Muriel could not believe it. "I thought I knew the ins and outs of the Teachers' Union contract," she said later, "but this was a first. I came from a school where the staff and I would sometimes go until 9 P.M. on a Friday evening!" The Shaw culture was totally new to her. How could teachers leave when students were still cruising the halls?

The Robert Gould Shaw Middle School, named after the Civil War commander of the historic African American 54th Massachusetts regiment, was located in the colonel's hometown, West Roxbury. Shaw, the heroic subject of both a large relief sculpture on the Boston Common and the 1989 movie *Glory*, symbolized the kind of leadership the Shaw Middle School's new principal, Muriel Leonard, would need to possess in order to turn the school around.

A Change-Maker

Muriel came to the Shaw as a designated school-turn-around artist, though she had only done it once before. Boston's newly appointed superintendent chose Muriel to lead the Shaw because she had spent four years transforming an apathetic school into a fully functioning elementary school at Boston's Trotter Elementary School. She managed to do so in such a way as to win the staff's affection and loyalty during a tumultuous transition.

With an educational and instructional background in speech and language pathology, Muriel had earned a reputation as a talented administrator in two previous assignments leading both a middle and high school. Her reputation as a hands-on teacher's teacher preceded her; she was known in the educational community as a principal who demanded excellence and was ready to provide support for anyone who aimed to reach her high bar. Always listening intently to others' stories, Muriel came across as empathetic and authentic. She was a formidable change-maker.

The school that Muriel Leonard took over in 1994 was in trouble, trouble that went beyond teachers' lack of commitment to after school work. The school was in chaos, and students were unruly. The year prior to Muriel's arrival, the Shaw was evaluated and deemed to be performing below standards. As a BPS-designated Intervention School, it was put on probationary status and slated to be dissolved.

Academically, there was solid evidence that the school was not adequately preparing its students. Each year, Shaw students fell further behind grade level. Scores on the district's norm-referenced MAT fell below the fiftieth percentile for two years running. The seventh grade reading and math scores were astoundingly lower than those of the sixth graders. Similarly, the eighth grade reading and math scores were lower than those of the seventh graders. The declining grade-level scores raised an extremely grave question: Was the Shaw actually effecting a regression in the skills and performance of its students?

The school would most likely have been closed had the school department not assigned to it a disproportionately large number of special education students. Eighty-four of the approximately 400 total students were assigned to substantially separate special-needs classrooms. Another forty-six students were "mainstreamed" into regular education classrooms but were determined to have special needs necessitating Individualized Education Plans (IEPs). Of the total school population, just over half of the students were black, with the other half fairly evenly divided among Hispanic and white students. Almost 90 percent of the Shaw's students were eligible for free or reduced-price lunches, and one-third received federal aid as Families with Dependent Children.

The majority of students attending the Shaw was bused in from all over Boston and had no connection to the local community. What had once been a strong neighborhood school was now without the support of a community. It was a school in chaos. Local stores were actually intimidated by the "imported" student population. They closed their doors between 1:35 and 2:00 P.M., when school let out, nervous about shoplifting and altercations on their properties.

"Lack of involvement was the norm for the teachers, parents, and community," Muriel explained. "After 2:00 P.M., teachers were gone, students were gone, and administrators, too, would leave when they could. There was a downward spiral of students not doing homework, teachers assigning less homework because students weren't doing it, and so on and so forth."

In her first year, Muriel gave high priority to providing a safe and stable environment and engaging the school community in the change effort. Her first step was to make sure that students came to class. "You will take attendance," she ordered teachers. "You will give tests, and you will patrol the halls."

Nevertheless, the absence of academic standards at the Shaw was dramatic. Early that first fall, Muriel received a call from an exasperated parent of a previous spring's graduate complaining that her daughter had been duped. Beaver Country Day, an elite suburban private school, had offered her daughter a high school scholarship on the basis of the girls' basketball prowess and straight-A average at the Shaw. They had rescinded the offer, however, in light of the girl's atrocious performance on the school's placement test. It was determined that she would not only have to repeat the eighth grade but portions of the seventh as well.

The incident prompted Muriel to discover that many of the Shaw's teachers gave grades based on student behavior rather than student performance. Students who were not discipline problems earned high marks. Muriel recognized that if problems of discipline were of top concern to teachers, these issues would need to be resolved before teachers could to move on to the "real" work of educating students and evaluating them fairly on the work they produced.

When it came to the English class with a reputation for "chewing up and spitting out substitutes, as if there were no tomorrow," Muriel decided it was in her best interest to teach that class herself. What she learned about her students from that experience was invaluable. One student had never seen the mark for a new paragraph before. ("What are these dollar signs on my paper?" he had asked.) Another student had filled Muriel in on the "schedule" the class had been used to: "Monday, we do spelling; Tuesday, vocabulary; Wednesday, spelling test; Thursday, vocabulary test; and Friday is a free day." "You can't ask us to do writing on our free day!" a student had protested as Muriel passed out a new writing assignment one Friday. "I'm changing that," Muriel had immediately replied. "This will help you to become a better writer."

One day, a first-year faculty member whom Muriel frequently counseled on her teaching, came to her at wit's end. Her class had organized against her and refused to complete their final project, confronting her with a dare: "You wouldn't fail all of us!" Muriel knew that Shaw parents had a history of calling city council members, or even state representatives, to have them intercede on their children's behalf. When it came to maintaining academic standards, however, Muriel would never tolerate strong-arming of this kind.

Students were ready for her when she strode into the room. "There are forty of us," they reminded her. "You can't possibly fail all of us. If you do, Mrs. Leonard, you're going to be in trouble." Muriel surveyed the room coolly. "Try me," she dared them. "Everyone who deserves an F is going to get one."

With no intention of letting them fail miserably, Muriel put together a daily afterschool support service that gave students the chance to revise their work and seek extra help if they needed it. After having given students every opportunity to succeed, Muriel was prepared to call their bluff—and they knew it. For the first time, when the grades went home, the phones remained silent.

Looking back, Muriel reflected on how she had changed the culture at the Shaw. Her message was,

> School is really a place where you come and do hard work. If you were not satisfied with whatever you produced the first time, there was always room to grow, and that went for teachers as well as students. I wanted this school to be recognized as a place where you do hard work and learn. The teachers had really gotten pulled into being satisfied. "Hey, I gave this assignment and half of them turned it in." Never mind what the students handed in was garbage, thank goodness they did it.

One of the most significant things we accomplished was a focus on developing an effort-based culture. We said to students, "If what you handed in wasn't good enough, this wasn't a comment on how good you are." We were saying, "We'll work with you to make sure you can do it."

Diffusing Standards

Muriel could not continue to be the sole bearer of standards; teachers had to take on the mission, too, but they would have to prove themselves first. During her first year, Muriel observed, coached, and assessed every one of Shaw's thirty-five teachers. Her approach differed from conventional supervising protocols. Rather than pigeonholing herself as a standards watchdog, she wanted teachers to be responsible for improving their own instructional practice.

She believed that every teacher knew whether or not they were delivering quality instruction to their students. Muriel saw her role as challenging teachers, not just evaluating them. "When I sit down and look them in the face, I say, 'Let's not have the administrator-teacher discussion. Let's be two adults talking here about whether you would send *your* child to your class, and are you preparing the night before the way you would want to be prepared if your child were there? Think about it: what should your child's teacher be doing the night before walking into the room?'" Some reacted cynically; some wanted to "wait and see." But a critical mass of teachers saw Muriel's approach as a welcome opportunity to explore and actualize their own dormant potential.

Muriel's initial invitations to teachers to redouble their efforts in order to bring high standards to their instruction were followed by a flurry of visits by her to classrooms to offer advice on how to improve teaching and learning. "When I first started to look at teachers in the classroom," Muriel commented, "it was clear some basic things weren't working, including basic classroom management issues. From there I looked for the learning opportunities teachers created for their students. This was relevant to their subject matter." She was not interested in seeing a lot of lecturing and note taking. "I wanted students involved in inquiry."

She wrote down reactions from the classroom visits and left feedback for teachers in their mailboxes. Sometimes reactions were positive, sometimes not. Muriel might jot down a request for a teacher to come to see her in her office to talk about observations she had made in the classroom. Or teachers might stop by her office of their own accord to address issues or concerns mentioned in her comments. Because teachers found typed comments intimidating—it reminded them of a formal evaluation—Muriel started writing on yellow notepaper instead. In the early years of her tenure, her "yellow papers" were a famous artifact of the culture she was creating—feared by some, coveted by others. All teachers knew that regardless of the particular feedback, this would not be the last they'd see of Muriel in their classrooms; she would be back.

When Muriel observed instruction that was below her standard, she gave teachers an opportunity to improve, and many did. But during her first two years, she identified six teachers out of a faculty of thirty-five who had been given "excellent" evaluations by the previous principal but whom Muriel repeatedly deemed "unsatisfactory." After extensive documentation, four left voluntarily, including one who agreed that his retirement was long overdue and another who even invited Muriel to his retirement party. Two teachers, however, "dug in their heels and stayed another two years before leaving, which was miserable for them and us." The Shaw's Boston Teachers Union representative protested the dismissals, taking their cases to the district despite Muriel's strong documentation.

Ultimately the openings allowed Muriel to recruit six new teachers vetted by a team of Shaw veterans. They brought needed expertise and experience to subject areas in which the Shaw was particularly lacking. All six agreed to Muriel's additional conditions of employment: demonstrating a willingness, even an eagerness, to become hearty collaborators and putting in extra effort well beyond the contracted hours.

Engaging the Faculty

By the end of her second year, Muriel had succeeded in offering faculty a credible vision of hope for the Shaw. When she asked them to answer a simple question—"What can you contribute to create more opportunity for our students?"—there was a positive response, even without a stipend to work the extra hours.

She invited everyone to lead after-hours nonacademic activities. The first month she didn't have many takers; by the end of her first year, however, fifteen teachers had begun to offer after-school activities and clubs.

"Can you do anything?" Muriel would appeal to the rest of the staff. "Yearbook, chess, something fun?" By the end of the second year, just about everybody in the school offered a recreational activity to students, with a commitment of at least an hour after school two days per week. Muriel had primed the pump for real change to follow at the Shaw. "We were becoming available to students," she recalled.

Muriel the Entrepreneur

The superintendent had charged Muriel with the task of turning the Shaw around but had left her on her own to garner the resources needed to do the job. She ended up taking advantage of the opportunity to apply for the school's membership in Boston's Plan for Excellence 21st Century Schools Cohort 1. Seventy-five percent of the faculty had to agree to participate, and the Shaw's faculty voted unanimously to begin the application process. The Shaw was selected for Cohort 1 on the basis of its potential for improvement. The $50,000 funding was contingent on the Shaw agreeing to implement the 21st Century Schools Six Essentials for Whole School Improvement. The Shaw, soon after its acceptance into the program, started working on the first two essentials: developing a schoolwide instructional focus and initiating a process of Looking at Student Work. The funding was used to hire a consultant to assist the school in raising the level of subject-area expertise as well as a facilitator to assist in knitting the school together through teaming.

Boston Public Schools' Six Essentials for Whole School Improvement

1. Use effective instructional practices and create a collaborative school climate to improve student learning.
2. Examine student work and data to drive instruction and professional development.
3. Invest in professional development to improve instruction.
4. Share leadership to sustain instructional improvement.
5. Focus resources to support instructional improvement and improved student learning.
6. Partner with families and community to support student learning.

Muriel succeeded in landing several other financial and academic resource supports as well. The Shaw qualified for a U.S. Department of
Education Chapter 1 grant, allowing for the hiring of additional staff. A
Harcourt grant brought in a math coach (at the time, the Shaw had only
one certified math teacher), and Muriel received faculty support to apply for inclusion in a middle school systemic change project sponsored
by the Massachusetts DOE Education Reform Restructuring Network
(ERRN), called the Carnegie Turning Points Initiative.

By engaging in the Turning Points program, Muriel and the Shaw
committed themselves to reforms that had proven records of positively influencing student achievement. Research from a number of Illinois
middle schools that had embraced and implemented the program demonstrated accelerated student achievement. Turning Points, not unlike
the 21st Century Schools, prescribed a change agenda. Both would provide valuable guidance in the Shaw's change efforts.

Turning Points Process for Change

1. **Develop a Common Base of Knowledge.** For schools to improve,
   members of the school community need to develop a common base
   of knowledge about the school change process, as well as research on
   learning, teaching, assessment, and restructuring. Study groups are an
   especially valuable way of accomplishing this goal.
2. **Strengthen Shared Decision Making.**
   - Create a coordinating committee for the school restructuring
     process. Ensure the committee has sufficient representation of the
     school community. The coordinating committee is a facilitative
     body, not a gatekeeping body.
   - The entire faculty becomes the decision making body for significant
     decisions to be made.
3. **Create a School Vision.** Develop a school vision statement, a set of
   guiding principles that is created by the entire school community and
   that reflects the ERRN program philosophy and principles. *At the heart
   of any school vision should be improving learning, teaching, and assessment
   so that all students achieve at high levels.*
4. **Take stock.** Gain an accurate picture of where the school currently stands
   using as much data as possible. This can include:
   - Staff, student, and parent surveys and/or interviews
   - Student work, including portfolios, exhibitions, and writing
   - Analyze the taking stock data, identifying major strengths and
     challenges.

(continued)

Turning Points Process for Change *(continued)*

5. **Use the Inquiry Process to Tackle Key Changes Areas.** Create 3–5 inquiry committees based on the major challenge areas identified by the taking stock results.
6. **Develop and Use a School Improvement Plan.** Effective school improvement plans are:
   • Driven by hard data that indicate a school's strengths and challenges;
   • Developed by school consensus, rather than by the principal or a committee.
7. **Continually Assess Progress.**
   • Develop authentic forms of assessment and implement them school wide in order to continually measure progress and shape the learning and teaching process.

Teams as Building Blocks for School Change

The Shaw that Muriel stepped into had minimal infrastructure. The Faculty Senate was dominated by high-seniority, pro-union teachers and had little representation by other constituents. The School Site Council was made up of parents and teachers who went through the motions of policymaking but who were relatively ineffective. There were grade-level teams, but only the sixth grade cluster had coalesced into a real decision-making body.

That team had warmed to Muriel's school change overtures and responded by peppering her with additional suggestions. Thinking that class periods were too short with five periods per day, the team suggested to Muriel that they try out a four-period schedule the next year. After the initial struggles with discipline issues were behind them, they wondered if maybe it wasn't time for teachers to stop patrolling the halls like prison guards and instead begin to engage in some productive work, like planning together.

Muriel could not have been more delighted with the latter recommendation and set about making a new schedule that would allow each grade-level cluster more common planning time to coordinate instruction. The sixth grade team's eagerness for collaboration fit right into Muriel's plans for change. Knowing that she could not turn the Shaw around all at once or by herself, Muriel saw teams as the building blocks of the change process. The Shaw, in Muriel's mind, would become a churning, self-governing beehive of interconnected teams, each one dedicated to some aspect of school improvement. Through team membership, each teacher would gain both a voice in the school and support for her own work. Eventually, teams, not Muriel, would be the keepers of the standards.

Unfortunately, not all of the clusters used their time as Muriel had intended. Instruction was not every team's main focus. Some spent their planning period complaining about students; others met with parents. Muriel could not let their misuse of time continue. "Planning means *planning*," she told them. "If you need assistance, ask me and I'll help you. But please use the time for talking about teaching." Muriel assigned a topic to be discussed during the planning time. Teachers were charged with defining high common standards.

Developing Common Standards by Looking at Student Work

A process specified as a condition of participation in the 21st Century Schools, Looking at Student Work, brought teachers together during their common planning time to work on the Shaw's schoolwide instructional focus: establishing common standards for assessing students' written work. For the first time, Shaw teachers would jointly calibrate standards for students' written performance. Though common planning time had brought teachers together before, instructional issues had been discussed only incidentally.

Now, teachers were required to use student work to develop common assessments, with the goal of raising the level of student performance. Grade-level clusters of teachers developed rubrics for scoring student writing—not just in English courses but in any course where written work was required. The aim was for the writing rubrics—which would address style, mechanics, voice, content, and organization, each on a four-point scale—to reach across all subject areas.

The initial work was done in grade-level and SPED department clusters. Teachers asked each other, "What are we expecting from students? What makes this content a 4 versus a 3 versus a 2?" Unfortunately, this segregated means of discussion led to nonalignment across rubrics. What constituted a 3 in one cluster was very different from what it meant in another. Muriel noted that the standards of her bilingual teachers were higher than anyone else's. Sixth grade teachers were more demanding than those in eighth grade. It became apparent that the Shaw would need to look at the rubrics subject-by-subject to see where the discrepancies were across the grade levels. When they had agreed on a final product, they posted them in large format on the walls of each classroom—ensuring that expectations were clear across all subject areas and at every grade level.

The Spirit of Inquiry and the Turning Points Survey Feedback

The Turning Points feedback survey program required the annual administration of a 200-item questionnaire to students and teachers at the Shaw. The questionnaire surveyed student attitudes, teacher attitudes, and comparisons between the two. The results were returned in the form of user-friendly bar charts. (For examples, see Tables 3.3 and 3.4.) Teachers studying the data were asked to look at themselves through a powerful mirror that reflected how their own attitudes and beliefs affected the students and the Shaw as a functioning school. This annual survey and feedback session would prove to be significant in helping the staff confront what was blocking the Shaw's progress and endeavor do something about it.

When data from the first administration came back, Muriel gathered the staff together to interpret the scores. She had the survey results displayed on large sheets of butcher paper that she'd pinned around the unused classroom that served as her office. Small cohorts of teachers dotted the room, some animated by what they saw. "Look here—the little sweethearts don't think we talk to each other enough!" one teacher exclaimed. Some groups huddled together, murmuring disparagingly about the scene, but a critical mass of positive attitudes energized the process and enabled teachers to move forward and begin to identify problem areas for the school. A new teacher and enthusiastic participant in the process recalled, "I don't want to say that everyone was ready to join forces and was on the same wavelength, because that was certainly not the case. It was the mix of teachers that Muriel had brought in, plus some old-timers, that jumped onboard. We were the ones that were doing most of the noticing."

Through that year's first survey review and the iterations of the process that followed each year, the Shaw was able to develop an annual, comprehensive school plan complete with committee assignments to address the various aspects of the work. In any one year, the faculty would identify five to six challenges and form a committee around each for targeted school improvement. One teacher noted,

> We actually changed our committees based on the data from the survey. It was pivotal in terms of how we focused for the next year, because the data would come out right towards the end of the year. We'd analyze it and say, "Where have we come from? Where are we going? What are we missing? We'd look at our [teacher] data and compare it with the students. We had teachers from different grade levels and different disciplines, and it gave us a chance to get together and decide what we wanted to do. We would take our recommendations back to the Leadership Team and the full faculty for their reactions.

For example, early on the faculty decided that the repertoire of assessing students was quite limited. A committee was formed to develop options. Muriel recalled how "the committee visited schools that were experimenting with portfolios and student exhibitions. Within three years, the Shaw teachers had developed a portfolio and exhibition presentation that was a requirement for grade eight promotion." She thought that "the beauty of the Turning Points data was that it was a staff report. They were looking at what they, themselves, had said. It confirmed the outcomes that we were seeing in our student achievement data. Now we could talk about the disconnect between instruction and outcome data."

Analysis of the survey results set the yearly agenda for the Shaw's move forward. Six committees convened to deal with the issues highlighted by the data analysis. By collectively examining the survey data, proposing hypotheses about the meaning of the patterns in the data, and then making an implementation plan, Muriel trained the staff to identify and solve schoolwide problems and simultaneously reinforced a spirit of inquiry in the Shaw's culture.

The Tipping Point

It would be difficult, if not impossible, to pinpoint exactly *when* between Muriel's second and third years the cultural changes at the Shaw reached a tipping point. Muriel's work to develop a community of practice began to have enormous implications for student learning. Teachers were no longer isolated in their classrooms; they teamed with their colleagues to improve instruction. An effort-based culture where second and third tries were always available was the norm for teachers and students alike. An intellectual vacuum had been filled with consultants who were sharing their expertise with the teacher corps. Instructional performance standards had been lifted to new heights, exceeding those of the district.

Muriel demanded high performance from her new hires, and these candidates were eager to embrace the challenge. She was not shy about the criteria for being a teacher at the Shaw: one had to be damned competent and willing to work long hours. For teachers who had the talent and desire to be first-rate, who wanted to be engaged in a vibrant learning community, and who delighted in being challenged to operate at the limit of their capacities, the Shaw was the place to be.

Striving for Excellence Tuesdays

By identifying an improvement agenda and agreeing to work toward it, Shaw's faculty, perhaps inadvertently, signed themselves up for more work outside of school hours. They had learned that 21st Century Schools required two hours per month after school to follow the standards of Looking at Student Work. The majority of the faculty agreed to spend every other Tuesday meeting in committee to discuss agreed-on challenge areas. These additional four hours were in addition to other after-school commitments already assumed by the Shaw staff. If this wasn't enough, the BPS superintendent had negotiated a new teacher contract that required teachers to participate in eighteen hours of after-school professional development each year. Many BPS teachers had balked and refused to take on the added districtwide time requirements. Most of Boston's other 21st Century Schools did not demand the extra two hours per month.

At the Shaw, this time was christened Striving for Excellence Tuesdays, and close to 90 percent of the faculty volunteered to log in more than forty hours over the course of the school year on after-school professional development. Tuesdays were not just given to committee work. On the last Tuesday of each month, the meeting time was extended by yet another hour, and the entire faculty came together to hear each workgroup report on its progress and challenges it had encountered. Minutes from the weekly meetings were distributed to the larger group, and discussions frequently culminated in the identification of additional areas for Shaw improvement. Striving for Excellence Tuesdays came to symbolize the faculty's commitment to making the Shaw a better school.

Teams, Teams, and More Teams

Muriel had made good on her promise to use teams as the building blocks of the new Shaw. Not only had she provided a rationale for coalescing cluster teams around Looking at Student Work, she had brought teachers together to work on broader school issues. Only a minority of teachers chafed at these intrusions into their nonclassroom time. A growing number of teachers welcomed the opportunity to participate in the broader range of school activities. One new teacher recruited by Muriel said the multiple-team structure encouraged communication, teamwork, and creativity across disciplines:

> There were two different ways of getting us to work together and open the doors of our classrooms, if you will. The clusters could be as closed as an individual teacher in her own classroom because it was only a group of five, and if you stayed only with that group of five, your perspective was limited—you couldn't see the big picture of the school. The committees allowed you to interact with maybe a special education teacher or a bilingual teacher, or, if you were a dance person, like me, you'd be able to interact with a language arts teacher. It opened you up and forced you to think outside of your own discipline. . . . Organizationally, committees were probably one of the strongest aspects of the school because they really did get people to collaborate.

Cluster teams and improvement committees were making some headway at the Shaw, but the school still appeared disorganized. Muriel was doing her best to hold the center together, but with so much of the decision making decentralized to teams, her capacity to provide realistic direction was challenged. She wondered if she could impose a more sustainable organizational structure without dampening the creative energy.

Muriel was more than ready to implement an organizational design that would diffuse decision-making power throughout the school's network of teams. In receiving support from the Carnegie Turning Points Initiative, the Shaw had been "strongly encouraged" to implement a representative governance network and create a vision statement that represented the school's core values. None of the other twenty-three 21st Century Schools in Boston took on such an ambitious, full-scale revamping of their organizational infrastructure. The Shaw's undertaking, however tumultuous, was subsequently justified by the voice and power the new structure gave to the whole school's staff.

At the time, Muriel had an operational Faculty Senate and School Site Council and a series of grade-level clusters. What the Shaw lacked was a Leadership Team that would represent the entire school in each subject area at each grade level. With such a team in place, ad hoc committees could research topics of concern and make recommendations to the Leadership Team. The team would in turn take its recommendations to the full faculty for a vote.

Muriel's intentions were good, but implementation of the new plan was chaotic. Staff had no prior experience with school democracy and found it confusing that Muriel was imposing another set of teams; no one really understood the role the new team would serve in contrast to the existing teams. To clarify responsibilities, Muriel encouraged the development of a flowchart that outlined who made what decisions (see Table 3.1).

The flowchart provided a model for all to see. It set clear decision-making expectations and made explicit the relationship between the Shaw and the Shaw's stakeholders. Over time, the document became established enough to prompt challenges when teachers believed decision making was not in accord with the agreed-on governance structure. In Muriel's mind, "This tool established an accountability system that significantly decreased the level of subjectivity for everyone."

Muriel would need teacher volunteers to put in thirty extra hours per year to serve on the leadership team. Despite the fact that faculty members were now putting in an average of forty extra hours per year, five teachers came forward and were willing to put in the total of seventy extra hours by serving on the Leadership Team.

With the new self-governance structure in place, Muriel was now sharing much of her decision-making power. She was more than willing to do this, but she still proceeded cautiously. Although she could "pretty much live with" what the Leadership Team and faculty decided, she had enough influence that if she felt strongly about something, she could still get the faculty to go along with her ideas. Her institutional power, wisdom, and expertise still allowed her an influence that could be used when the situation demanded it.

Table 3.1 Governance and Decision Making Flow Chart

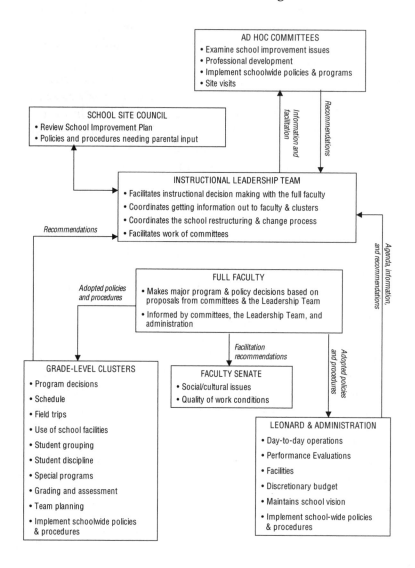

The Shaw Vision

With the newly minted decision-making structure came a test: constructing a consensually agreed-on vision as prescribed by the Turning Points model. Muriel was skeptical about whether or not the vision would have any intrinsic influence after it was developed, but she strongly supported any process that would encourage collaboration among Shaw's teachers, students, parents, and administrators.

The Leadership Team engaged the school community in the process. A teacher-led Parental Involvement Committee was created to engage parents. The School to Career Committee, also led by faculty, had meetings with representatives of the Shaw's business and nonprofit community partners to ask for their input. Extensive efforts were made to include student feedback as well. Students were surveyed and asked such questions as, "What would your dream school be like?" and "What would you do to make the Shaw School better?"

After a laborious process that included drafting, debating, and redrafting, a vision emerged—one that upheld Muriel's core belief that all students should be academically challenged in a supportive community.

The Shaw Vision

The Shaw Middle School community believes that each student should be academically challenged in a safe, supportive, and nurturing environment. At our school, staff and parents collaborate to improve learning for each and every student. The Shaw Middle School provides:

- A school culture that promotes respect by and for all students, teachers, and parents, and in which students are expected and taught to become responsible members of our school community and society
- A curriculum based on high standards and meaningful instruction rooted in comprehensive and diverse methods of teaching which enable all students to compete in the world
- An environment for adults and children which demonstrates sharing, innovation, risk-taking, and professionalism

---

Intellectually, Muriel knew that if the Shaw was to sustain and build on her efforts, the school needed the staff's pluralistic involvement. Emotionally, Muriel found it difficult to participate in the tedious give-and-take of the participatory process. However, nothing superseded her conviction that the Shaw had to have multiple forums in place through which every voice could be heard.

Building Instructional Capacity: Teachers Taking Responsibility

Establishing a school governance structure was a necessary step, but it was merely a warm-up for the marathon yet to come. Muriel thought it was relatively easy to prescribe who decided what and when and to even hammer out a common purpose. But the Shaw was not just a governing body; it was a school, and its end product needed to be highly educated students. To attain that goal, high-quality instruction would make all the difference.

Muriel had started her assault on poor teaching early in her tenure. Her presence in classrooms was constant, with each visit reliably followed by written feedback. The work she had asked teachers to do in developing a set of clear standards, in the form of the writing rubrics, was a giant leap for the Shaw, both in terms of teacher collaboration and in stating and raising student expectations.

In her third year, Muriel wanted the teachers to take a deep look at their students' academic performance. The district superintendent had just replaced the relatively obsolete, norm-referenced MAT with the Stanford 9, another norm-referenced assessment, but which had four categories to measure degrees of proficiency. The Shaw's Stanford 9 scores were the perfect vehicle with which to present teachers a preview of the work ahead of them. Stanford 9 scores calibrated the degree to which student performance fell below or above grade level.

Muriel's orchestration of the Stanford 9 data feedback session was a freewheeling, informal session, but one with all the drama Muriel intended. She had the scores presented on large paper posters mounted on the walls of a classroom. Teachers were invited to walk around and call out what they noticed in the data. A studied silence followed the invitation, but then the room began to buzz as teachers tried to comprehend what the data was telling them. One teacher noted, "This wasn't a blame session. We were trying to figure out what the scores meant."

Muriel facilitated this initial session, identifying where work was needed. Thereafter, committees were charged with further analysis and asked to bring back recommendations for curricular redirection and instructional change. The staff review of the Stanford 9 data was a first step for teachers in owning and taking responsibility for their students' academic performance. However, the data they were examining were not exactly current. Stanford 9 tests had been administered in the spring, but scores were not returned until the following fall. "My eighth graders didn't get a very high score on the open response section in math," one teacher reflected. "But by the time we had looked at the data, they had graduated!"

Timeliness of data was critical. But while it may have been too late to remedy skill deficits at the individual student level, there was certainly plenty of room to make more general assumptions regarding areas that needed attention. In retrospect, Muriel was orchestrating what proved to be a tectonic shift in how teachers assessed their own work: looking at student performance data to evaluate their own instructional effectiveness.

Digesting the implications of the Stanford 9 data was just the beginning for the Shaw's teachers. More feedback was on the way, and it would be more personal and more intimidating. It was one thing to inspect curriculum and abstract methodology; it was another to confront one's own attitudes and practices.

Do You Believe In Me?

The implications drawn from the 1996–1997 Turning Points data took a while to sink in; but when they did, it was distressing. Students, particularly those eligible for free or reduced-price lunch, calculated their chances of graduating from high school as greater than the perception of their teachers' expectations. This made it clear that students believed Shaw teachers, on average, had less confidence in their students' capabilities than the students did themselves. Moreover, these students saw their parents as having higher academic expectations of them than did either their teachers or they themselves. (See Table 3.2.)

Table 3.2 Turning Points Survey from Shaw Students on Government Supported Free or Reduced-Price Lunch

	Definitely or probably will	Might	Probably or definitely won't
Self: Do you think you will graduate from high school?	80%	13%	7%
Parents: Do your parents/guardians think that you will graduate from high school?	83%	9%	8%
Teachers: Do your teachers think that you will graduate from high school?	67%	20%	13%

Source: Turning Points Survey © 1997, Robert D. Felner, PhD, National Center on Public Education and Social Policy

The Consultancy Protocols: Professionals Critiquing Professionals

Muriel realized the Turning Points survey and Stanford 9 feedback served, and would continue to serve, as critical tools for calibrating progress in student outcomes and could serve as means for improving instruction. But she was reminded daily that there was an enormous gulf between teachers making meaning from data and doing something about it. How could she help them modify their instructional practices for improved student learning?

Muriel chose to initiate a lesson plan improvement process using a Consultancy Protocol model; teachers would have to critique each other's unit guides and ask one another to account for achieving the unit's objectives. It was an enormous and unprecedented psychological leap for teachers. Within any profession, it is unusual for colleagues to critique one another; it is even more unlikely that colleagues would be asked to make a public commitment to incorporate outcomes of the session into their professional work.

Consultancy Protocols

Step 1. The presenter gives a quick overview of her work.

Step 2. The consultancy group asks clarifying questions of the presenter.

Step 3. The group then asks probing questions of the presenter—these questions should be worded so that they help the presenter clarify and expand his/her thinking.

Step 4. The group then talks with each other about the work and issues presented.

Step 5. The presenter then responds to what he/she heard.

Step 6. The facilitator leads a brief conversation about the group's observations of the process.

Note: Developed as part of the Coalition of Essential Schools' National Re-Learning Faculty Program and further adapted and revised as part of work of the Annenberg Institute's National School Reform Faculty Project

---

The beginning sessions were strained. Nervous, sometimes even perspiring, teachers would tentatively explain the prepared written outline of their lesson plan to a group of same-subject peers, usually six to eight other teachers. Behaving as if the presenter wasn't present, the assembled faculty would dissect the lesson plan to draw out what they felt was useful and what they thought should be changed or eliminated. "This is what you need to do in order to move forward," the facilitating teacher would summarize.

The process was difficult for all involved. "They were putting their souls on the line," Muriel noted. "They hadn't done that before, but they got used to it. We began to see some payoffs in the classrooms. We had to learn as a faculty to step back and give some candid feedback to each other." The rising level of comfort the Shaw staff felt in giving honest feedback was obvious. "They got to the point where they could say, 'Hey, this lesson really stinks; that's why your students are doing so poorly.' Or, 'You didn't prepare adequately; this is what you need to do now.'"

"They were tough on each other," Muriel reflected. "I had a teacher that really made the team very angry. He came in 'half-stepping' with his plan. They let him know that they resented his slipshod presentation and poor preparation for his students." Subsequently, the teacher came to Muriel to admit what had happened at the Consultancy. "My team really laid me out on the assignment that I planned to give to my students," he told her. "They're upset with me. I feel even more embarrassed than I would be if you had sat down and told me the same thing. I'll never make that mistake again." Before his next presentation, he ran his ideas and unit plan past Muriel to make sure they would meet the approval of his peers.

Roundtables

By the 1997–1998 school year, Muriel had a significant number of teachers who really knew their work in the classroom. Not every teacher at the Shaw was highly competent, but there was a critical mass of teachers confident enough to push back at Muriel. They had had their fill of coaching from outside experts and were ready to showcase and learn from the Shaw's in-house talent. They approached Muriel to ask, "What about the expertise of our own faculty?"

In response, Muriel organized a roundtable forum for good classroom practices. "Has anyone something to share?" she asked. She invited those who felt they had something relevant to share, based on goals they'd previously outlined, to tell the group about their successes. Sometimes a teacher would report that she had benefited from the expertise of a colleague who had been helpful in a particular area. Other times Muriel would bring up something she had observed during her classroom visits.

With the help of a committee, Muriel began to select four or five people to share at each roundtable. She would name a topic, such as "conferring," and teachers had the opportunity to sign up if they had something to share about it. One person would lead the discussion, but everyone who attended the session would bring something to share. The model allowed for recognition and appreciation of the work that teachers were doing. It also left people with a plan for alternatives that they could implement the following day in class. Teachers were comforted by the fact that there were several other colleagues in the building who would be working with the same techniques. They could observe in one another's classrooms and share ideas back and forth.

Shaw teachers were beginning to assist and support each other, as well as candidly critique each other's educational products (e.g., lesson plans). They had started to reduce their dependence on Muriel and, thus, lay the groundwork for a self-sustaining improvement process.

Engaging Families

When Muriel arrived at the Shaw in 1994, the number of involved parents could be counted on one hand. Early on, she had sent out the word that parents were partners in the education of their children. But despite her efforts, in 1997 the school's Leadership Team, motivated by results from the Turning Points Survey, identified parental involvement as a continued area of challenge for the school.

The faculty went to work. Teachers received lists of fifteen to twenty homes to call and make personal solicitations for parental attendance at Shaw events and to engage parents in helping their children with their schoolwork; they also established a daily homework hotline and sent home a weekly parent newsletter. The Shaw developed a home-school compact that evolved from a series of focus groups with teachers and parents. The compact, signed by all students, parents, and teachers, made explicit the responsibilities of each party and symbolized joint commitment to students' education.

The number of events for families focusing on student work increased as well. The long-standing curriculum night in October and the traditional winter holiday social event were supplemented with an evening science fair, an exhibition of student work, and an evening performance. Shaw students, trained and certified as babysitters, provided childcare for parents bringing younger siblings to these events. Staff found that not only were these new events well attended by parents, they were also largely enjoyable experiences for the faculty.

At the suggestion of the School parent council, parent workshops were held at the Dudley branch of the Boston Public Library, a location more accessible than the school for many families. The well-attended workshops focused on the MCAS and Boston's new learning standards. Additionally, at the request of the parent council, teachers prepared curriculum overviews of topics to be covered in the upcoming quarter, along with major assignments, tests, and standards against which students would be measured.

The Alternative to a "Get By" Mentality

In the academic year 1997–1998, Muriel faced a problem. She was learning that her school could have the best instructional system; but unless students had incentive, internally and externally driven, high student performance could not be attained. Traditionally, parents' expectations motivated students, but this was only beginning to occur at the Shaw. It could take years for parent involvement to truly take hold, and Muriel didn't have the luxury of time. She needed to act now; to wait was to sacrifice the education of Shaw's current students.

When she thought about the problem of student motivation, she couldn't help but think that there was something wrong with the way the Shaw, and the district in general, structured its reward system for students. The hell-raisers were having all the fun, she realized. The kids who ran around skipping classes all the time were the ones who were having the best time at school. It wasn't right.

Muriel found that students were more motivated to get Ds than As. The school system, with the Shaw as an unintentional coconspirator, was training students to "just get by," rather than encouraging them to aspire to higher achievement. They were reinforcing the lowest expectations: "If you don't do this, you won't pass." By sending warning notices to parents of students in danger of failing, the school and the district focused on failure. Muriel felt it was time to turn the attention toward a positive outcome; sending home progress reports might encourage students to try for the honor roll.

The Shaw's Leadership Team developed a Comprehensive School Plan that argued that the system was out of whack. It pointed out that the Stanford 9 scores were structured in terms of numbers of students performing at the lowest level rather than the students performing at higher levels. The Leadership Team argued that both the Boston Public Schools and the Shaw had not nurtured a culture of academic achievement but, rather, advocated a mentality of "getting by."

One solution was to embrace and implement a program that had originated at the district level but had withered in the absence of follow-through. In each subject area, for each marking term, students would be required to complete a culminating piece of work, a Milestone Product, which would meet at least a Level 2 standard as defined by the Stanford 9's four-point scoring system (4 being the highest and 1, the lowest).

Students who failed to complete or adequately revise a Milestone Product would not only receive a failing grade for that marking term but also fail for the year, unless the Product was satisfactorily completed. Some Products were course requirements, proposed by the district; but most were designed by teachers. No longer would it be sufficient for

Shaw students to just pass a course; they would now have to demonstrate their capacity to produce a Product of superior merit.

What Is a Milestone Product?

These products are significant projects or pieces of work that require students to think and use ideas, information, and skills in creative ways to demonstrate what they know and are able to do. Milestone products must be completed to a satisfactory level of quality in order for students to receive a passing grade for the term. At the R. G. Shaw Middle School, each student is required to complete a milestone product in each subject each marking term. All four products must be completed in order for a student to pass a given course for the year. Students are given feedback from teachers on the work they have done and have multiple opportunities to revise, expand, and improve their work.

For the teachers, it meant a great deal of planning before the semester started. They were accountable for giving students, at the beginning of a class, examples of a Milestone Product to serve as a model of what was expected, as well as the knowledge base required to complete it. Shaw teachers had to be much more intentional in setting explicit academic goals for their students, keeping them motivated throughout and teaching to a standard that would allow students to achieve an exemplary Milestone Product.

Milestone Products alone, however, would not motivate students to aim for higher achievement. The assignment provided an avenue of expression for those who wanted to work, but to other, less motivated students, it was just another burden. The Shaw had another idea about providing incentives for academic achievement for students who were not intrinsically motivated to get their work done.

The New Report Card

The Shaw drew up an Eligibility List, which, for qualifying students, would serve as a ticket to all cherished extracurricular activities, such as the dance program, chess club, or basketball games. The idea came from a group of teachers responding to Muriel's challenge to build the school of their dreams. They wanted a robust program of extracurricular activities for their students, but the competition for students' attention and time posed a problem. One teacher's prized basketball star could be held hostage, not allowed to play in the big game because he had not completed his Milestone Product for another teacher. A dancer for a major student production could be denied rehearsal time by a math teacher who said that the student "was acting badly in my class, so he can't perform."

New Eligibility Rules for Extracurricular Activities and Athletic Programs

As part of our effort to boost student learning at the Shaw School, we have adopted a new and higher standard for student participants in after-school activities. Here are some highlights. A more complete statement of the new policy is included in the Parent Handbook, which will be distributed at the October Open House. Students must:

- Attend school regularly
- Exert maximum effort in class work
- Be familiar with and follow school rules
- Make up tests or products missed due to absence within two days
- Maintain a C (or 2.0) average for all subjects
- Have no more than two warning notices during a single marking term
- Have no more than one failing report card grade
- Not fail the same subject more than one marking term
- Not be suspended more than one time during the school year.

This policy is stricter than required by the Boston Public Schools and represents just one part of our plans to become one of the best middle schools in the city academically. Our motto is NO SURPRISES. NO EXCUSES.

Out of this conflict, the Eligibility List emerged. For interschool athletics, the public schools already had an eligibility policy: in order to practice and play, students had to maintain at least an overall C average. In addition to the fact that the policy did not cover nonathletic extracurricular activities, there were too many loopholes; with an F in one class and an A in another, a student could still be eligible for participation.

The Shaw's Eligibility List, in combination with the Milestone Products, was just the right remedy for raising the school's academic standards. Together, the two programs provided incentives for students to strive to meet standards. Eligibility came from passing every course, which meant delivering, at a minimum, a Level 2 quality of work. Contingent on this achievement was participation in *any* Shaw extracurricular activity.

Such a radical change in school policy demanded vetting by the Shaw's major constituencies. The Leadership Team pointed out that the Boston Public Schools' performance on the Stanford 9 tended to differ from the norm-based tests, such as the MAT, *not* by a greater number of students performing at the lowest level but, rather, by a lack of students performing at the highest level. Using their argument that neither BPS nor the Shaw had cultivated a culture of academic achievement and had instead encouraged a mentality of "getting by," the Leadership Team argued its case to the Boston Public School Committee, which agreed. The proposal was debated by the Shaw's parent council. Parents signed off and agreed that they would support the initiative.

Teachers expressed a concern that the policies might make students feel pressured, but the Shaw was overwhelmed with enthusiastic student response to the new policies. The Eligibility List was published every four weeks in the parent newsletter. The timing of its publication was not arbitrary. There was considerable discussion about the mindset and development of preadolescents. The consensus was that the traditional eight-week semester was too long a period to provide an opportunity to "fix" what needed to be fixed in order to become eligible. Muriel, speaking for a majority of the teachers, advocated for more frequent publications. "If we wait eight to nine weeks," she argued, "many kids will give up, figuring, 'Forget it, I messed up. I can't get back on track,' thus beginning that downward spiral." Muriel's argument won out, and the four-week Eligibility List cycles were introduced.

Publication of the Eligibility List was a big deal. Students, discovering their names in print, felt proud of the acknowledgment of their work and academic status. Many circled their names and carried the list around in their pockets. The list soon superseded report cards as a status symbol of accomplishment. Muriel was succeeding in creating a new cultural artifact that visually symbolized hard work and academic achievement. "I can't begin to tell you the impact," Muriel observed. "We discovered that students didn't necessarily know what they got on their report cards, but they knew if they were on the Eligibility List."

Besides serving as a gatekeeper for maintaining academic standards, Muriel was pleased to see that the list reinforced her idea that at the Shaw "you work hard, and if you didn't get it the first time, you try it a second time, and a third—whatever it takes to meet the standard."

On one occasion, students came to Muriel to ask, "Mrs. Leonard, what's he gonna do? We need him on the basketball team. Could you help us out?" The inquiry began a very worthwhile discussion with the student in question. "Where is the problem?" Muriel asked him. "Where'd you break down here? What is it that you didn't do?" Suddenly, students had to identify and figure out what sorts of strategies to use to get themselves back on track. It was up to them to determine whether or not it might be worth it to spend more time with the math teacher, who typically had a room full of students after school who came for extra help. Students began to understand that they had "blown it" but that they would have another opportunity to get themselves out of the hole.

Crash on the Horizon

In the spring of 1998, the Shaw was in a self-congratulatory mood. The system of Milestone Products leading to Eligibility Lists made perfect sense to everyone—at first. One parent, representing the beliefs of many, told Muriel, "God bless you for making sure she does her work." But it soon became clear that the Shaw was rapidly accumulating a backlog of students who had not successfully completed their Milestone Products. Teachers had failed to allow adequate time for students to revise the Products, precipitating a large number of first-term Incompletes. Parents, who had initially endorsed the idea of Milestone Products, panicked and deluged the school with phone calls.

Consistent with Muriel's self-reported modus operandi of "ready, shoot, aim," the implications of the new assessments had not been fully realized. The Shaw was a school that, in 1998, had 87 percent of its students scoring in the Warning category (Level 1) on the math portion of the MCAS. The introduction of Milestone Products anticipated the whole school reaching Level 2 by the end of the term. Muriel's unwavering optimism that the school and its students would rise to the occasion had infected the Leadership Team.

With 350 students, each in seven classes for four marking periods, there were twenty-eight Milestone Products per student. After the April vacation, it became clear that they would need to institute summer school for at least 200 students. Since there was no available financial support from the district, the Shaw had to self-fund a summer school program and mobilize the faculty to staff it. Muriel was able to do it.

As time went on, students fell into two groups. A few students gave up, thinking, "I've blown it. I'll never be able to dig myself out of this hole." The majority of students, however, began to modify their behavior and take advantage of the supports that the school was now providing. Muriel recalls,

> We really struggled with making sure that we had plenty of entrance and exit opportunities for students, because we didn't want them to fall into the first group. We agreed that we had to have attainable goals that would contribute to a climate where students really improved their performance. At midterm, we gave students the opportunity to get on the Eligibility List. We have a nine-week recording period, so roughly every four weeks students had an opportunity to get back on, and those who had not met the standards in the first four weeks could rise to the occasion with a little more effort.

During the second year of the Milestone Products, it became clear that the new practices demanded different teacher attitudes. The faculty needed to support students "where they were" to give students a chance to understand that their first attempt wasn't their last. Students were not expected to write perfectly the first time they picked up their pencil. They needed to be taught to revise and improve their work. Muriel wanted teachers to understand that they should not spoon-feed their students but, instead, should nudge them to improve their work by first looking at it with them together and then engaging in a conversation about what needed to be done to make it better.

Shaw Improving

The Shaw was definitely showing progress. Teachers were teaching to higher standards, and a communal sense of hopefulness had blossomed. Most teachers were staying late, two or three hours past dismissal, some of them three or four afternoons per week. Extra effort on the part of both staff and students was becoming the norm.

In the Turning Points survey, teachers reported assigning more homework. The percentage of teachers who reported assigning less than an hour of homework per week dropped dramatically to 5 percent from 20 percent the previous year. Not only were students assigned more homework, but they were actually completing more assignments compared with the year before. And significant increases in the percentage of completed homework were reported by students who qualified for free and reduced-price lunch. Students were spending more time on their homework; over half devoted at least an hour per night to their studies. Students in all three grades were reading more books, both for school assignments and independently.

Although teachers had initially expressed concern about "pressuring" the children, student reports in the Turning Points survey calmed this fear. Despite the increased work load, students reported a drop in both teacher expectations that were "too high" and in teachers "assigning too much homework." Reports on the Turning Points survey also indicated a distinct reduction in the incidence of problematic behavior. Fewer students were rated as presenting "serious or very serious problems."

There was yet another piece of good news from the 1999 Turning Points data. Students now perceived their teachers as more confident that their students would graduate from high school. From the 1996–1997 school year to the 1998–1999 school year, there was a 6 percent gain in reported teacher confidence, paralleled by a 9 percent increase in the students' own beliefs in their potential for graduation.

Muriel could see the real payoffs of her assault on teachers barricading themselves in their classrooms, dishing out worksheets for rote memorization, and delivering mind-numbing "chalk and talk" lectures. By the teachers' own self-reports on the Turning Points survey, their classrooms were now wholly different places. The Shaw engaged students in intellectual challenges that demanded not only problem *solving* but a better understanding of what the problem was. (See Table 3.3).

Isolated teachers alone in their classrooms were now gone from the Shaw. Teachers were out and about, mixing it up with each other as well as with parents. By their own self-reports, these transactions were increasingly educational and primarily involved the coordination of curriculum assignments and assessments. Muriel's efforts to decentralize instructional decision making and structure integrative forums for debate and mutual support were pushing the Shaw ahead. Parents, teachers, and students were coming together to reach their educational goals. (See Table 3.4.)

Table 3.3 Teacher Perceptions of Their Own Classroom Practices—Question: How often, on average, do the following take place in your classroom?

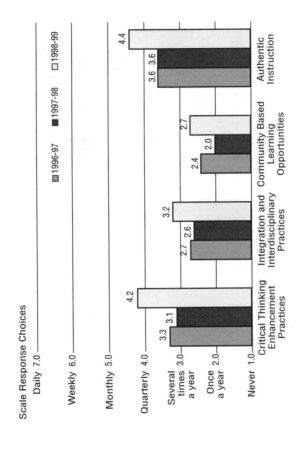

Source: Turning Points Survey © 1997, Robert D. Felner, PhD, National Center on Public Education and Social Policy

Table 3.4 Teacher Perceptions of Team Practices—Question: How often, on average, does your interdisciplinary team or grade level team do each of the following?

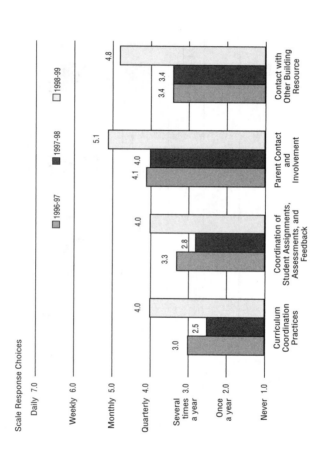

Source: Turning Points Survey © *1997*, Robert D. Felner, PhD, National Center on Public Education and Social Policy

Massachusetts' MCAS performance tests were first administered in 1998, three years into Muriel's tenure at the Shaw and one year prior to her departure. The trajectory of the Shaw's scores in both math and English language arts during her principalship and subsequent to it evidenced a school that was gaining traction in educating its students. The record was still poor, but the direction was decidedly positive. (See Tables 3.5 and 3.6.)

Table 3.5 Grade 8 Shaw ELA MCAS Scores Compared to Other Boston Schools

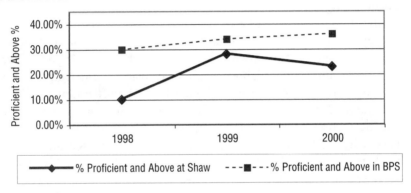

Source: www.doe.mass.edu

Table 3.6 Grade 8 Shaw Math MCAS Scores Compared to Other Boston Schools

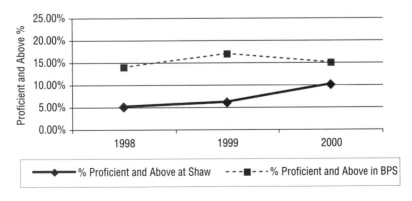

Source: www.doe.mass.edu

Epilogue

In June 1999, Boston's superintendent of schools, Dr. Thomas Payzant, in recognizing Muriel Leonard's competence as a principal leader in light of her accomplishments at the Shaw, promoted her to Cluster Leader of eleven schools and reassigned her to one of them, the McCormack Middle School. Muriel fought to stay at the Shaw, asking if the composition of the cluster could be reshuffled. But Payzant believed that the geographic integrity of the cluster was too important and denied Muriel's request to stay at the Shaw. She began her term at the McCormick the following fall.

The Shaw greatly missed Muriel. Her departure, after only five years as principal, was premature, and the school was not ready for her to leave. Despite a great deal of progress, she was still the animating force necessary to maintain the high expectations of teacher leadership and improved student performance. Teachers who had truly internalized Muriel's methods were able to move forward on their own, but those who had merely been going through the motions came to a grinding halt after her departure. The problems were exacerbated by the mass exodus of new teachers that Muriel had brought in who chose to leave when she did.

The positive outcomes of Muriel's leadership endured for two years after her time at the Shaw. The subsequent administration could not maintain the momentum. The critical elements that Muriel had created were there, but teachers, students, and staff were not prepared to bear the burden of self-sufficiency and could not sustain the model without her. The Shaw limped along with dismal student performance until 2003, when the middle school was closed.

Chapter 4

Michael Fung
and Charlestown High School
1997–2007

When teachers at Charlestown High closed their classrooms at the end of the 1997 school year, they knew they would return in the fall to a new headmaster. Angela O'Neil's resignation was public knowledge. But it was unclear whether Walter Restuccia or Betina Jones, the two assistant headmasters under O'Neil, would be named her successor. Both had made it through the elaborate screening process of teachers, parents, and community members, as had two other former headmasters who were less likely candidates.

It would be the superintendent's choice; and with that choice, he would not just select a new headmaster but symbolically endorse both a leadership style and a school-based constituency. Restuccia, passed over in previous attempts to land the top job, represented the pragmatic, steady hand and carried with him a loyal following of Charlestown senior faculty. Jones, O'Neil's hand-picked assistant, was still an unknown, but had proven to be a clear advocate both for students and higher instructional standards. The newer, younger Charlestown teachers were rooting for her.

At the end of the summer, the staff received a letter from their new headmaster. To their surprise, it didn't come from Restuccia, Jones, or the long-shot candidates. It was a letter from Michael Fung.

August 25, 1997

Dear Colleagues:

As the new headmaster of Charlestown High, I wish to welcome you back for the new academic year. I look forward to working with all of you to make Charlestown High the leading district high school.

Charlestown High must change. Like *all other* BPS district high schools, we did very poorly in the Stanford 9. In math, for instance, almost nine out of ten students were performing at Level I, showing little mastery of the subject. In SAT I, the mean scores for Charlestown High students last year were 334 (Verbal) and 432 (Math), while the national mean scores were 505 and 511, respectively. It was once said that insanity is to do the same thing over and over again the same old way and expect a different result. If we want a far better result, if we are to succeed in our endeavor, we must rethink our purpose and our way of educating our students.

We are here to educate—to teach *and* to nurture. The time is now to reinvent a new Charlestown High, a high school with graduates that are *educated*: literate, with a sense of the past, a vision for the future, an appreciation of the arts, a feeling for the suffering of the less fortunate, a commitment to decency and honesty, and a willingness to serve the community.

After the announcement of my appointment, one of my first tasks was to examine the then current master schedule. That schedule required three additional positions. As I was not prepared to request those additional positions, I worked with John Smith to create a new master schedule and introduce a new organizational structure. The attached one-page flyer summarizes the key features of this new structure. It also provides you with the latest room assignments.

For the moment, this is my plan and my vision. Within a few weeks, I hope this will become *our* plan and *our shared* vision. In time, for Charlestown High to be an exemplary high school that staff, students, parents and the community can be proud of, this has to be *your* plan and *your* vision. I look forward to those days.

Sincerely yours,

Michael Fung

Michael's letter hit Charlestown with tsunami force. Even in his introductory message, the new headmaster had managed to alarm senior faculty by disregarding both the sanctity of their classrooms and their denial that Stanford 9 testing was a valid measure. Michael had succeeded in putting Charlestown teachers on notice that their cozy, comfortable, unexamined way of life was in serious jeopardy.

Charlestown High

Charlestown, one of Boston's oldest public high schools, is located in a traditionally white, working-class neighborhood. A large percentage of the faculty was approaching retirement, and while there was strength in the teachers' extensive experience, wave after wave of failed reform efforts, a stream of changing superintendents, cynical assignment practices, and broken promises had left their mark on the school. Energy and hope were scarce.

The 1,000-member student body at Charlestown in the 1990s was a rich cultural and racial mix: 44 percent of students were African American, 26 percent Asian, 15 percent Hispanic, and 14 percent white, the majority of which were bused to and from the school. In 1996, slightly more than half of Charlestown students participated in regular education classes, while the rest were participants in the Chinese bilingual, Spanish bilingual, and special education programs. Because of the lower student-teacher ratio in these areas, fewer than half of Charlestown's teachers taught in regular education classes. The school was informally divided into four relatively separate subcultures that paralleled the four different programs. The majority of staff had many years of seniority; of the eighty-five teachers, fifty-seven had more than twenty-four years of service.

Angela O'Neil, like her predecessors, had failed to successfully address the school's many problems: discipline, attendance, and some of the poorest achievement scores in the city. Under her tentative leadership, the faculty maintained a lumbering, dutiful pace. They were not necessarily resisting her efforts to engage them; they were just not responding to her suggestions for change.

O'Neil was messianic in her belief that bottom-up management was intrinsic to successfully sustaining school change. She firmly believed that restructuring into clusters was the secret to overcoming the anonymity that plagued urban schools. Reluctant to put any actual mandates in place, she found herself lost in a quagmire of languishing committees and lackadaisical staff. During her short tenure at Charlestown High, despite her good intentions and progressive agenda, little progress was made. She resigned after a year and a half, realizing "how much more work needed to be done, and how difficult it was going to be without being able to bring at least some new faces and some new ideas into the building."

The New Headmaster

Michael Fung was not a typical public school administrator. For years
he had balanced two worlds as educator and entrepreneur. He was passionate about educating children and setting them on the road to a better life. Despite the availability of other choices, his personal and cultural
values placed public education and service in the Boston Public Schools
at the center of his life.

Michael had been a teacher in Boston for eight years, and a highly regarded principal of the Taft Middle School for ten years, where he had
mentored at least nine administrators who had gone on to become leaders in Boston schools. Given his distinguished administrative record, a
previous superintendent had chosen Michael to be his deputy superintendent, responsible for all of the district's secondary schools. In a subsequent superintendent's reorganization plan, Michael was made lead
technology administrator. When that position was abandoned in a cost-
cutting move, Michael returned to the classroom, where he had begun
his career.

When talking about his influences, Michael is quick to explain that
many of his most powerful lessons did not come out of his master's degree from MIT but instead from the challenges of starting a business.
Michael had joined family members in creating a technology consulting
firm. Struggling to respond to entrepreneurial challenges, he had discovered some answers in business literature and, in doing so, noted clear
parallels between issues faced by businesses and those faced by schools.
An avid reader of the *Harvard Business Review*, Michael strongly believed
that schools needed to adopt management practices, such as reengineer-
ing (the concept of redesigning an organization starting from a clean
slate) and performance measurement. He would come to recommend
and periodically distribute articles about management to the Charlestown faculty.

Negotiating a Headmastership

Taking a page from a how-to-succeed-in-business book, Michael saw
a unique opportunity to redeem his well-honed educational leadership
credentials and land the Charlestown headmastership.

The district Cluster Leader was responsible for overseeing Charlestown High and presenting candidates to the superintendent. Michael, on hearing of Angela O'Neil's resignation, lobbied the district Cluster Leader to nominate him as a more viable option than the four candidates presented by the screening committee. The choice between Restuccia and Jones pitted Charlestown's older and younger factions against one another; selecting one over the other risked further dividing the already estranged school. The superintendent, apparently captivated by Michael's aspirations for radically changing the failing Charlestown High, made Michael the permanent headmaster, not subject to the screening process. Michael said he made a deal with the superintendent to serve at the latter's will; like his counterparts in industry, if he did not produce, he was out. The superintendent offered to reassign Restuccia and Jones to start Michael with a clean administrative slate, but Michael refused, saying, "I always work with whoever is there." He felt that he was quite capable of managing Restuccia's and Jones's disappointment and potential resentment. He knew, however, that "if I alienate one of them, I lose about 40 percent of my staff; if I alienated two of them, I might as well give up."

Back to School

Michael dominated the first faculty meeting that fall. He explained the rationale for his Charlestown vision, first introduced to staff in his August letter. He wanted a specific measurable goal for the school and had already decided that that goal would be raising student test scores on the Stanford 9. Michael believed that in the first year, 50 percent of Charlestown students could reach Level 2. The goal was improbable to anyone studying Charlestown students' previous scores. The previous year, 90 percent of students scored at Level 1, the lowest of the four score levels on the Stanford 9. A Level 1 score indicated that the students had "little, if any, mastery" of fundamental skills in the tested subject area. Michael viewed Level 2, denoting partial mastery of fundamental skills, as the minimum acceptable performance for the majority of Charlestown students. Seemingly stunned by Michael's decisiveness, or unable to appreciate his argument, no one objected to the goal or asked for further clarification.

Michael Fung's Rationale for His Charlestown Vision

- A study of local high schools showed that 15 to 16 percent of students failed each subject.
- Only 2 to 3 percent of these failures resulted from poor performance; 12 to 13 percent were due to attendance (students who miss 15 percent of classes fail the term).
- Teachers often gave a low pass (D) to keep students out of their classes the following year. If D's and F's were combined, then 25 percent of students failed due to performance.
- If two out of every three of the 75 percent of the students who passed each year scored at Level 2 on the Stanford 9, then the school's scores would improve by 40 percent.
- Thus, 50 percent of students will reach Level 2 on the Stanford 9 in a year.

Michael lost no time in beginning structural changes at Charlestown. He decided to reconfigure the school into six units, and he welcomed teachers back with a new master schedule requiring approximately 40 percent of them to move to new classrooms. Many of those teachers had taught in the same classroom for over twenty years.

Saving the major structural decisions for himself, Michael was more than happy to let others decide on the details. He believed that implementation and day-to-day operational decisions should be handled by those closest to the issues. In the days prior to the teachers' return, he had delegated the task of assigning teachers to units and selecting unit leaders to the assistant headmasters, who knew and had worked with the staff.

Each unit consisted of 120 to 150 students and would be run by a small group of teachers who would enjoy considerable freedom in creating their own educational policies. The goal of the units, which combined regular, bilingual, and special education students and teachers, was to create "six independent mini-schools, each with a shared vision and common purpose." To facilitate coordination among unit teachers, Michael grouped unit classrooms and teacher offices together in the same physical area of the building and provided unit teachers with common planning time.

Preoccupied with packing and moving, teachers paid little attention to the actual reorganization plan, not realizing the dramatic effect it would have on their professional lives. It was the fall of 1997, and Michael was taking the first steps to implement small learning communities, an organizational concept that would not appear on the local, or national, secondary school reform scene for another five years. Michael's thinking was way ahead of his time. But was the Charlestown staff ready for his vision?

Acting as a self-described "dictator," Michael justified his swift, unilateral action: "I knew that I had to create a sense of urgency. It is undemocratic to begin with, but once people accept it, they will find they'll have more power over subsequent decisions and more independence."

Among most teachers, there was little overt resistance; some vented their frustration privately. One teacher noted, "I was mad. We got a brief, unwelcoming letter from the School Department telling us when to arrive, and when we showed up, we had to start changing rooms. This school has five floors and only one elevator." Another said, "We could have been better prepared. We were asked to buy into this plan without really understanding why. I think we all have a better [sense of it] now, but at the time, he only briefly touched on the goals."

A handful of teachers openly resisted what they perceived as an incursion on their implicit entitlements and were prepared to fight. Mrs. Jordan, a longtime leader of one of the grade nine clusters, announced at the first day's staff meeting that she had been in her classroom and office for twenty-five years and would move "over my dead body." Walter Restuccia, the assistant headmaster, leaned over to Michael and whispered, "Look, I told you this could happen. A lot of unhappy people have been by to talk to me. I've known them for years and have never seen them this bent out of shape." Michael appeared unperturbed. He let the comments pass in the meeting, but afterward he moved swiftly, arranging to meet with Mrs. Jordan in private.

Behind closed doors, Michael, demonstrating his mastery of political persuasion, was matter of fact, explaining that he could not let Mrs. Jordan damage his credibility and authority by refusing to move—especially as she was an influential person in the school, a real "opinion leader." He asked point-blank for her resignation as unit leader if she could not support him. If she agreed to move, he would work with her in other areas and do what he could to ease the transition for her. He very much wanted her support. Mrs. Jordan reluctantly agreed.

Michael reflected on his strategy.

> You really have to think strategically. Changing the classrooms is a very good example. Wanting groups of students together so they can work as a team with a teacher was the reason. But there was another reason. I wanted to see if I asked the teachers to do something that was unpleasant, I wanted to see how much resistance there would be, and that would dictate my strategy. I wanted to see who will openly oppose me. When I found out it was just Mrs. Jordan, I said to myself, "This is a piece of cake. I can now impose the new master schedule on the staff."
>
> By [reassigning thirty classroom teachers], I sent a message: "I'm coming in to change the school." Obviously, there was a rationale for changing those classrooms. But the important thing is that when you go into a situation, you have to send a strong message. It's very logical to move fast when you are first appointed—when you're first appointed, you are the strongest.
>
> . . . The other thing is that minor change will result in as much resistance as major change. That's one thing that if you read all the literature on change, that's generally what they say. If you make minor changes, there will be people who resist it. If you make major changes, there will be people who resist it. You may as well do the major change.
>
> I think as a [principal] leader the most important thing you can do is show people what direction you are going. That's what the master schedule and the reorganizational structure are. I know that doesn't deal with instruction which I have to deal with, but at least you show people what direction you are going, and probably that's the most important thing. So the master schedule and the restructuring are very much like creating a constitution. Within the constitution we all work a certain way. It provides the latitude for instruction.

When the units were assigned, one of the grade nine clusters from the previous year, headed by Mrs. Jordan, continued intact with special education and bilingual additions. In contrast, teaching groups in other units were working together for the first time. Each unit was comprised of six to eight teachers from Group I subjects (math, English, social studies, and sciences) and was headed by a unit leader with administrative experience. Restuccia and Jones each headed a unit, as did two former deans of discipline and two department heads.

Michael gave authority for most decisions to the units and unit leaders. The unit system was designed to give teachers the flexibility to experiment with new ways to achieve educational goals. In October, the teachers in one unit set aside Monday, the day with lowest attendance, to experiment with block scheduling. Students were split between math and English during a double period. This gave teachers more time to reinforce basic concepts and provide enrichment activities.

Michael also provided each unit with $5,000 to spend any way teachers desired— no strings attached or additional approvals required. "I gave each unit $5,000, and one group of teachers wanted to buy a Xerox machine," Michael recalled. "I said, 'This is nuts. This is crazy. This is not what I intended for you to do. But since I promised you, go ahead.' Within three weeks, they got their machine. They said, 'Wow! That has never happened to us. A headmaster keeps his promise and was able to deliver.' So this is something that you have to do along the way to create credibility."

Consistent with Michael's view that operational issues, particularly those around discipline, needed to be handled more effectively, the unit system gave teachers new resources and authority to deal with discipline. Now that teachers within a unit all had the same students, they could work together to solve problems with particular students and implement solutions in a consistent manner. For example, when a disruptive ninth grade student continued to wear a Walkman in class, the teachers in his unit met with his mother during their common planning time to discuss ways to handle the problem.

Michael strongly supported teachers' decisions in discipline cases and discouraged second-guessing by other staff. When Michael was approached by staff and teachers who were critical of a "harsh" disciplinary decision from another unit, he refused to intervene, saying, "I gave them the authority. The kid was their student, they knew him best, and they did what they thought was right."

Straightening out discipline issues was not proving simple, however. Each change incurred a new round of discussions and brought new problems to light. Unit leaders, the majority of whom seemed to spend the larger portion of their day on discipline issues, were frustrated with the system of sending students to detention in the auditorium after school. The student behavior reports required for detention lacked a section asking teachers to outline what they had already done to try to solve the problem. This encouraged teachers to think of detention as a first resort. Several unit heads felt that teachers were avoiding their discipline responsibilities by simply sending students to detention, and all agreed that most problems were best handled in the classroom by teachers themselves, with support from the unit leader when necessary. Unit leaders proposed that only when intervention within the unit failed should teachers look beyond the unit for solutions to discipline problems. Teacher reaction to the proposal was mixed.

Michael said that he would not make the final call and told the unit leaders that they had the power to decide this issue. If they wanted the discipline policy changed, it certainly could be. The burden was now on the units to reach consensus, and it was up to the unit leaders to take on the job of justifying an unpopular change and urging recalcitrant teachers along.

Despite Michael's idyllic vision of self-contained mini-schools, his restructured unit system did not seem to be producing the successful, self-sufficient bodies he envisioned. Discipline issues, lack of cohesion within units, minimal support for unit leaders, and confusion and chaos surrounding the new system hindered the units' success. In addition, teachers felt Michael intentionally manufactured "competition" among units, discouraging collaboration and sharing of best practices and encouraging a culture of secrecy and isolation.

Midterm Reflection

The holiday break gave Michael Fung a chance to take stock of his progress. As the end of the second marking period approached, he had to admit that he had mixed results. He had accomplished some important goals: The school was restructured—a task that had thwarted two previous headmasters—and he was on speaking terms with all of the staff. Even Mrs. Jordan, after discovering that her unit and staff really did have *more* freedom, was succumbing to his tireless outreach; the week before, she had even sought him out for advice.

Michael's early intervention was not limited to restructuring. He ordered and made safe the school's hallways and public areas. Previously, many of the upper floors of the sixties-era open plan were not safe, and false fire alarms were a common occurrence that disrupted classes and the school's overall decorum. In response, Michael implemented a variety of stringent, remedial policies. He rescheduled classes to minimize the number of students in hallways at any one time. Class attendance was carefully monitored, and no one was allowed to exit during scheduled class time. Michael personally monitored lunchroom behavior, establishing a policy of no standing except to enter, find a table, or exit. Fire alarm vandalism was eliminated with severe prosecution of perpetrators.

Now there was evidence that the teachers were coming around and were more accepting of the change. The physical reorganization of classrooms, though perhaps not propelling teachers into instantly cohesive clusters, did make it easier for teachers to discuss common students and speak with parents together. One teacher noted, "We can be more on top of the kids because we know them, we know who should be out of class and who shouldn't. Last year, you'd see kids in the hall and you didn't know why they were there. The halls are a lot quieter this year—it's less disruptive." Students seemed to have the opportunity to get to know their teachers better and now had the freedom to go to their teachers or unit leader, all of whom had the authority to address many of their concerns, instead of going to the school office.

The overall atmosphere of the school had improved. In spite of this, problems remained. Michael knew the hardest part of the change effort was still ahead, and he needed the support of the faculty to make progress. In February, they would vote on issues critical to the next stage of restructuring.

He felt that the structure of the units was working but that they were not having the impact on instruction that he had hoped. Few teachers had been persuaded to adopt different, more effective instructional practices. When he had entered the school, he had seen only one teacher who regularly used a cooperative, project-based learning approach. Now there were three or four who did. He wryly noted, "At this rate, it will only take me ten years or so to change the habits of my eighty-plus faculty members."

Michael could not wait for the Class of 2008, not with more than 200 graduating students each year unable to demonstrate eleventh grade math skills. A 10 percent improvement every year would only add up to twenty students next year. He needed to find a way to reach his staff, push instruction to the forefront, and maintain continued momentum with his structural changes.

The Teachers' February Vote

Michael walked through the halls of Charlestown High on a gray day in early February 1998. Looking at the bright Chinese New Year banners posted on the walls, with gold characters proclaiming "good luck" and "great fortune," he hoped that it was a fortuitous sign that the vote was coming just as the New Year was starting. Perhaps it would bring better fortune for him and for Charlestown High.

Michael certainly felt he could use luck now. On February 13, the faculty would vote on yet another school reorganization plan, first presented to them in November. The reorganization was important, but perhaps even more significant to Michael was the provision that would allow him to open-post for five new positions. If the faculty granted him this authority, this would be just the beginning. He would be able to make significant, long-term changes in the faculty, bringing in new blood to replace veteran teachers less interested in following his lead.

Michael's newest reorganization plan called for a two-tiered structure, with a lower school and an upper school. The lower school, made up of ninth and tenth grades, would focus on providing students with a strong foundation in the major subjects of math, English, social studies, and sciences. The lower school would be divided into four units, similar in structure to the units he had put in place that fall.

The upper school, made up of eleventh and twelfth graders, would be structured into "Pathways," with curriculum in career fields such as communications technology, advertising, desktop and web-page publishing, and finance and economics. In a memo to the faculty, Michael wrote that these Pathways would "provide students with the opportunity for hands-on, project- and portfolio-based investigative education." This would help students use learning techniques that were more relevant to the working world as well as link content knowledge to career fields.

Michael tried to make the plan as clear and complete as he could. He discussed the school system's long-term plans and showed how Charlestown's plan would fit in. He told teachers that if they had questions they should ask; no question was unworthy. He encouraged the units to discuss the plan and said he would welcome their input or questions. He made it clear, however, that *he* would make the large-scale decisions. He would rely on faculty and staff to work out the details and help bring the plan to life. His ideas were a broad-brush sketch; the faculty would turn these ideas into a working school.

February 13: The Results

The day before the vote, February 12, Michael sat uncharacteristically silent through a two-hour faculty meeting in which the school's union representative delivered a bitter harangue directed at Michael, accusing him of vastly overstepping his authority. With the call for open-posting five positions, she felt Michael was poised to render the Boston Teachers Union powerless. Michael, confident and calm, told her at the end of the meeting, "I think you have great ideas, but let's see what the faculty thinks is a good idea tomorrow."

Few staff could disagree with the reorganization. It was imbued with a rationale that they were hard-pressed to make serious arguments against; however, the five open-posted positions were raising serious concerns. There was no precedent for the Boston Teachers Union to allow such latitude. The basis of the union contract was to protect seniority in positions. If Michael were allowed to hire at will, the union would be severely undermined.

Michael chose a high-risk strategy. He had never heard of a headmaster being granted the authority to open-post for so many positions, but he had to follow his instincts. If the school was to make breakthrough gains, it could not keep "shoe-horning" people into positions for which they were marginally qualified. Explaining this to his faculty, he implored them to trust his experience and judgment. This vote would be a clear referendum on his leadership thus far.

The staff and administration at Charlestown High woke up on the morning of February 13, 1998, unaware that the day would symbolize a watershed moment in the school's history. On that day, the faculty would ceremoniously surrender their allegiance to Michael Fung, and he would capture the school. He had led the school for only five months.

Michael had delivered a swift, preemptive strike with his letter to the faculty in August, and his subsequent master schedule had reorganized the faculty into six units, giving them a degree of autonomy they had never experienced before. On February 13, the faculty was unprepared for Michael's brand of power politics. Fung, the organizational master, outmaneuvered them and left them with little choice but to give him the vote he so desperately wanted. Whether or not they agreed with him, there was no question that Michael certainly now had their attention, as well as their respect.

"The way I approach change is to try to get as many people on board the train as possible and then the train will leave the station. I will try to make the train go eighty miles per hour, and if you try to jump off, you will get hurt."

Michael grinned at his assistant headmasters as they walked into his office. "No one will even believe it. Complete approval for the plan and five open-postings. No one has pulled this off before. That's a real mandate."

The faculty, in giving Michael their vote, humiliated the union representative, who resigned the following year, writing to her union leadership that the teachers at Charlestown had essentially given up on their own union.

Already in the Bag

The vote had been overwhelmingly in Michael's favor, 67 to 11; more than 85 percent of the faculty had agreed to the reorganization plan, and more than 72 percent to the open-postings. Michael confided that he had been rather surprised at the margin but not the outcome. He lamented, "It was probably only a few hard-line unionists who opposed me."

He had not left the outcome of the vote to chance, however; he had been busy individually targeting key players at Charlestown. From day one, he had made an arrangement with Walter Restuccia: Walter's freedom to carry on as he always had in exchange for his loyalty to Michael. Michael instinctively knew Betina Jones was not given to playing politics; he could count on her loyalty simply because he was the headmaster. Mrs. Jordan's allegiance had been secured the first day of school when he put her position as unit leader on the line. Other informal leaders, such as long-serving varsity coaches, were reminded, not too subtly, that their added pay for extracurricular activities was at the discretion of the headmaster.

Prior to the vote, Michael framed the choice to the school's opinion leaders, most of whom had secured special financial extras from previous headmasters: "Look, I'm trying to reform the school for the kids. All I ask is that you give me a chance to hire five new teachers. If you won't allow me to do it, you are basically picking a fight with me, and I'll accept the fight and I'll change all of the positions. Think about that. You lose, and that means the faculty loses." He told them he didn't care who was responsible, "but if the faculty works against me, I'm going to give those positions to someone else, and I don't care who gets them. You want to fight it that way; I'll fight it that way."

The faculty decided it wasn't worth fighting. Michael had his own idea as to why this was the case. "The teachers know that [at that time] I have probably dismissed more tenured teachers than anyone else in the school system. So there's that factor," he posited. "What you need is to have the illusion that you are the strongest; to have the illusion that you have the support from the superintendent, the support from other people. It may not be real. I know that I need to have the support of the faculty. If somebody challenged me I would be in trouble."

Bursting with Pride

Michael could not contain his pride over his success and had to let the superintendent know what he had accomplished in such a short period of time. He knew, "If you don't show some improvement in your first year, you're in trouble." So, in an April 13, 1998, memorandum to the superintendent, with the subject heading "Self-evaluation," Michael highlighted the 85.9 percent victory of the reorganization and his new capacity to open-post five new positions. In the letter, he boasted that he had accomplished four of the five goals he had set for himself in assuming the leadership of Charlestown:

1. Win the trust and the support of the faculty, both administrators and teachers.

2. Create a sense of urgency and send a strong message that, to improve student achievement, Charlestown must change.

3. As a part of the budget process for FY99, create a new academic structure that addresses various internal and external demands and expectations.

4. Develop a new master schedule for FY99 that allows teachers to work as teams with a shared vision and common purpose.

Notice of Michael's four achievements reached a wider audience. One of the featured columnists for the *Boston Globe* ran an op-ed piece recognizing the forward-looking Michael Fung, who had restructured Charlestown into smaller units "without one additional dollar or one additional teacher."

In his memo to the superintendent, Michael went on to admit that he "had not been completely successful in accomplishing [his] fifth goal, persuading teachers to adapt a more relevant and effective instructional practice." Closing his memo, he set out three major goals to be completed by the end of the academic year:

1. Prepare students for the standardized tests (Stanford 9 and MCAS) and ensure that more than 90 percent would take the tests.
2. Seek funding and external resources to support the development of new instructional practices.
3. Build a technology infrastructure in support of restructuring and establish better procedures to improve the operations of the school (addressing chronic absence and tardiness, cutting of classes, and other disciplinary issues).

Michael's prompt for this latter goal came straight from Charlestown's data; the school had the highest dropout rate in the district.

The Money Flows In

Angela O'Neil had brought some significant foundation support to Charlestown, but when Michael mounted a major fundraising effort, his business and technology background clearly wielded a major influence. The Treffler Foundation promised $50,000; NEC and Cetrix both chose Charlestown as a technology demonstration school and installed network servers and software worth about $30,000; Cisco selected Charlestown for a $14,000 hardware gift. The largest and most influential support came from the international management consulting firm Bain & Company, which Michael had courted for three months, trumpeting at every opportunity his successful restructuring of the school. His presentations were cloaked in business terminology and packaged in PowerPoint slides.

In May 1998, with the celebration of Bain's twenty-fifth anniversary, the firm's managing director presented Michael with an offer of 20,000 hours per year for three years of pro bono consulting for Charlestown High School. Michael calculated the gift in terms of teachers' overtime salary of $30 per hour and arrived at an estimated value of $750,000 of free consulting service each year for three years. If the actual hourly rate of Bain Consultants was used, the gift was astronomic.

Michael wasted no time in utilizing Bain's largess. He had the company develop a model of project-based learning to supplement his initiative to change the teaching practices of Charlestown's faculty.

The Failure of Project-Based Learning

Emboldened by his successes in reorganization and garnering external support, Michael was at last ready to tackle Charlestown's instruction. The school's pathetic test scores signaled that something was seriously amiss in the classroom. Michael had an answer: project-based learning. He could personally attest to its effectiveness. Two years earlier, banished to another of Boston's high schools as a classroom teacher, Michael, by his own account, had had enormous success with eleventh graders training themselves to master Microsoft's PowerPoint software in the service of presenting their life stories. Michael was not alone in his belief that project-based learning would be key in revamping Charlestown's instruction. In a speech made a month earlier on structural reform, the superintendent had called for an increased emphasis on project-based pedagogy.

In the spring of 1998, Michael invited the entire Charlestown faculty to attend, at his expense, a month-long summer workshop on project-based learning. Forty percent of his faculty took him up on the offer, and Charlestown had more staff in attendance than the entire BPS district combined. By the following fall, however, follow-through of the new pedagogy was lacking. Some teachers told Michael, "Ok, if you want us to do project-based learning, we'll do it." Others simply couldn't warm to the approach. They complained, "The kids are so noisy; I can't take it anymore," and pleaded to be allowed to return to their old ways. In any case, the effort proved short-lived. As far as Michael could determine, of the thirty-one teachers who attended in the summer, only three or four made any attempt to incorporate project-based methodologies into their teaching.

The failure of Charlestown's veteran teacher core to embrace project-based learning was a defining moment for Michael and the school. Disturbed by their lack of response, he gave up on most of the veteran teachers. Michael would not allow them to be a part of his equation to transform Charlestown High.

In a June 1999 report to the superintendent, in which Michael laid out his change strategy for Charlestown, he wrote, "I plan to aggressively recruit an energetic, committed, highly-skilled new teacher force. . . . There is no point in telling veteran teachers that what they have been doing for the past twenty-five years is all wrong. In fact, one can argue that most veteran teachers, indeed, believe that what they have been doing in the classroom is fine. Otherwise, they would not have survived during all those years."

His blanket dismissal of veteran teachers was in part a consequence of his impatience with basic supervision and evaluation. By his own account, sorting good apples from bad was not his strength—unless the apple was grossly rotten, and then he could be unrelenting. Michael prided himself on flunking the district's required coaching program for administrators, John Saphier's *The Skillful Teacher*. He wrote performance evaluations rarely, and only when prompted by the need to dismiss a teacher. Instead, he delegated the task to other administrators. Michael could recognize skillful teaching and gaps in instruction, but he was reluctant to engage in the interpersonal give-and-take that inevitably arose when delivering feedback. He did not have the interpersonal dexterity to sort through the veteran teacher cadre, resurrecting the talented ones who were willing to improve and letting go of those beyond his redemption. Save for a very small number who exhibited exceptional teaching skills, the great majority of veteran teachers were allowed to continue their work, essentially "shelved" for the remainder of their careers and isolated from the mainstream of Michael's change efforts. Their lackluster performance and the absence of any engagement with the school was a reflection of the instructional limbo to which they had been relegated.

A New Goal

In 1998–1999, just a year after his arrival, energized by several new faculty members and a major redistribution of staff resources, Michael set about charging Charlestown with a new mission. Because of his unorthodox change strategy, he knew he must demonstrate unquestionable performance results. His timing was strategic. Boston's superintendent had made no secret that he was committed to student performance results, and potential success could now be captured by a new state-mandated, high-stakes student performance assessment that every tenth grader would be required to pass in order to graduate, the MCAS. This would become Michael's new goal for Charlestown. It was a clear, measurable marker toward which Michael would focus the school's efforts and turn it upside down to achieve. To consistently and continually improve tenth grade MCAS scores would become Michael's obsession, and thereby Charlestown's, for the next eight years. It would drive how resources were allocated within the school, how teachers and units were assessed, and how Charlestown's success was measured against Boston's other nonexam high schools. The tenth grade MCAS scores would be Michael's measure of success in presenting evidence of his leadership to the superintendent.

Determined to use every resource at his disposal to improve Charlestown's MCAS scores, Michael began using the consulting hours awarded by Bain & Company. Using highly sophisticated analytic techniques to deduce how Charlestown students could be trained to improve their MCAS scores, Bain crunched every student response and drafted a remedial protocol for the next set of tenth graders. Unheard of in 1998, the analysis demonstrated an unprecedented degree of sophistication in both interpreting MCAS scores and presenting student performance as feedback data to improve subsequent performance and align curriculum with state standards. Charlestown was one of the first, if not the very first school, to perform this type of disaggregation.

Anything that was not making a direct contribution to the improvement of tenth grade MCAS scores would be cast aside. Inherently, this meant a dangerous flipside to an otherwise worthy goal of improving student scores: What is there left to do in eleventh and twelfth grades after students have passed the MCAS? Does preparation for and passing of the MCAS account for all that high schoolers should know and be able to do? And would English language learners and special education students be penalized by this single-minded goal to improve school MCAS averages?

Michael did not waste time pondering these larger questions; instead, he went on a shopping spree for new teaching faculty. The primary search was for those who could teach ninth and tenth grade mathematics and English language arts, the two subject areas tested on the tenth grade MCAS.

Unit Reorganization

Prior to Michael's arrival, Charlestown had failed its freshmen miserably. Only the truly self-motivated had been able to piece together a high school education of any substance. Now the organizational structure to focus attention on ninth and tenth grade preparation was in place. Michael had inherited some semblance of ninth grade units, and his first year's reorganization laid the groundwork for a more broad-based use of self-contained units schoolwide. Working from his first year's plans, Michael had only to rethink who would comprise each unit. Whereas the original plan had intended units to include a sampling of all four grade levels, the new units would be broken into lower and upper school units—ninth and tenth graders in one and eleventh and twelfth graders in the other.

Michael Fung's Charlestown's Unit Structure

- Each Unit is accountable for the well-being of its students.
- Each Unit is independent. It adopts its own administrative rules and policies, including disciplinary and grading policies. (Certain decisions, such as the suspension of students or fiscal expenditure, must be unanimous decisions.)
- Each Unit is responsible for the "Unit administrative duties." Unit teachers will not be assigned other administrative duties.
- As much as possible, the classrooms of each Unit will be located in the same area. Except for the two assistant headmasters, who are assigned additional duties and responsibilities, all Unit leaders will have their office located in the same area as the Unit classrooms.
- Each Unit determines its own instructional approach and curricular emphasis. (The headmaster encourages a project-based, investigative approach.)
- Each Unit can establish its own teaching schedule and will no longer be limited to the traditional 48-minute classes.
- Unit teachers share at least one hour (for most Units, two periods) of daily common nonteaching time.
- Unit teachers will meet with the Unit leaders regularly and with the headmaster at least once a week (on Mondays).

Michael's revised unit structure certainly had the potential to give freshmen a better education. But that was just the architecture; teacher teams had to make it work. Michael knew the lynchpin for the success of his rather unorthodox strategy to increase MCAS scores was highly dependent on the quality and dedication of the teams of ninth and tenth grade teachers. As there were very few veteran teachers Michael felt he could trust in this role, he placed his bets on an unlikely population: recent female graduates of Ivy League schools, most of whom who had little or no teaching experience but who wanted to make a personal contribution to improving the lot of urban students. A number of these women were recent graduates of the Massachusetts DOE–sponsored Massachusetts Institute for New Teachers (MINT), an accelerated teacher preparation program that offered $20,000 signing bonuses with a commitment to teach in urban districts for three years. Michael's goal was to hire highly motivated and enthusiastic teachers with strong content knowledge who were just coming out of college and didn't yet have families and who would be more willing to put in the time and work the long hours required to make real progress.

No veteran teachers with twenty-plus years of service were invited to apply, and only a few teachers with any professional tenure were assigned to ninth or tenth grade positions. Michael did not want his new breed to be "poisoned" by the culture and habits of Charlestown's veterans. He placed his bets for Charlestown's future on hiring and coaching a whole new cadre of teachers, not one of whom would come through the district's traditional pool of unassigned teachers. Michael had secured the freedom to hire at will, and hire at will he did.

Michael credited his leadership model to the highly successful internet firm Yahoo!: "You give creative people a lot of freedom and they will perform." Smart people will produce smart students, who will demonstrate high performance on the MCAS.

He already had the open-posting options given to him by the faculty vote in February 1997 and subsequent years. His ability to bypass the traditional hiring channels to search for prospects beyond the school system was further enhanced by a loophole in the union contract. If he added a stipend to any position, for example, $2,000 per year to fulfill additional administrative responsibilities, he could open-post the position without a faculty vote.

Funding was not an issue; he had more than enough coming from outside sources. Besides the five new teachers authorized by the faculty vote that Michael hired in his first year, he hired ten new teachers in his second year, fifteen in his third, and eighteen in his fourth. They were

Michael's hires—exclusively. Any pretense of a parent-teacher screening committee was abandoned when Michael threatened the use of his statutory veto power if he did not get his candidate.

Only two of the new hires were the result of dismissals. Some positions were prompted by retirements or Charlestown's extraordinarily high turnover rate. But Michael's creative budgeting choices facilitated the majority of hiring. He budgeted almost entirely for teachers instead of reserving a substantial portion of his budget for administrative positions, as most principals did. On a mission to improve the quality of teaching, he was creating a dangerously lean administrative organization, one that left large gaps in traditional student and teacher support. Michael retained only two guidance counselors for a student body of 1,200. When the two long-tenured assistant headmasters announced their retirements, he replaced just one of them. Subject matter department heads were eliminated. There was only one dean of discipline.

It wasn't that Michael regarded the functions served by eliminated positions as unimportant. He believed that one should "never do something for someone that they can do for themselves"; it was his favorite administrative motto. He determined that these abandoned functions would be vested in the units; teams would carry the *complete* responsibility for educating ninth and tenth grade students and ensuring their success on the MCAS. They alone would be held responsible for everything from subject matter decisions to disciplinary actions.

The new hires would bring energy, if not instructional competence, to the units. Michael arranged to have experienced teacher-administrators appointed as unit leaders to provide administrative support and assist new staff in coordinating their efforts. He sparingly sprinkled experienced faculty into four of the five units but designed Unit III to be made up of totally new teachers. Michael strongly believed that with his coaching, Unit III could be propelled to excellence, and so he appointed himself unit leader. Michael would use Unit III to model unit leadership for his other administrators.

With the exception of only one school year between 1998 and 2005, Michael maintained this role with units exclusively staffed with his new, young, female hires. Welcoming the new teachers with flowers and off-site lunches, Michael went to elaborate lengths to distribute written guidelines to these first-time urban teachers. The "Charlestown High Classroom Procedures," based on current research, went so far as to prescribe a checklist for correct instructor behavior from the time students entered the classroom until they left. He also had some advice for new teachers: Don't go to the veterans for help; many are poor teachers and will lead you astray.

Although the actual time Michael spent with teachers on his team averaged only two hours per week, the new teachers welcomed his offers of help and resources and tried to follow his directions without question. Unfortunately, their lack of experience could not always be overcome by their intelligence or Michael's coaching. First-year teachers who had never worked with high school students before in any environment, let alone an urban public school, struggled endlessly and were often shocked and devastated by their failures in the classroom. With a turnover rate more akin to the high-pressure, corporate environment of a large investment banking firm than an educational setting, Charlestown was a revolving door for new teachers. Though there were notable exceptions, a vast majority were simply unprepared for the task.

Michael was unfazed. If those who couldn't hack it quit, it merely provided him with an opportunity to fit someone else in their slot. Believing firmly that getting "the right people" in place would be the key to his success, Michael was not deterred by the casualties his policies were leaving in their wake and was not inclined to change his hiring strategy. Ever suspicious of veteran teachers, he was committed to the idea that smart, young, inexperienced teachers could be "molded" to suit Charlestown's needs.

The fact that Michael constantly sought new teachers was not lost on veteran faculty who were left the thankless task of instructing the remaining eleventh and twelfth graders. Resentful that they were not included in Michael's plan for success, they silently went about their business, doing not one thing more than was absolutely required and leaving the school promptly each day at the final bell.

The resulting organization reflected Michael's need to have the school revolve around him, with few intermediaries to get in his way. Although most units had administrative heads, it was clear that they were very much under Michael's control. He was at the helm; it was he who controlled most of what happened at Charlestown High School. If a unit leader crossed him, or got in the way of one of his new, young protégées, he froze them out. Except for the initial return-to-school session, there were no faculty meetings, and no faculty senate. As a staff member at Charlestown High, you were loyal to Michael's vision or you left.

Charlestown: More Than Okay

In 2000, Michael's change process was well under way, and his efforts were beginning to pay off as evidenced by the ever-improving MCAS scores. But Michael now faced a new challenge: He was forced to confront a comprehensive district audit. At that time, several Boston schools were required to have an In-Depth Review (IDR), and Charlestown was one of them. Michael was resolute: Charlestown *would* pass with flying colors. To prepare for the review team's visit, he enlisted the help of the once-resistant Mrs. Jordan, whom he knew could command the attention of the veteran faculty. She was named chair of the Review Committee and was responsible for responding to the review team's questions in a voluminous written report as well as deftly orchestrating how the school would present itself during the two-day visit. The entire teacher corps was instructed on "proper" classroom technique and how to appropriately answer potential questions asked by the reviewers.

The results were astounding. The five-person review team, comprised of Boston headmasters, principals, and administrators, interviewed Charlestown teachers, examined records, and observed classroom instruction. Their resulting assessment exceeded even Michael's own estimate of Charlestown's overall performance at that time. Of the twenty items on which Charlestown was judged, the team awarded the school ten "Demonstrating Effectiveness" ratings, the highest possible rating on the four-tiered rubric, and eight "Operational" ratings, the second-highest score.

Amazingly, there were fewer things that the team found "not to their liking" than Michael himself found. "The team saw a lot of good teaching from the new teachers. That's what swayed them to give us high ratings," he explained. "But I gave us a lower rating because the ratings have to translate into significance in test results. Our test results are good, better than most of the district's high schools, but we can do better." Michael was clearly buoyed by the glowing, positive external assessment, which reinforced his view that his strategy was paying off.

The Iconoclast

By October 2002, Charlestown's rapidly improving MCAS scores were the envy of Boston headmasters districtwide. At administrative meetings, his peers asked Michael, only half-jokingly, if he had some secret weapon. Michael couldn't resist the chance to show off his own irreverence toward the district and quickly put together a satirical chart outlining the areas where he chose to depart from the district prescriptions and chart his own course for success. (See Table 4.1.) His comparison of Charlestown with Boston Public Schools' ideals put his unorthodox position on the public record, solidifying his standing as the iconoclast of the Boston Public Schools, a status he greatly enjoyed.

Table 4.1 Michael Fung's Answer to Why Charlestown's 10th Grade MCAS Scores Are Higher Than Other BPS Non-Exam High Schools

Relevant Items	Charlestown High 2002–03	BPS Ideals
Headmaster	Poorly-behaved, frequently failing to follow directives or meet deadlines	Well-behaved, scrupulously following central office orders
Instructional Leadership Team (ILT)	Conscientiously irrelevant: showing little instructional emphasis or leadership or teamwork	Where the actions are and where the hope of school transformation lies
School Change Model	First (and quickly) the structure, then the people, then the culture	The Six Essentials for Whole-School Change
Looking At Student Work	Still unstructured and informal	Structured, formal and regular
Classroom Instruction	Teacher-led, learning-centered	Student-centered
Readers' Workshop	Not officially implemented in 2002	Do it with heart and soul
Writers' Workshop	Not officially implemented in 2002	Do it with heart and soul
Staff Evaluation and Supervision	Encourage the heart	Improvement in teaching through rigorous annual evaluations; removal of non-performers

(continued)

Table 4.1 Michael Fung's Answer to Why Charlestown's 10th Grade MCAS Scores Are Higher Than Other BPS Non-Exam High Schools *(continued)*

Relevant Items	Charlestown High 2002–03	BPS Ideals
Best Practice High Schools	Not a Best Practice high school and probably will never be one	Brighton High, Burke high and Snowden International
Managerial Emphasis	Results; Execution (getting the right things done); Learning in action; Substance; Having the right people in the right places	Processes; Formal planning & implementation; Measurement; Form; Proper training and credentials

Inside Unit III

By April 2004, the atmosphere in Unit III of Charlestown High was quite different from that in the other units. Elsewhere teachers continued to grapple with discipline issues, and unit leaders had to fight for respect. The units struggled to establish common ground among an ever-changing staff. Students in the eleventh and twelfth grades were dispassionate and indifferent learners.

In contrast, on the fifth floor, Unit III students were in their classrooms hard at work. The ninth and tenth graders were struck by the differences between their present environment and other urban schools to which they'd been exposed, even the rest of Charlestown High. They could be heard saying, "This is like the good schools you see on TV, isn't it? People are quiet, pay attention, do homework." Unit III had successfully created an effort-based culture in which students succeeded because they regularly attended school and completed assignments thoroughly and carefully.

A year and a half earlier, a September 29, 2002, *Boston Globe* article described Charlestown High as "one of a handful of Boston schools that stands out in MCAS" and went on to note that Charlestown's 53 percent tenth grade passing rate on the 2002 mathematics MCAS exceeded that of fourteen Boston Public High Schools, outranking all but three (not including the city's prestigious exam schools). By 2003, the passing rate was up to 70 percent, and in May of 2004 a full 84 percent of

Charlestown High tenth graders would pass the mathematics portion of the high-stakes exam. Charlestown was making a major difference in the education of its ninth and tenth graders, whose hard-working teachers put a high demand on their students and received a high return.

It was an unlikely success story. The five members of the Unit III teaching team came together for the first time in September 2000, making them, by 2004, the only unit at Charlestown High whose teachers had been together for four consecutive years. Two teachers, responsible for science and English, had never taught before. The math teacher had taught a single year of calculus in a university setting, and the history teacher had taught a single year at Charlestown High (in another unit). Only one Unit III teacher, Karen Loughran, had significant teaching experience behind her, and her five years were spent almost entirely outside of Boston. All five members of Unit III were women, predominately from Ivy League schools. One was African American, and none were from Boston. Together, their lack of urban, public school experience was surprising. They perfectly fit Michael's profile for new hires.

Though each was intelligent, hard working, and knowledgeable in her content area, and each entered Charlestown with only the highest expectations for success, Unit III got off to an understandably rocky start. The opening months of their first school year together were not just difficult; they bordered on hopeless. With Michael as unit leader, the rookie teachers were left virtually on their own. Not interested in micromanaging, he had put structures in place that gave units the potential to thrive but left all implementation decisions entirely to the team. Michael Fung was interested in theory and results, not the daily struggles of new recruits.

Karen Loughran was recruited by Michael when the two met at a citywide math meeting while she was covering for a teacher on maternity leave at one of the city's exam schools. Michael did his homework, learned that she had excellent teaching skills, and decided to bring her aboard at Charlestown.

A charismatic salesman, Michael exploited the opportunities available at Charlestown to potential teaching recruits by delivering a picture of working with a hand-picked crew of new, young, energetic colleagues. He worked hard to recruit those he wanted, but he was not willing to meet anyone's demands. Karen explained, "After he offered me the position and gave me a couple of days to think about it, I called him and said that I needed more time because I had just been offered another position. He said, 'No, you need to decide today, right now.' I took it."

Karen, with a background in social work and more classroom experience than her peers, suggested to her team that they put into place an old-fashioned, don't-even-think-about-it-cause-you'll-never-get-away-with-it discipline system. Karen's five years of teaching deemed her an expert in the eyes of her teammates, and they readily agreed. Collectively, they managed to construct a set of ideals and rules for student behavior and discipline. With Karen taking the lead, they established long lists of acceptable and unacceptable behaviors and pledged to hold each other accountable for all student behavior, agreeing to support one another when it came to suspending students.

Michael strongly supported teacher-determined student suspensions; but until the teachers of Unit III defined and outlined the unacceptable behaviors, they did not know how to use the power Michael had given them. Once they did, they began to send the message to their students that things were going to calm down. From that initial conversation, the team emerged. "Teachers were given total authority to dictate the rules and consequences for the unit, provided that all decisions were unanimous," Karen reflected. "[We] took advantage of this latitude. To change student behavior, clear rules with harsh consequences were posted and followed carefully. Every student was expected to be in school every day, on time. A first time tardy resulted in a forty-five-minute detention. Skipping classes was an obvious problem; any student who skipped class—even one—would be suspended for a minimum of three days."

Because Charlestown traditionally had a very high ninth grade dropout rate, Unit III felt it was especially important to aggressively reach out to the ninth graders. They used a cell phone, designated to the unit, to call the parents of any student absent on a given day. Each of the five teachers was assigned one evening of the week to call the homes of all students absent that day. They also implemented more serious interventions, working closely with a Boston Police officer who would visit, at least once a month, the homes of students who did not show up for school. They pressed charges for truancy against students who had missed more than twenty days of school.

The team's disciplinary rules were viewed by other units as draconian, but the five teachers of Unit III went to great lengths in explaining to their students why they had implemented such strict rules. What they had to offer their students as educators was instructionally important and could not be dismissed, "not even for one day."

Karen quickly became the informal teacher leader of Unit III. The special rapport she developed with students encouraged them to speak candidly with her. Other teachers came to view Karen as their pipeline to the students.

The unit's science teacher had a Ph.D. in biology but was not the typical academic. As a teenager, she had dropped out of high school and struggled with substance abuse issues before straightening herself out, earning her GED, enrolling in community college, and eventually completing her graduate studies. When watching kids struggling, she had the unique perspective of really knowing what it was like to be in their place. Telling her students her story was a powerful means of getting their attention, and as she gained more classroom experience, her high expectations and enthusiasm for her subject matter kept them engaged.

The English teacher was a graduate of Smith College. An African American, she grew up in a housing project on "the mean streets of Maine," as she liked to joke with her students. Her strength was her commitment to exposing Charlestown students to the idea of college and their future, something many of these ninth and tenth graders had never thought about before. During her time at Charlestown, she planned extensive, overnight trips to colleges with which she had developed and nurtured partnerships. In turn, she also arranged for college students and mentors to speak to her students at Charlestown High. She made her students understand why their education really mattered and motivated them to open their eyes to "life after high school."

A "natural disciplinarian," the math teacher always had high expectations for Charlestown students. She kept Unit III on track, never allowing them to back down from the commitments they'd made to enforcing student behavior and consequences. She held all Unit III teachers accountable, reminding them that they had already agreed on what was acceptable and had to stay the course. She was terrifically organized and soon became known as an expert on "classroom management." Several years down the road, visitors to her classroom observed her teaching AP calculus to inner-city students for an hour and finally "believed that it could be done." Her well-run classroom served as an inspiration to those around her.

The history teacher was a graduate of Harvard and had an unbelievable wealth of content knowledge. Because she was so knowledgeable, she had a certain amount of flexibility in her lesson plans, which enabled her to engage in deep, complex conversations with her students, many of whom had never been asked to adopt a truly historical mindset. She exuded a love of history, and her students quickly responded to her insights and enthusiasm.

A Plan for Success

Late in the fall of 2000, when the palpable chaos in the classrooms and hallways (a manifestation of the team's inability to manage their students' horrendous behavior) became too much to bear, the teachers of Unit III realized that something would have to change. The way things were going, it was unlikely that many of their students would even make it through the year, much less emerge prepared to pass their MCAS exams. Desperate to salvage their first year, the five Unit III teachers began to focus on high expectations for student behavior and attendance. They believed that by concentrating on the "whole child," rather than exclusively on classroom academics, they would be able to set the foundation for student success. Unlike much of the veteran faculty, all of the teachers in Unit III truly believed their students could excel. They understood, however, that unless the expectations were clear and high, students would not be motivated to live up to them. Karen mused,

> Part of it was a real genuine conviction that the kids could learn. And I think a lot of it came from [the teachers'] personal upbringings and the schools that they went to. A genuine belief that the kids could learn at a high level and that we weren't going to lower the bar; we are going to bring the kids up. I mean, we did do a lot of scaffolding, but we said, "This is what BPS expects from ninth grade, for example, math, kids. So we are going to follow curriculum." Whereas a lot of people would say, "There is just no way these kids can do algebra; they can't even add." And we gave them calculators and said that they can do it, and they did. So, it was really all about having high academic expectations.

The teachers of Unit III developed five mutually agreed on structures that they supported across the board; this contributed to their eventual success with their ninth and tenth grade unit.

1. Strictly enforced attendance and discipline policies (e.g., skipping class results in automatic three-day suspension; parents are contacted with each absence).

2. Teaching curriculum aligned with BPS and MCAS.

3. "Advisory" group meetings once a week on Fridays. (During this time, one academic class would sacrifice academic content and two unit teachers and two school counselors would split students into four groups of seven to eight each and give them a "future orientation," in which they would discuss the importance of graduating, what to do after high school, etc. Each student would build their own portfolio of goals for during and after high school.)

4. Two-hour, academic after-school program taught by all unit teachers (with greater than 50 percent student participation).

5. One hour of homework each night in all subjects (a good portion of which could often be completed in the after-school program).

Unit III teachers were committed to these structures and believed in their importance. They worked together tirelessly to ensure that they were upheld.

Many of their students came to school lacking the self-discipline, impulse control, and readiness to learn demanded of Unit III's structure, culture, and academically challenging environment. The teachers believed they were the single-most-qualified team of people to address all aspects of their students' education and discipline. Their approach differed from the other units, which had a leader who often spent a significant portion of the day attending exclusively to disciplinary matters.

As they sought to get their students acclimated to their new learning environment, the five Unit III teachers went out of their way to explicitly recognize student achievement. They held awards ceremonies, named students-of-the-month, and planned field trips as rewards, along with subtle and demonstrative encouragement sprinkled throughout the school day. One teacher would affix little paper stars to the hands of those students who had excelled during the period. Despite the obvious childishness of the act, it was not uncommon for recipients to proudly display these simple reminders, which served as a record of their accomplishments in the halls after class. That academic achievement was so valued was a testament to the high expectations the team had created among its students.

"A huge part of our success," that teacher insisted, "was our respect for one another as teachers. We all believed that our students deserved to have really good teachers, deserved a good education, a positive environment.

We agreed on ways to enforce policies. We were very consistent. So the experience that they are having in my class was not that different than the one they were having in the next class. A culture develops that is very positive and focused on them."

Looking back, these teachers recalled that their positive attitude, and perhaps naivete, helped them achieve success. They actually believed that they could solve all of Charlestown's problems, and they were willing to give it a try. Much of this could be attributed to their youth and idealism, just as Michael Fung had hoped. Some of it was the result of their combined personalities. "Michael is very busy," Karen explained,

> so we've all had to take on leadership roles. We all feel accountable and proactive. We are all, by default, more proactive and [interested in] problem-solving, and because of that we get more done. We are very fast-paced and action-based. Solution oriented. We spend less time talking and more time on real-life solutions—finding them immediately. The positive side to that is that we get a lot done. The negative is that we spend less time reflecting on our actions. I think a lot of that has to do with me being the unofficial leader. My style is to identify the problem, find the solution and implement it immediately.

Without a great deal of guidance from above, and with the freedom to create policies and structures that they believed in, Unit III felt a great deal of ownership for their small learning community. During one year when Michael stepped away from leading the group and assigned in his place a unit leader willing to involve herself in a more hands-on fashion, the team rebelled. Vigorously defending their independence to Michael, he ceded to their resolve and removed the unwanted unit leader. As one Unit III teacher described it, "Our unit loves operating on our own. We like being able to set up our own things and not having interference. We set up our own discipline policy, for example."

The team bonded and worked long hours together. Even though it was extremely difficult, the teachers insisted on holding each other to the academic and behavioral standards they had created. It would have been easy to back down when one of them really liked a particular student or felt intimidated by a demanding parent, but their shared commitment was strong. They agreed that they were going to send a message to the students about how important it was for them to be in class, on-task every day. They asked for commitments to both academics and high standards for student behavior.

The teachers met daily for an hour to evaluate and discuss student behavior and academic progress. Michael required structure to their meetings but let them determine that structure themselves. Unit III held fast-paced, ambitious, and results-oriented meetings. They made a point to always treat one another respectfully and courteously and came to rely on these meetings for encouragement and support. Often they used the sessions to brainstorm about different solutions to difficult or ongoing problems, such as the lack of parent involvement or the ever-growing list of teacher responsibilities. Karen explained:

> During our common meeting time, I would present my classroom, just so that people had the understanding of my approach, my organization, etc. We had different themes—like we'd talk about organization, and so I would spend the whole time presenting how I organize myself, and then I would present issues that I am having. And we would go back and forth about [possible] solutions. And then the next week maybe we would talk about discipline and classroom management. I'd talk in general about my approach with kids and then specifically outline one recurring issue that I noticed. So, we would problem-solve around that, come up with some strategies as a group, and all try and implement that same strategy.

Michael occasionally attended these meetings, dropping in and out as it suited his full schedule. Unit III teachers were welcome to go to him if they needed him, and they were well aware of the easiest times to catch him. But for the most part, the team found itself without a regular unit leader, making decisions on its own, under the guidance of the informal leader, Karen Loughran. For these new teachers, this ownership and control was very empowering. It motivated them to work harder, to prove that their ideas would work. For these teachers, the unit came first—before the school, before their individual classrooms, before themselves. "I think that in any small, learning community, the Unit has to be the priority in order for it to work," one teacher reflected.

Time on Task

According to Karen,

> Michael was really clear about the urgency around the work. There was no "movie day," like some of the other schools in Boston; there was none of that. It really felt like an academic environment. He set the tone by

continually talking to teachers like they were intelligent, asking on a daily, weekly, monthly basis, "What topic are you teaching? What's your approach?" He wasn't asking to see my lesson plans to make sure I had done them; he was genuinely asking to give me some suggestions and wanted to just engage in conversation about the curriculum, which no one had ever done before that. It doesn't matter if he is talking to a physics teacher or a math teacher or a science teacher or an English teacher—he is constantly talking to people about what they are doing and just making people feel like what they do is serious and important.

Emboldened by their understanding with Michael, Unit III teachers felt comfortable approaching him about Charlestown's method of scheduling more time on task, which they felt was not working. When the Unit was first formed, Michael had in place a system whereby students who had done poorly in English would receive two hours of English instruction each day. Students passing English would receive two hours of daily instruction in mathematics instead. Two Unit III teachers, one of whom was teaching mathematics, and Karen Loughran, who was teaching the second hour of both English and mathematics, went to Michael and said, "You know, in terms of their skill deficits, they *all* need two hours of math—all of them—forget two hours of English because they have history; they have science; they can practice their comprehension, reading, and writing skills in other rooms. There is no way these kids are going to learn the math unless they have two hours of math every single day."

Michael said, "All right; try it next year," and the two coordinated and taught two hours of math to all of their students. At first, they spent at least two hours planning together for each week's math lessons. They talked about how to meet the objectives, how to split up the curriculum, how they would inform students about the additional hours of math, and how they were going to do everything they needed to do. They planned all of their lessons together and talked about what worked and what didn't, retooling their instructional strategies as they went along. They engaged in peer observation, giving each other feedback to improve the quality of their instruction.

The hard work paid off, and Unit III began to see results. The number of students failing the math MCAS dropped 10 percent from 1999 to 2000. In 2001, the number of failing students dropped an astounding 45 percent. In just two short years, the number of students at Charlestown High failing their mathematics MCAS exam went from 90 percent in

1999 to 35 percent in 2001. By 2004, only 15 percent of Charlestown tenth graders failed the mathematics MCAS exam. (See Tables 4.2 and 4.3.)

Table 4.2   Grade 10 Charlestown ELA MCAS Scores Compared to Boston Non-Exam High Schools

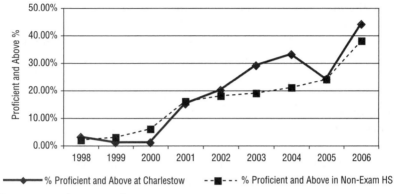

Source: www.doe.mass.edu

Table 4.3   Grade 10 Charlestown Math MCAS Scores Compared to Boston Non-Exam High Schools

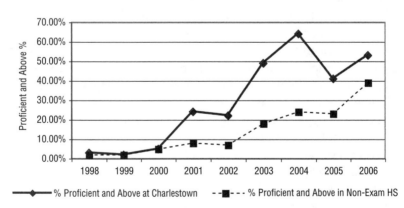

Source: www.doe.mass.edu

The unit attributed much of its success to the after-school program they had developed. Students now had two hours of math during the day and a solid hour of homework after school. This meant three very intensive hours of math every day for two years. All Unit III kids were welcome to come to the after-school program, and about 60 to 70 percent took advantage of the opportunity. These teachers stayed after school most days for a minimum of two hours—informally teaching a ninth grade component and then a tenth grade component. It was their commitment that so drastically improved student performance.

By the third year, the team had refined and defined a small learning community that was yielding spectacular results and improving MCAS scores. Unfortunately, up to a fourth of the students were still not qualifying for promotion to the next grade level.

As a solution to this problem, Karen suggested that each student be assigned a "promotion adviser" who would ensure that the student could move on to the next grade level. All team members and four other staff members quickly affirmed the idea and volunteered. Assignments were made to each of the at-risk students. These promotion advisers became the students' confidants, problem solvers, and adult advocates. Advisers checked their students' academic progress weekly, and sometimes more often. In the first year of the focused promotion effort, eighteen of the twenty-five students improved enough to be promoted.

What price did Charlestown pay for putting such a singular premium on the measure of MCAS scores? The education of the eleventh and twelfth graders at Charlestown languished. Subjected to only spotty teaching and with little attention paid to their lives outside the classroom, upper school students, like the senior faculty that taught them, were abandoned and left to their own devices. Many dropped out when they had had enough; the number of graduating Charlestown students going on to accredited institutions of higher learning was comparatively low. Concerned that this measure might be held up for scrutiny, Michael Fung decided once again to reconfigure the Unit structure. In 2004–2005, he incorporated eleventh and twelfth grade students and teachers into the already-successful ninth and tenth grade units.

Looking back at his successes, Michael Fung is more than satisfied with the changes he brought about at Charlestown High and the methods he used to make those changes. "That's why I adopted the strategy of bringing in new teachers," he explains, "so that, eventually, I hoped for a critical mass. Because in terms of change in the long run, if you want the change to be permanent, that has to be the culture of the school. Bringing in new staff is [the best way] to try and create a new culture."

Chapter 5

Kathleen Flannery and Edward Everett Elementary School
1994–2006

Kathleen "Lite"

Four months into Kathleen Flannery's first year as principal of the Everett, a fifth grade teacher who had acted as second-in-command during most of Kathleen's predecessor's sixteen years as principal, knocked on the door and asked to see her. After some awkward pleasantries, he got around to the reason for his visit. "I don't think you understand the gravity of the situation here," he said. "This is really a serious job. I think you're too 'lite' for it and, quite frankly, you laugh too much."

Kathleen wasn't sure how to respond to the charge. She laughed too much? She did laugh a lot. Her infectious giggle had been heard throughout the hallways of all her previous schools and had, at times, drawn knowing smiles from her coworkers. She liked to laugh at herself, and her breezy, slightly self-deprecating demeanor made her easy to warm up to. She thought of herself as an approachable, upbeat, glass-half-full sort of person. It was a sad commentary, she thought, that a woman's cheerful disposition could actually be seen as a flaw, that it could be mistaken for an indication that she was not serious about her work.

Kathleen had been in urban schools for twenty-two years and had spent ten of them as assistant principal of the Burke High School, one of the toughest high schools in Boston at that time. Most recently, she had spent two years as principal of a school in Lynn, Massachusetts, that boasted 700 students, without so much as an assistant principal to support her. Kathleen knew that she was not naive. "But," she thought to herself, "it's okay if he wants to presume that I am. Whatever he wants to believe about me is fine. It's what I *do* that matters." Indeed, modeling exemplary work would be Kathleen's signature strategy for bringing about change at the Everett. She may not have taken herself too seriously, but she took her job incredibly seriously. Kathleen was simply unwilling to compromise when it came to hard work and excellence.

She looked at the teacher, smiled, and took in a deep breath, thinking to herself, "You really don't have a clue about who I am or what I can do." With a wan smile, she replied aloud, "Time will tell."

Looking for a Place to Start: Breaking Out of the Bubble

Kathleen looked forward to the job of building a small community at the Everett, where she would have the opportunity to really know her students. Although it was a small school, it felt just the right size. With approximately 375 students and two classrooms for most grade levels, the Everett was small enough to allow her to develop personal relationships with students and their families but big enough to allow for scheduling flexibility and grade-level colleagues, unlike some of the truly tiny schools in the district.

Everett students were, for the most part, well behaved. They obeyed the rules and spoke respectfully to their teachers and to each other. Everett staff felt proud of the culture they had created. Despite their successes, however, Kathleen felt that the school climate at the Everett was missing something. She saw a school that was isolated from the world. It was known only to its students, teachers, and the occasional parent; very few outsiders came in. There were no student teachers, few after-school programs, and no financial resources beyond the school budget.

Kathleen knew the sad truth: An urban school could not make ends meet on its allocated budget alone. She decided to begin her work by opening up the Everett to the larger community, contacting businesses and universities in an attempt to form partnerships that would bring funding and resources into the school. This was a safe place to begin making changes. The outcome would be vitally important to the future of the school but nonthreatening to Everett teachers. She would show teachers what *she* could do for *them* first, before asking them to change things for her.

Feeling strongly that a university partner interested in sending student teachers to the Everett would be an incredible asset, Kathleen began to bring representatives from local colleges and universities through the building. She spent a great deal of time on this difficult project, and it was not easy. Universities were looking to send their student teachers to an environment where they could practice the techniques they learned about on campus, but teaching at the Everett looked a lot like it had forty years ago, in the 1950s. The desks were in rows, the classroom doors were closed, and the children were passive learners, sitting quietly and attentively.

"Well," Kathleen told them, "some things are working at the Everett and some things aren't. Just like all of the other places that I've been." It was going to be good, she convinced them; the Everett was going to be a special place.

Kathleen was smart, savvy, and, perhaps equally importantly, likable. She was able to make the most of the contacts she had and could effortlessly recruit others. She had a way about her that allowed people to trust her, to feel safe and optimistic about their investment in the Everett School.

Putting Relationships First

Kathleen's first priority had been to build a trusting relationship with her staff. Especially cognizant of the maxim "know your audience," she carefully considered how the Everett teachers would react to the things she said and did. She knew that if she got them on the defensive, the Everett would suffer.

She knew that many principals arriving in new schools made sweeping, dramatic changes that reflected the ideas and practices they thought made education work. Frequently, new principals attempted to get rid of uncooperative staff and hire their own team of supporters. Teachers who already agreed with the principal's methods would feel comfortable doing things "their way." Kathleen considered this "my way or the highway" leadership and did not think it was a constructive way to create a healthy, dynamic working relationship, particularly with a staff whose knowledge and expertise she respected. In a school that had many things going for it, the slash-and-burn method would certainly do more harm than good, and Kathleen already felt that her presence at the school was perceived by the community as a threat to the status quo. She would have to find another way to push the Everett to aim higher.

The staff at the Everett had not experienced a real instructional leader before Kathleen. The teachers were their own instructional leaders and they took that job seriously. The previous principal was well liked and had developed positive relationships with teachers, parents, and students. He had viewed his principalship as a managerial position. He was first and foremost a building manager, and his attitude toward curriculum was laissez-faire. He relied on teachers, particularly those with backgrounds in reading, to make curricular decisions.

He had chosen to move to a larger school as a means of increasing his salary before retiring in three years. He had not informed any of the Everett's teachers or parents about his intentions, and they did not learn the news until the superintendent assigned Kathleen to the Everett in August. Parents and teachers were not given a voice in the selection of their interim principal.

Because of their hands-off leader and the tremendous responsibility that they bore in his stead, the hard-working, close-knit Everett teachers were one of the best things the school had going for it in 1994. Kathleen could not believe how many teachers came in early and worked late.

She marveled at the hours the Everett staff devoted to planning, especially as the staff was comprised primarily of experienced teachers, who, in other schools, were generally set in their ways. The culture at the Everett was different than what she had previously experienced. Teachers expected each other to plan and to work hard. Kathleen had always been a hard worker, but she had never led a school where "overworking" was the norm. She recognized this as a remarkable asset.

The Everett staff was already involved in many challenging initiatives. The teachers wanted to reconsider their reading program, so they went out and looked at programs other schools had in place. Kathleen had never seen teachers doing that kind of research on their own, yet she could see that they were not looking at the full breadth of available programs. She was impressed that they wanted to explore options before making their final choice. There was no doubt that Everett teachers really wanted their students to achieve.

Less evident to her was whether or not teachers were doing the "right" work. Privately, she questioned much of their methodology; publicly, she was hesitant to criticize. After all, they were working—and they were working hard. They took their jobs seriously and thought of themselves as professionals. Most importantly, they were *convinced* that they were very successful and felt good about the school and proud of their accomplishments. What good would it do to disparage their efforts?

The teachers were apprehensive about Kathleen, an outsider in their insular community. They questioned her qualifications and were distrustful of her ideas. To incur animosity by pushing her own agenda against the wishes of the staff seemed imprudent. It would be better to build on and tap into the already-present pride that Everett teachers felt for their work and for the school.

So Kathleen decided to spend her first year listening. She didn't want to make changes for change's sake. She found it more sensible to gather as much information as she could and then move forward strategically as an informed insider, rather than an axe-wielding reformer.

She was already formulating ideas about the particular directions wanted to take the school but was committed to hearing teachers' arguments. She saw herself as a professional and respected the integrity of teachers as her colleagues. Disinclined to declare that hers was "the right way," Kathleen felt that she had no more proof than the teachers to support the instructional effectiveness of her ideas. Kathleen respected evidence as the only empirically decisive argument.

More Than Just a Memo

Kathleen felt lucky to have Kim Marshall as her BPS mentor. He was a rare individual who was willing to openly share his plans and ideas with Kathleen. He honestly felt that it was important for her school to be as successful as his own and did not judge or interfere with Kathleen's unusual approach to leadership.

Aware of what a powerful tool Kim's *Mather Memo* could be, Kathleen made the decision to create her own. She did not want to lead a school in which certain people were "in the know" and others had to depend on the informed to pass the knowledge along. A more inclusive community would provide access to the same information for all to use in making informed decisions. The *Morning Memo* would also provide Kathleen with a medium through which she could communicate her views and hold her staff responsible for schoolwide information. Teachers could not come to her saying, "I didn't know. . . . I hadn't heard that we were supposed to do that." It would all be in the memo. Not only was it available to all staff members, it was the obligation of the faculty to read it and familiarize themselves with its content.

A Matter of Equity

There were some practices that Kathleen felt she could not let continue in her school. One was "tracking by ability group," or simply "tracking." At the time of Kathleen's arrival, Everett used the tracking method to teach reading. Students were pooled across grades and then pulled out of their classrooms in groups according to their reading level. Each teacher taught only one reading group. Some taught "high" readers and others taught "low" readers. In this system, teachers had just one lesson to prepare and the freedom to gear their teaching to the specific needs of the group. But children would miss some instruction in their own classrooms while they were out of the room at their reading groups. Additionally, the groups were static, branding students with predetermined expectations for their achievement.

Tracking by ability group was something that Kathleen simply did not believe in. Data from the state Department of Education supported her views, citing definitive, negative consequences of the practice. Kathleen diligently distributed this research to her staff, but it didn't turn their heads. They had decided to implement this grouping methodology themselves after observing the practice at other schools. They were quick to point out that it was their visit to the Mason School, led by exemplary principal Mary Russo, which had convinced them that this was the road to success. They firmly believed that tracking provided the most efficient structure to teach reading. The teachers maintained that this was what the school's most vocal parents wanted.

It was true. There was a political and cultural aspect to the debate that went beyond the structure of the Everett's reading groups. The Everett was an ethnically diverse school, a rarity within the system, and it boasted parents of a variety of racial and economic backgrounds. The dichotomy between the highly involved, "active," white parents and the practically invisible families of the students that made up the rest of the Everett population bothered Kathleen tremendously. Most of these active white parents were not working and had the time and opportunity to walk their kids to school, participate in fundraising, and work on committees. Kathleen thought of them as good people who wanted to do their part and give back to the school community; however, she also saw that in exchange for their loyalty, they felt they deserved certain favors.

Toward the end of her first year, Kathleen began to receive letters from parents indicating the teachers to which they wanted their children assigned. Kathleen was confused. If parents were permitted to request teachers, why did only *some* of them know about it? Letters regarding classroom assignment came to Kathleen exclusively from parents of high-achieving, white students. When questioned about the letters, these parents explained that the previous principal had always acted in accordance with their wishes. Kathleen was uncomfortable with the policy and shortly afterward announced that she would be holding "promotion meetings" with each grade-level team, during which teachers would determine classroom assignment based on a number of factors, including race and achievement and, if they'd like, sibling preference (children who had older siblings pass through the Everett before them would have preference for the teachers that their siblings had).

It was against this backdrop that Kathleen made the decision to temporarily side-step the tracking issue in the interest of building rapport and demonstrating good faith. But she would not let the issue go for long. When she called Mary Russo at the Mason School to listen to her reasons for promoting the method, what she heard surprised her: The Mason had abandoned ability grouping across grade levels. "Oh God," Mary exclaimed. "We left that behind five years ago. Yes, we were doing that when the Everett people came to visit, but now we've moved on."

What Reading Recovery Was Covering Up

Two teachers were responsible for referring students to the Reading Recovery program, the special one-on-one reading intervention program for first graders who were having difficulty learning how to read. Because these teachers had undergone a great deal of special training, and because the program was provided as a one-on-one service, it was considered an exceptional and expensive option. Traditionally, Reading Recovery programs were offered exclusively to students in the bottom 10 percent of their class.

Conversation about the referral process revealed that the teachers in charge of choosing were not referring certain students who fell into the lowest tenth percentile. These excluded students were almost entirely special education students or those presumed to have "low IQs." Kathleen had not heard people speak of IQ as a legitimate way of categorizing kids for quite some time and felt that the discussion of IQ might be a red flag indicating an entirely different issue—one of race.

Flagrant acts of racism were certainly not taking place at the Everett, but Kathleen sensed that there might be an elusive, unspoken racial undercurrent in the building. "No one discusses race in the open, certainly not in Boston," she said. Kathleen wanted to get a second opinion about her suspicions and went to an Everett teacher she greatly respected and asked, "You don't think it's based on paternalistic, racist stuff, like, 'I don't believe these kids can do any better,' do you?" The teacher's response neither confirmed nor denied Kathleen's suspicions: "I don't know. I never thought about it."

During Kathleen's investigation, one of the Reading Recovery teachers began demonstrating a new method to other schools in the district. The literacy group was a specialized type of reading program where teachers worked with six to eight students at a time. Kathleen recognized the innovative new method as a unique opportunity to efficiently eliminate the biases of the Reading Recovery program.

She took decisive action and boldly discontinued Everett's Reading Recovery program, figuring, "If we were not going to provide the service to the bottom 10 percent of the class, to whom were we providing the service?" In its place she began literacy groups. Students from each first, second, and third grade classroom were now taught in groups using the new methodology. She faced dissent after this decision, but results were indisputable. She was quickly able to say, "Look at these kids. We've got kids reading who have never read before."

Action Through Hiring

When Kathleen came to the Everett, there were approximately twenty teachers on staff. She had a school that was 70 percent minority (primarily comprised of students of Cape Verdean, African American, and Vietnamese descent) and a staff that was 12 percent minority, represented by three black teachers. Even the age range was narrow. Most teachers were similar to Kathleen herself: female, white, middle aged, and middle class.

The Everett staff was comprised of the highest-quality teachers with whom she had ever worked, a group of good people who had chosen to work in urban schools. Yet she believed that the only way to change racial undercurrents at the Everett was to hire more people of color. If a more diverse group was part of the dialogue, Kathleen theorized that everything would change—views, politics, and understanding. She didn't want to hire people who thought like her; she wanted to hire people who thought for themselves and brought a range of diverse opinions and experiences to the table. If everyone's life experiences were uniform, there would be no new paths to explore in finding out what could work best for the Everett. Everything would continue as it always had.

When she was interviewing, Kathleen looked for hardworking teachers. She didn't want to hear things like, "I don't do meetings," or "I don't stay after school." Her goal was to find people who were willing to work as hard as they needed to in order to get the job done. Kathleen resolved to only hire new teachers who could uphold Everett's core values and high standards. She would say to her candidates, "You would want to work here because this is a school where we accomplish things—where we're successful. But we're only successful because we're willing to do the work. You don't want to work here if you really like to get in at 9:00 and leave at 3:30, and, truthfully, you wouldn't be *able* to work here successfully. I'm looking for people who are willing to put in the time."

For a while Kathleen interviewed *only* people of color. Believing that one should always hire the best teachers for the job, she felt it her responsibility as a principal to be sure that her staff reflected the diversity of her student population. She thought it extremely important that students be exposed to a variety of adults from different backgrounds working together and treating each other with respect. In time, she diversified her staff through new hires, bringing the percentage of minority teachers from 12 percent to 40 percent and ensuring that they represented a full range of ages and experience levels. And after ten years, Kathleen was ultimately successful in her quest to hire a talented Cape Verdean teacher. She had long imagined herself in the place of her Cape Verdean students: attending a school where people did not speak their language and did not come from the kind of background they had come from—would they really feel a part of that school? The Cape Verdean students would finally have a role model who was like them, and Cape Verdean families at the Everett would have a staff member with whom they could communicate in their own language.

The Reading Wars

Whole language was an up-and-coming reading program in which structured methods of teaching reading, such as texts that introduced controlled vocabulary and phonics-based methodology, were abandoned in favor of a literature-based curriculum. Kathleen had overseen the implementation of a whole language program during her previous principalship. Although she had seen very rich anecdotal evidence that a whole language program produced good writers and avid readers, she was not able to claim particularly good test scores as a result of it. Kathleen was of the mind-set, however, that with good, solid instruction, achievement would inevitably improve. An undue focus on scores did not seem especially valuable.

Even though she could not reference any data-based results from her personal experiences, Kathleen felt confident that the whole language approach was stronger than the old structured approach that Everett had been using (basal readers). Wanting to introduce the more progressive model and bring literature to the Everett, Kathleen began to talk about whole language at curriculum meetings. Sharing her concerns about the existing reading program, she distributed articles to staff to keep them abreast of the current research.

Everett teachers were largely unimpressed by the whole language research and took exception to Kathleen questioning the way they taught students to read. They had been teaching for a long time. Several of them were experts specializing in literacy. For what reason should they believe that programs through which they had achieved success for years were useless? Why should they reform a system that was working? Everett students were reading. Kathleen's denunciation of tracked ability groups and enthusiastic espousal of whole language methodology appeared to them naive and simplistic. They saw no reason to make the switch or to allow Kathleen to give them a unilateral order to do things differently.

What made the situation worse was that it was not just the method of teaching that was in dispute. It was that their current methods had come from their explorations, had not been mandated by their previous leader. It was their "baby." They had instituted it after conducting research at other schools. Not only was Kathleen was throwing darts at their methodology, she was also threatening their autonomy to make curricular decisions at the schoolwide level.

Kathleen found herself wondering how it was that teachers thought their students were doing "just fine." In 1994, the only kind of data that existed at the Everett was MAT data. Though achievement data was not considered all-important in those days, the Everett's scores were clearly low, falling in the thirtieth percentile. Kathleen knew that there were other schools in the district with comparable student demographics which were scoring higher. She considered whether sharing this data with her staff would assist her in conveying the sense of urgency to consider alternative reading methodologies.

She was able to see the problem for what it was; low test scores (and the credibility of the MAT as an accurate calibration of student achievement was seriously in question) were not an indication of a "bad" school. She knew that the effectiveness of any school was far more complex than a single day of testing could capture. Nevertheless, she felt compelled to bring the MAT scores into the discussion. "Our test scores on the Metropolitan are quite low," she finally said. "The thirtieth percentile. Do you think the thirtieth percentile is good enough? Would you send your child to a school with scores that low?" The teachers brushed off the implication. "We never pay much attention to reading scores," they shrugged. "If they're low, it's probably because we have many second language learners. Let's not forget, all of our students are reading at the end of first grade!"

Kathleen continued to advocate whole language with gentle persistence, but she did not mandate the switch. It was her nature only to plant the seeds of an idea and then step away, giving others the opportunity to come around on their own. At every opportunity she extolled the program's virtues, stuffing teacher mailboxes with article after article. At the same time, she maintained that the teachers were the experts. After all, some of them held degrees and extensive training in reading instruction. She was not a literacy expert herself. She would defer to their better judgment even though the direction in which the faculty was going did not seem right to her. Kathleen knew that if the Everett was to continually improve its teaching capacity, she would be dependent on the teaching staff, and they would have to rely on her. It was their collective instructional wisdom that would eventually make the difference in student performance.

Although Kathleen was not going to back down from her personal mission to ensure that student learning was the Everett's first priority, she was not yet ready to mandate change just because *she* believed in it. She wanted the evidence to speak for itself. She envisioned her school community as a place where she would act as an equal participant in the educational process, not as a disengaged managerial figure or a stubborn bully. She would never be able to engender mutual trust with such ineffective approaches.

With this philosophy in mind, Kathleen was determined not to fight the consensus; instead, she would build on the collective energy of the faculty and cultivate strong relationships with them. The "wait and see" strategy was risky; the debate could last for months without resolution. What if Kathleen's credibility began to erode as a result of her choice not to act decisively?

Tipping the Balance

In the midst of the debate, the district suddenly came through with a new mandate: Boston schools would move to a literature-based reading program. No longer was this a matter of a "naive" principal following the latest fad; it was a clear initiative from the city. Kathleen had anticipated what was coming and had been trying to keep the Everett ahead of the game, a pattern that would repeat itself throughout her tenure.

With this BPS mandate, professional development to implement the program came as an unexpected and welcome gift. The teachers would be trained to use the new program and would be obliged to instruct all of their students in their own classrooms—regardless of reading level.

Implementation was not without resistance. Teachers retrieved the old basal readers from the cabinets in the basement, claiming that struggling, lower-level readers needed the controlled introduction of vocabulary words that the basal provided. They insisted that the range of reading levels within each classroom was so great that they could not rely on a literature-based text alone. Furthermore, they felt that higher-level readers needed more challenging material and sought to put these students back into upper-grade classrooms during the reading period.

Teachers were not just questioning the district mandate; they were testing Kathleen as well. She chose to sidestep the confrontation. As long as teachers were using the new text, she did not stop those who were supplementing it with the basal readers. Nor did she confront those teachers who continued to track the higher-level readers by sending them to an upper grade for reading instruction. She knew that there were also some parents who wanted the tracking system to remain in place. Accordingly, she put a time limit on the practice so that parents and teachers would know that this would not continue forever. Kathleen mandated that by the start of the next year, all students would be taught by their classroom teachers.

Although ranks were divided, some teachers started to come around. Kathleen was encouraged. One teacher noted, "It's not like all of our kids were getting admitted to advanced work classes under the old system. We're a pretty professional group, so I think we know that we have to keep looking at what we're doing to see if it can get better."

One third grade teacher decided to monitor the naturally occurring research experiment that this split in methodology had brought about to compare the effectiveness of the two approaches in teaching reading. Several of her higher-level readers stayed in her classroom during the reading period, while others, because their parents had insisted, were sent to a fourth grade class. At the end of the year, the teacher told Kathleen that both groups stood out for improvement in reading. "The Stanford 9 data I have," she reported, "shows that the children who remained with me got the same high nineth percentiles as the children who went to the fourth grade. And, they all went off to the same advanced work classes at the end of the year."

Apparently, the literature-based, whole-group structure had worked as effectively for higher-level learners as the old grouped-by-ability tracking system. Significantly, Kathleen chose not to broadcast the results of the informal study to the Everett staff. Instead, she allowed the findings to travel through the teacher network. Would they be moved by this new evidence?

Almost a Member of the Faculty

The philosophy of the literature-based series that replaced basal readers was whole-group learning. If a child struggled, they were to be given extra support, such as reading with a tape recorder or another approved method. Flexible guided reading groups from which students could move up or down according to their level of skill and understanding *in that moment* would replace the static, leveled groups. Phonics would be embedded in the curriculum, taught incidentally rather than explicitly.

Everett teachers were nervous about the program. They were concerned that even if higher-level readers could transition without trouble, lower-level readers would be left behind. They considered the methodology "scattered" and feared that there were going to be gaps.

Soon after the literature-based series had been adopted in the beginning of Kathleen's second year, one of the reading teachers, a very knowledgeable and serious woman, approached Kathleen in her office just after dismissal. "We're having a faculty meeting on the reading program upstairs," she informed Kathleen. "We're really upset about the new curriculum."

Kathleen went upstairs to the auditorium and took a seat at one of the tables. The teacher leading the meeting began to state the various problems with the literature-based series. It was immediately obvious to Kathleen that the problems were real. Children did not have access to controlled vocabulary, and they did not have a phonics component. Kathleen had assumed that teachers would be able to include the phonics on their own, embedding it in the curriculum of the literature-based series. She began to appreciate that they needed a system to do that. She asked them, "So why don't you know how to teach phonics? You've been teaching phonics all of your life—why is it that you need a structured phonics program all of the sudden?" But she began to realize that the basal readers had phonics already included in the text. The staff did not know how to teach phonics independently of the material; it had always been prescribed for them. They believed that if phonics was not taught in this structured and defined way, the program would never work.

The meeting was uncomfortable. Everett teachers were, for the most part, polite and respectful and did not like to make scenes. Kathleen listened to the meeting organizer begin to speak about the way teachers at the Everett liked to approach the methods they had found effective over the years, but she knew there were teachers present who did not adhere to the old approach. She had been in every classroom, and she knew who did what. She was surprised at the generalizations the meeting organizer made, thinking to herself, "They have this belief about how things are that is not at all grounded in the reality of classroom instruction."

She decided to speak up. "There are people in this room who don't do things in the way you describe. I don't know why they're not speaking. I don't know why they aren't voicing their opinions." The room was silent.

Kathleen looked around and finally said to one of the teachers, "What about you? What do you think about this?" The teacher looked at her with an icy stare. "I'm not really a literacy expert," she declared, "and she is," nodding to the organizer. "I defer to her." "Except in your classroom," thought Kathleen, "where you do everything entirely differently." Kathleen knew she had made a misstep. The staff was clearly choosing to present a united front, and she was on the outside. She had challenged them, and it had served only to strengthen their resolve against the program she had advocated.

Respect and Restraint

Shortly after the meeting about the reading program, the reading teachers came to Kathleen to let her know that they had begun to investigate options for a structured phonics program. They justified their actions to Kathleen: "How can we give our kids this test? They don't know what the words are. They don't have the phonics strategies, and their vocabularies aren't controlled. The literature program is a nice thing to do a of couple times a week, but we have to teach *reading*. We have to *teach* our children to *read*. It isn't going to work." They told Kathleen that they were looking at a program called Won Way Phonics.

Kathleen knew all about Won Way Phonics, part of the Bradley Language Arts curriculum. The program was not respected in Boston. Kathleen had run the *only* school in the Lynn Public School system that did not have Won Way. Because everyone else in the system used it, she was criticized for turning it down.

Kathleen pleaded with her teachers to choose any program but Won Way, but they were adamant. "We've looked into it and it's absolutely the best program," they insisted. "We've gone to the Marshall School and we've seen it. We'd like to bring some other teachers over there to see for themselves."

"Well, that's a good idea," Kathleen conceded, "but what else are you going to look at?" "What else do you want us to look at?" they asked. Kathleen wasn't sure. She called several principals to see what structured phonics programs they used, but this was the first year of literature-based instruction in Boston, and schools were not using structured phonics. A few people told Kathleen that they were using the old basals to build phonics in.

Kathleen decided to advocate another program, the Literacy Collaborative, which her colleague Casel Walker was using at the Manning School. It had everything she liked, and the reading and classroom teachers at Everett seemed to think highly of it. Kathleen thought it was a shoo-in; she was thrilled. But, the day after she had discussed the program with the reading teachers, they came to see her with concerned looks on their faces that said, "It's not going to work."

"We can't do Literacy Collaborative," they said, listing the reasons why. Kathleen was dismayed, "What are you talking about? You didn't go to a school to see it; how can you just stand there and say we can't do it?" In response, they organized a committee to observe the Literacy Collaborative in action, along with the Won Way program. At the end of their investigation, they chose Won Way Phonics.

Kathleen felt that she had not truly been heard, but she deferred to her staff. She had tried to introduce them to the Literacy Collaborative programs, but they felt strongly that it was a waste of time for their students to be in learning centers. These classes were not well prepared and not individualized; the teachers believed it would be better to have a structured phonics program alongside a balanced reading program. In the end, there was such a groundswell of support for Won Way that Kathleen acquiesced. She trained her entire staff in Won Way but let them know she also wanted them to include other practices of a balanced literacy program. Won Way would be just one component; she did not want to see a literary program built around phonics.

The team worked together and, with the help of coaches, developed its own balanced literacy program. The teachers were able to include what they liked about the literature-based program along with Won Way for structured phonics. The balanced literacy model evolved over time. They stepped into Writers Workshop first, far ahead of the eventual mandate by the district to do so, and ultimately Readers Workshop as well. The initial program relied on guided reading groups, examination of students' scores, Writers Workshop, and Won Way.

The adoption of the new program was hard for Kathleen, because at the time the city was truly resisting phonics. Other principals would come up to her, smirking, and say, "Oh, you're the one doing Won Way Phonics, right?" At the time, she did not really respect the idea of structured phonics; but looking back, Kathleen was pleased that she listened to her teachers rather than insisting that the whole language approach was the only way to go. By listening to her staff, she took great strides in building her relationship with them. They developed the Everett literacy program themselves rather than purchasing a packaged program, so there was a tremendous sense of ownership, and the teachers were able to grow and change the program as needed.

Everett teachers were given the freedom to do what they thought was right, and they were successful. Won Way became a positive aspect of the Everett's literacy curriculum. It worked and was part of the reason that Everett students did well. Within just one year, scores jumped dramatically. Won Way helped transform Everett students into good readers who could concentrate on comprehension without having to worry about phonics. The teachers had been right; their students had needed a structured phonics program.

It would take nearly a decade for the research to come out stating that structured phonics should be integrated into every literacy program. The Everett was ahead of the game again, and this time it was the teachers who had made it happen.

Nothing Less Than Excellence

Early in her tenure at the Everett, Kathleen, as well as the rest of the teaching staff, could see that one fourth grade teacher was not performing up to her high academic standards. This was a problem that demanded her attention. It was also a symbolic issue: How she dealt with him would be a clear sign that teachers would now be judged primarily on measured student performance. The question was how fast to move knowing that she risked losing the faculty's allegiance. Letting go of a hardworking veteran because of poor job performance would be a first for the Everett. This teacher, like everybody else in the school, had always received an "excellent" on his performance evaluations from the previous principal. Would classroom performance now trump seniority?

The teacher was a courteous man of about sixty years. He was well respected and liked by his fellow teachers, and parents loved him. But he could not do the literacy work. Before Kathleen had come to the Everett, when reading was taught through tracking by ability group, the principal and teachers had covered for him by giving him the high-level group. But as the work got harder, demands on him ratcheted up. Now that they were not tracking by ability, it was increasingly apparent to

Kathleen that he really did not know how to teach reading to a diverse group of students. The children in his class just weren't learning.

Kathleen spoke with him. "I gave you a 'satisfactory' last year, but I'm really worried now that you can't do the literacy work. Don't we both agree on that?" He agreed, explaining that he didn't have a background in reading. He also told Kathleen that he planned to retire in a few years.

But Kathleen couldn't wait that long. She told him, "I'm going to take a couple of areas in your evaluation, write them up as 'unsatisfactory,' and add an instructional prescription." Then she asked him about his retirement situation. She learned that his wife did not work and that his retirement pension would be their entire income. She was worried that he would not be able to afford to retire sooner, as every extra year he taught would increase the amount of his pension.

Kathleen met with him four times that year, going over the prescription. She required him to plan for ninety extra minutes, forty-five minutes with his colleague and forty-five minutes with the content coach. But he could not implement the plans laid out for him. Kathleen spoke to him about how worried she was. She didn't want to interfere with his retirement and asked him if there was anything she could do to support him, explaining that he might need to go back to school and actually take some courses in teaching reading. He said he understood, but the meeting was tense. In April, he told Kathleen that he would retire, acknowledging that staying on would not be good for the students.

Kathleen knew that if she really had had to "go after" him through the evaluation process, it would have caused a tremendous rift in her relationship with the rest of the staff. "We made common ground when we agreed that his teaching wasn't good for the students," she said. "It could have been a very messy situation, but I believe that all of the work I had done with him along the way made the difference. He *chose* to go."

The Teachers Come Through

Opening her mail early in her second year, Kathleen came across a notice from the district offering an opportunity for schools to apply to be a part of Cohort I, a program that would bring resources, money, and consulting expertise to assist in implementing a whole-school change effort. There was no question in Kathleen's mind that the Everett could use the help. The school was isolated, and opportunities like this could not to be taken lightly. However, Kathleen would need 80 percent of the faculty to agree to apply for the program and abide by the specifications. She wasn't optimistic—she couldn't get 80 percent of the staff to agree to anything!

Although she felt that she had pushed her staff too much already, Kathleen figured that she didn't have much to lose. She put the application notice into all faculty mailboxes, believing all the while that nothing would come of it. The next day three teachers came to her with the notice in hand. "We saw this," they said, indicating the paper in their hands, "and we were wondering if you thought it was a good idea for us to apply." As much as she wanted it, Kathleen resisted a plug for the proposal. "It's up to you," she said calmly. "If you mobilize the faculty, we can do it."

They did. With Kathleen's assistance, the faculty team wrote a winning proposal that brought a change coach, a content coach, and $12,000 to the Everett to work on a district-prescribed, whole-school change plan. "We were ecstatic," Kathleen remembered. "We thought we had hit the jackpot; there was great excitement. The school had never won anything like this."

The Wrong Coach

As a part of initiating the Cohort I process, Kathleen had been asked to select a "change coach." She chose a familiar figure at the Everett who had assisted her in developing an instructional change strategy and periodically facilitated teacher meetings.

Everett teachers respected expertise. They considered themselves experts in their fields and felt that the only people worth learning from were other professionals, people who possessed an even deeper knowledge in a designated area. The coach's team facilitation skills were not recognized as legitimate expertise, however. In the eyes of the staff, she had no public school experience and was not a literacy expert. Her attempts at team process orchestration went unappreciated. Kathleen saw what was happening and did not want to lose the precious opportunity to move instruction forward at the Everett. She let the coach go and replaced her with someone with considerably more literacy background who was capable of doing hands-on work in the classrooms.

Kathleen's decision to switch coaches would prove a watershed moment with the Everett faculty. Not only did it indicate that she agreed with their views of what an "expert" should be, but, more importantly, her decision showed that she respected and valued her teachers' work and that she was willing to listen to what they had to say. From that point on, a new trust developed between Kathleen and the teachers. Kathleen was now a part of their team. The faculty for the most part, had always liked Kathleen personally; but disputes over reading had forced a wedge between them. By acknowledging their concerns, she broke the tension, and the faculty began to respect her as a leader.

The Tide Turns

Kathleen had been in schools where progress was difficult because teachers simply could not do the work. She was hopeful that she could make real improvements at the Everett because she knew the Everett staff was capable of it; Everett teachers understood the issues.

Confident in her strong staff, Kathleen worked tirelessly to push them forward, though they often resisted her efforts. As their relationship grew more familiar, teachers began to joke with Kathleen about her hard-driving ways. She was relieved when this began to happen: "Once they make fun of you and it's on the table, that's a good thing. At meetings, they began to say, 'Oh god, she read another book; what are we going to have to do now?'" Eventually, the staff took to giving her the benefit of the doubt when it came to making changes at the Everett. "We know, Kathleen, that it isn't you," a staff member would say, "that the district is making us do it." "No," she would insist, "I *believe* in this. This is the right thing."

Kathleen had taken a lot of time to build strong relationships with her staff. They did not agree with her about everything, but they had grown to respect her and believe in her. They knew that she wanted to be the principal of an excellent school and was committed to making the Everett the very best place that it could be. The once-hesitant Everett staff became willing to attempt new ideas and approaches.

One of their new initiatives was the Instructional Leadership Team (ILT), a new system of organization the district was piloting. With this approach, a teacher from every grade level would sit on the ILT, and together they would make instructional decisions for the school. Kathleen would have a voice on the team as well, but only equal to that of the other team members. Everett teachers were not accustomed to this kind of formalized leadership, but they stepped up to the task. At times they were nervous to speak for their colleagues; at other times they were quick to challenge Kathleen and speak their minds.

Everett on Display: Were They Ready?

While Kathleen had won over the teachers personally and proven herself as a leader they could trust, some of her other goals had reached a dead end. She was frustrated in her attempt for greater instructional and curricular reform and was discouraged when comparing what she felt was possible with the reality of what she saw as too much "chalk and talk" at the front of the classroom.

One Tuesday evening, Kathleen's deputy superintendent called to ask her whether it would be possible for a group of forty administrative leaders (including BPS deputy superintendents, cluster leaders and coordinators, and Dr. Thomas Nardone, former principal in the New York City Public Schools) to do a "walk-through" at the Everett the following morning. The walk-through had been scheduled to take place at another Boston school, but that principal's mother had passed away and she would be out of the building. They were looking for another school that had succeeded in improving students' academic performance.

Kathleen was honored that they had thought of the Everett—but *tomorrow*? As employed in educational circles, a walk-through was not merely a guided tour through the hallways and back to the principal's office. The entourage would spread out, observe instruction in the classrooms, question the staff and students, and assemble a full-scale critique of the Everett. Though she was excited by the prospect, Kathleen wondered if she should take the risk. There was, after all, a chance that they would see and hear the worst of the Everett.

With no time to consult her staff, Kathleen agreed to the walk-through on one condition: the team would have to provide feedback about what they saw in classrooms. Always looking for a fresh perspective and anxious to push her staff forward, Kathleen hoped that the feedback would make the experience worthwhile. She felt reasonably confident that the Everett would be able to hold its own in the limelight.

In the early afternoon of the next day, after the walk-through had been completed, Kathleen sat in the middle of the auditorium to receive the feedback she'd requested. She would be the focus of a "fishbowl" exercise, with the administrative leaders arranged in a circle around her. "It was amazing how much they got from just one day," she recollected. "It was positive and negative— but I thought that they were fairly accurate. Because it was my school, my baby, it was little hard for me to hear what they had to say. But hey, I knew that what they said was true. I understood the things that they were criticizing."

Everett teachers were scheduled to receive their feedback after Kathleen had received hers. Dr. Nardone, the walk-through facilitator, took Kathleen aside before she called in the staff. "Okay, it's *your* school," he reassured Kathleen. "What do *you* want to accomplish?" Kathleen did not need time to think about the answer to that question. "Well," she replied promptly, "I think that there's too much direct teaching going on in classrooms. And although it's done incredibly skillfully, I think the kids need more time to experiment and discover. That's why we're not scoring at Levels 3 and 4 on our assessments. We are doing all right moving students out of Level 1, but they're not reaching the more advanced levels of achievement." He asked her, "So, what is your answer?"

Kathleen's prekindergarten program was run by a teacher who believed strongly in a constructivist curriculum based on encouraging critical thought and student ownership of the learning process. Her science program also addressed the Massachusetts Curriculum Frameworks through experimentation and hands-on discovery, and her highest MCAS scores were in science. Observing in those classes, Kathleen could not help but feel that constructivism was the way to go. "Constructivism is like what whole language was to me," she told Nardone. "I sense that it is right, and there's a lot of evidence for it, but I'm having trouble getting the faculty to believe in it."

Nardone agreed with Kathleen that the principles of constructivism could help to push the Everett forward. As the head of the delegation, when he presented his feedback to the staff, he incorporated Kathleen's ideas, highlighting constructivist practices present in the school and implied that they should be incorporated into instruction throughout the school.

Kathleen knew that when people walk through a school, they don't really know what kinds of struggles the faculty is facing. They can't possibly understand the big picture in just one day. However, this was a rare opportunity. Feedback from an outsider—especially an expert—could sometimes help to drive home ideas that would otherwise not have been taken seriously. Kathleen knew that her teachers would not have listened if she had simply told them that constructivism was the answer. They were tired of her pushing and still proud of their success in shaping the reading program. She could use the credibility from the walk-through team to add to her own political capital.

She knew that if Nardone told Everett teachers that they were doing really well, it could be a bad thing. Teachers might be inclined to think, "Oh, we're doing everything right" and continue about their business, not even considering the prospect of making changes. She was hopeful that Nardone's presentation to the teachers would be positive but leave plenty of room for improvement. What he said was perfect; she couldn't believe what a powerful effect it had. There had been enough positive feedback for teachers to feel that their hard work had really been acknowledged, which made it a good time to say, "Ok, see this? We are really on the road here, but how can we take it up a notch? How do we accelerate the improvement?"

Fortuitously, the very next issue of *Educational Leadership* was dedicated entirely to constructivism, featuring an article entitled "The Courage to be Constructivist."[1] Kathleen copied and distributed the piece, commenting on it at the next ILT meeting. "I think this is the right road," she told them. "But that's just my take on things." "Although," she was quick to add, "I think that the team that just visited us believes in this also. Do you think that this is where we have been heading?"

It took several sessions for the ILT to embrace the pedagogy and forge five principles, adapted from the *Educational Leadership* article, with which to measure constructivism's application at the Everett. The team members, prompted by Kathleen and the journal article, could see that constructivism would assist their efforts in moving students on the MCAS from Levels 1 and 2 toward Levels 3 and 4. Level 3 performance required students to exhibit problem solving and critical thinking skills. The constructivist methodology would certainly prepare them for this. The Everett was also on the verge of implementing a new mathematics program, the TERC *Investigations* curriculum. Constructivism and *Investigations* were cut from the same cloth; both concentrated heavily on experimentation and hands-on learning. The timing was right.

The ILT went on to organize a professional development day around the *Investigations* curriculum. Kathleen immediately knew how important this first step was going to be for the adoption of constructivism at the Everett. She knew that if she got up and lectured about constructivism, no one would remember it. But if they worked in teams and planned out the content of their new math curriculum around the constructivist principles, it would become ingrained. Kathleen would have to keep it alive, of course, and she did. Into her daily classroom visits she incorporated a section for feedback about the constructivist principles she did or did not see in the classroom that day. She thought of her regular feedback as another way for teachers to monitor their own progress, putting what they had learned from the research into practice.

Constructivism in the Classroom: Basic Principles for Moving Students to Level 3

1. Teachers seek and value students' points of view. Knowing what students think about concepts (prior assessment) helps teachers formulate classroom lessons and differentiate instruction on the basis of student needs and interests.
2. Teachers structure lessons to challenge student suppositions.
3. Teachers recognize that students must attach relevance to the curriculum. Relevance grows interest in learning. The heart of the constructivist approach: learners control their learning (ownership).
4. Teachers structure lessons around big ideas, not small bits of information. Exposing students to wholes first helps them determine the relevant parts as they refine their understanding of the wholes (writing exemplars).
5. Teachers assess student learning in the context of daily classroom investigations, not as separate events.

Note: Adapted from Martin G. Brooks and Jacqueline Grennon Brooks, "The Courage to Be Constructivist," *Educational Leadership* 57, no. 3 (November 1999).

Providing Regular Feedback through Classroom Visits

The professional evaluation instrument used in Boston was cumbersome, and most principals agreed that it did not act as a real impetus for change. Kathleen knew that regular classroom visits were much more powerful.

She used a clipboard to keep track of her daily classroom visits. Without a careful grid with all of her teachers' schedules blocked in, she knew she would never be able to ensure that she was making her visits equitably. This maintenance of a systematic schedule to observe teachers was a lesson she had learned from her mentor, Kim Marshall.

Each visit followed approximately the same routine. She would begin by writing at the top of her notepad the teacher's name, the date and time, and the subject/topic of the lesson that she was observing. As she observed the lesson, she made notes on the context of the lesson (this was for her own reference later on, when she would use these notes to write up teacher evaluations) and feedback for the teacher. She used carbon-paper notepads so that on completion of the visit, she could leave one copy of her notes on the teacher's desk and take the other with her for her files.

One sunny morning during a January thaw, Kathleen slipped into a third grade class, carrying her notepad and her clipboard of constructivist principles. Evidencing a history of such visits, her presence went seemingly unnoticed in the classroom by both students and teacher. Small groups of students dotted the room. Their animated conversations were intermittently punctuated by questions for classmates or the teacher. Kathleen pulled up a chair and joined one of the groups. "Tell me, what are you doing?" she asked the children. "We have to figure out how many carts it will take to carry all of the groceries," one student explained.

Kathleen examined the work the group had done thus far and nodded her approval of their efforts. "It looks like you're making good progress. But tell me, do you know why [your teacher] has asked you to solve this problem?" The student's eyes lit up with his reply. "She says 'cause when we grow up, we'll know how to figure things out." Kathleen smiled at she stood up. "Thanks for letting me sit in. I'll let you get back to your problem."

Before leaving the classroom, Kathleen left a note on the teacher's desk, complimenting her on the open-ended framing of her assignment and commenting on how diligently the students were solving the problem. Kathleen did ask that she give a bit more thought to how she might provide students with better appreciation for why she was asking them to solve this kind of problem.

The teacher knew that Kathleen would follow up—she followed up on everything! "When she asks a question, as in the note I just received, she expects a response. . . . I like to get her feedback and suggestions. Her constant feedback keeps inquiry alive. It makes a big difference. I know that someone else in the building is aware of what I'm doing in my classroom."

The district eventually noticed the difference this feedback could make as well. Years after Kathleen had begun collecting documentation about her informal feedback; BPS implemented a new requirement that principals attach notes from informal visits to the formal evaluation document.

Common Planning: Taking Instructions to the Next Level

Kathleen was nervous. It was her third year at the Everett, and she was on her way to an early-morning meeting that she knew would be contentious. She was going to announce that teachers would have to plan their lessons regularly with their grade-level colleagues. Ninety minutes of their planning and development (P&D) time each month would be spent in common planning meetings. She had looked at the union contract and knew that she could do it, but she also knew that it would not go over well. Teachers at the Everett were fiercely independent, and she knew she would be treading on sacred ground by interfering with any of the four P&D periods they were allotted each week.

After experiencing car trouble on the highway, Kathleen pulled into the Everett parking lot five minutes after the scheduled start time of the meeting. She ran in, rushed to the front of the room, and started right in, out of breath, "I'm thinking of doing common planning, where the two classroom teachers [from each grade level] come together and meet for ninety minutes a month." They stared at her, wondering what in the world she was talking about. "So, I'd just like to go around . . . ." She interrupted herself. "It's hard for me—the same three people speak up and no one else tells me what they think. So, I'm going to go around the room and listen to what each of you has to say about this."

In her haste, she had not been clear with her staff that she had made the decision about common planning; teachers would be required to plan together for ninety minutes each month. Her plan to go around the room and share opinions on the topic was not actually a way of opening the issue up for discussion but was instead merely a tactic to get a read on how the teachers felt about the decision. After years of observing, taking consensus, making compromises, and letting her teachers take the lead, Kathleen had earned the privilege of making reasoned, unilateral decisions by repeatedly proving to her staff that she did not always intend to do so. But unfortunately, because she was frazzled, she didn't take the time to make this clear.

As they went around the room, teachers expressed their lack of interest in the idea. "You'll just take all that time from us," they objected. "That's our planning time, and if we do this, we won't have any time to plan." They argued that collaborative planning was not really planning; in order to be effective, they had to plan on their own.

Only three teachers said that they'd be willing to try it. One was a new teacher who mentioned that she might be able to benefit from hearing the ideas of her more experienced colleague. "She was one of the first to speak," Kathleen remembered, "not knowing that this was going to be the most unpopular idea on the planet." An experienced third grade teacher also thought it sounded like a good idea; she understood the value of collaboration. One other teacher admitted that common planning was a worthwhile practice, but she went on to say that she didn't like it, didn't want to do it, and didn't intend to change her schedule.

At the end of the meeting, Kathleen said, "The issue is collaboration and providing ourselves with time to be able to collaborate and to look at student work. I've heard everything that's been said, but I am absolutely sure that we have to be playing from the same deck. Without common planning, we can't even play the same game. Collaboration is what whole-school change is all about. So, I'm going to go forward with it." She knew that if she was going to be successful in school reform at the Everett, she had to provide time for teachers to sit down and have conversations with each other about their work.

The teachers, however, were furious. They couldn't believe that Kathleen had asked them to speak their minds and then ignored what they'd had to say. They were so used to her following their lead that they could not believe that she was going to have her own way. It was as though she had betrayed their trust.

Through manipulation of the school schedule, Kathleen created spaces for grade-level teams to meet. The question now was what they would talk about during this time. How would these meetings lead to high standards of student performance and an integrated curriculum? Looking at student work would be important in determining consistency across classrooms. Students in the two second grade classrooms would need to learn the same things to prepare them for third grade. To make this happen, teachers would need mechanisms for assessing performance across classrooms. Using a combination of assessments and samples of student work, common planning would help teachers to determine what they were going to teach and how. Looking at student work to identify student strengths and challenges would provide focus for teachers when planning lessons, and group discussions would give teachers an opportunity to get feedback from their colleagues about changing instruction to increase student achievement.

Teachers would bring samples of ungraded student papers and tests and come to agreement about the scoring. The introduction of "interrater reliability" would enable the Everett teachers to see beyond their classrooms and begin to look at the school as a whole. This format would eventually allow teachers to map a schoolwide curriculum where each grade would build off the previous one and prepare the students for the next grade. The issue was "next steps": changing instruction to reflect the outcomes of the data, building a belief that common planning sessions should be about looking at data and using that data to inform instructional planning.

Kathleen allocated 180 minutes a month for grade-level sessions, and she planned to participate in as many as she could. It was an incredible time commitment, but she believed that she would eventually be able to ease off as teachers began to really "land" the process. Somehow, it took a lot longer to land than she originally expected.

After an uneven start, the ILT decided to look at why common planning was working at some grade levels and not at others. They realized that teachers who were only participating when Kathleen was present were not achieving the same success as those who were truly planning together for ninety minutes a week. It worked when Kathleen was with them; but when she didn't attend, teams weren't as punctual or as focused.

Formal Looking at Student Work (LASW) sessions eventually came about after Boston's Plan for Excellence introduced them as one of their Six Essentials. Kathleen had begun common planning because she'd realized that there was no forum in which to discuss student work. When

LASW came down the pike, common planning was the means by which to do it.

MCAS Is Not Enough: Formative Assessments to the Rescue

In 1998, the benchmark of student achievement was the state-mandated MCAS. Relatively speaking, the MCAS was a good calibration of students' knowledge and problem-solving capacities, but it suffered from a major flaw: The results arrived a full six months after the May administration, well into the subsequent school year. By the time teachers found out where the gaps were, their students had already moved on to the next grade level.

Kathleen realized that if the school was really going to use data to drive instructional and curricular improvement, student performance assessments needed to be administered more frequently—say, three or four times per year—and have a quicker turnaround time. Formative assessments, designed to "inform" instruction, would generate interim student performance data and keep Kathleen and teachers focused on the pulse of student performance. This way they would be able to inform and modify their technique throughout the year to target struggling students and meet their goals, hopefully diminishing the potential for low MCAS performance in the process.

A full year before other schools in the district, the Everett began using formative assessments. Kathleen had always tried to implement programs before they became mandated. It was her way of building credibility with the district. When the suggestions became mandates, as they inevitably did, she would be able to inform the district about her experiences and hopefully prevent the mandate from being "too screwed up." It gave her the opportunity to have a conversation with the district and implore them to use the Everett's experiences to inform their parameters.

Though the district might have subsequently applauded Everett's methods, the teachers resisted Kathleen's early attempts at a formative assessment initiative. To them, it was just another instance of the ILT taking away from their teaching time. They were teachers first, planners and data-reflectors second.

Finding the right formative assessments was hard, especially for the fourth and fifth grades. Everett teachers decided it might be worthwhile to talk with other systems that were implementing formative assessments. For reading, they settled on a teacher-developed instrument being used in the Weston Public Schools. For the writing assessment they used Kim Marshall's Mather School writing rubrics. Because the teachers had to work together with Kathleen to find the assessments that the Everett could use, it became a team process. They still did not really want to do it, but now it was something that they had created, a piecemeal of assessments they had selected. By participating in the process, their resistance began to wear down.

Tackling two subject areas simultaneously was very ambitious. Teachers needed professional development to understand how to give a "cold prompt" and learn how to administer the reading assessments. The actual data that first year was less important than the process by which it was obtained. Once Kathleen had collected data from each teacher, she averaged it out by hand, writing down the percentage of students at each level. Not wanting to use teachers' names, she coded one room at each grade level "red room" and one "blue room." She didn't want anyone to feel scrutinized or singled out. While Everett teachers were not yet in a place where they could interpret the data, it was remarkable that they had put the tests and scoring methodology into practice.

By the next year, formative assessments were mandated by the district, and the Everett was once again ahead of the game. Teachers who had balked at the idea a year ago, now nodded nonchalantly at the news of the mandate. "Oh," they shrugged, "we're already doing that."

Now that the staff was not distracted by learning how to do it, they could use the data more effectively. They developed their own writing rubrics, and in January the ILT said, "Okay, these are our results for January. Now let's look to see if we are going to meet our SMART [specific, measurable, attainable, relevant, and time-bound] goals in June or if we're going to need to accelerate instruction." They began more sophisticated conversations about how to meet their goals. The Everett faculty began to look at data in LASW sessions and started to feel informed about their progress throughout the year.

Kathleen paid one of her staff members a small stipend to enter the formative assessment data into charts, making it a little more meaningful. The charts listed the SMART goal on the bottom, enabling Everett staff to easily compare their current standing with their ultimate objectives. The new data-charting system was effective and user-friendly. Teachers could see how many students met the goal and how many did not.

Data Doesn't Matter If No One Is Paying Attention

In January, when the formative assessment data arrived, Kathleen looked at the numbers for each class and was shocked at what she saw in the first grade. She knew these students to be an average cohort of children without many challenges. Their scores on the kindergarten formative assessment (the Observation Survey) were decidedly average, but their first grade formative assessment scores were frightening. The Developmental Reading Assessment (DRA) benchmark for the end of grade one was 16. Kathleen expected that by January most first graders would have reached at least a 10. In this group, there were a few students at 10, but the vast majority scored lower. Kathleen spoke to the literacy and content coaches and immediately arranged a meeting with the kindergarten and first grade teachers, inviting reading specialists as well.

She asked the group if they had any idea why the first grade scores were so low. Initially the first grade teachers were defensive about the data and quick to put the blame on the students themselves, saying, "These kids don't know anything. This kid here, for example, should really be in special education." The kindergarten teachers, who had the group the year before, disagreed. "They were doing okay on the Observation Survey," they said in bewilderment. "Why would they be having difficulty on the DRA in January?" They turned to the first grade teachers, only half in jest: "What did you do with my babies? What happened?"

Kathleen couldn't get the words of the first grade teachers out of her mind—"They belong in special education." She wanted the teachers to know that they couldn't dismiss students so lightly, putting more weight on who they were than what they had been taught. "Our job as educators," she said quietly, "is to figure out how to reach each student and teach each one the skills they need to learn. Even if they are kids who will eventually end up in special education, they are still going to take the MCAS. So what are we going to do to make sure they succeed?"

Gradually, the conversation grew more specific, focusing on teaching methodology. The reading teachers began to point to skill areas that students were struggling with, identifying how they could help them. In the end, it was a very productive meeting; they discovered that students were writing too often without getting regular feedback. Teachers were simply not conferencing enough. The meeting made Kathleen realize that formative data, averages, and graphs were not enough if teachers didn't own the data results. On their own, teachers were not inclined to discuss data or alter their instructional practice to improve student outcomes.

Kathleen asked each first grade teacher to show her their students' writing folders. "Let's look at the status of each kid," she said, opening the first folder. "How often are you taking a child's folder and giving them feedback? How often are you meeting with your students?" "But, there's not enough time," the teachers protested. Kathleen shook her head. The children were writing too often without getting regular feedback. Just as teachers needed constant feedback to improve and fine-tune their instruction, students needed steady and specific feedback to improve at their job, learning to read and write accurately and effectively. Teachers would have to provide this information through written comments on a student's writing or via targeted student-teacher conferences around a given piece of work.

By June, Kathleen had eight students who did not reach the benchmark. It was not great, but the intervention they had put together in January certainly saved many more students from the same fate. Teachers had looked at their data and developed ways to address students' misunderstandings. Specifically, the literacy specialist worked with classroom teachers on comprehension skills, and together they refined their learning centers to make them more focused and meaningful in meeting the needs of their students.

Parents as Instructional Partners

The staff had fine-tuned the literacy instruction with an excellent curriculum and pedagogy. But despite their best efforts, student reading scores had not budged from a three-year plateau. Kathleen and the ILT began to pay attention to research that indicated that the total amount children read directly affects their reading achievement. Only having their students for a limited number of hours each day, teachers did not have the time (with all of the curriculum they were now required to cover) to have students read for an hour each day—the time they agreed was necessary for students to reap true benefits. Teachers realized that their students would have to read at home to fill this gap. Teachers and parents would need to partner to make it happen.

At the next Back-to-School night, the Home Reading project was the only topic on the agenda. They had developed Home Reading contracts for all students, grades K–5, one for primary students and one for elementary students. Primary students must read, or be read to, for twenty minutes each day, and elementary students must read for thirty minutes each day at least four days a week; this schedule included weekends and vacations.

For the next several years, teacher interactions with parents were focused on Home Reading. They hoped that if they put all their efforts into one goal, it could be achieved.

The contract went home every Tuesday in the parent communication folder. The contract from the previous week was signed by parents and students and returned the next day. Of course, this was an honor system, and people could lie, so Kathleen did not consider the data gathered about Home Reading to be 100 percent accurate. However, she did see it improve greatly over time. (See Table 5.1.)

Table 5.1 Percentage of Students Reading at Home

Always completes weekly Home Reading	55%
Regularly completes weekly Home Reading	20%
Completes weekly Home Reading fairly often	16%
Rarely completes weekly Home Reading	10%
Never completes weekly Home Reading	0%

The Everett set a benchmark against which students were expected to measure: 75 percent of students in grades K–5 would regularly return their reading contract. ("Regularly" meant that a student returned his or her weekly contract anywhere between six and ten times per twelve-week marking period.) To ensure that families understood that the Home Reading requirement was as important as any work assigned during the

school day, the Everett included a Home Reading section on student report cards, and students earned a "grade" in Home Reading.

With 75 percent of students regularly returning the contract over the
course of the school year, Kathleen attributed the Everett's success to the
value that staff placed on reading in their own lives, which they made
evident to their students. Their fervent support of the Home Reading
program encouraged students and parents alike to take the program
seriously.

Teachers received compiled reports of their students' Home Reading
from Kathleen each marking period, enabling them to see where their
students fell in comparison to other students in the building. Kathleen
felt that this was a powerful way to encourage teachers to make Home
Reading an important part of what was expected in their classrooms. No
teacher at the Everett would want to look at the thrice-annual report and
see that the students in their classroom were not as responsible about
their Home Reading as students in other classrooms.

With the Home Reading program, Kathleen and the Everett had done
it again. Vigilantly observing what was blocking student achievement,
teachers took their cue from the research literature and formulated a plan
to address an area of weakness. Their innovation did not go unnoticed.

After assessing the efficacy of several Home Reading programs, BPS
subsequently required all schools to implement Home Reading contracts. To promote the mandate, they produced a video highlighting several successful Home Reading programs, the Everett's program among
them. The video, which featured interviews with principals and parents
involved in Home Reading, was sent to the home of every BPS child before the opening of school in August 2003.

One of the reasons that the Everett's Home Reading program worked
so well was its extraordinary library. The Everett was the proud home
of one of the best elementary school libraries in the district—the best,
Kathleen would often boast proudly, *automated* elementary school library in Boston. The library, dedicated in the spring of 2002, was the
result of extremely generous private donations and tremendous volunteer efforts from business partners and friends of the Everett, the likes of
which were virtually unheard of in Boston. The primary funders, Allen
and Nancy Clapp, had become involved with the school when Allen, a
retired businessman, was assigned to Kathleen as her "business mentor"
during an experimental program to match district principals with people

from the business world to see if corporate-sector knowledge might be useful in the district. Allen and his wife, Nancy, a retired librarian, were taken with Kathleen and the Everett community. Allen began volunteering his time, helping out with odd jobs and in classrooms. Once the school library was up and running, Nancy volunteered her time serving as librarian three days a week.

Kathleen knew that the high-quality, 8,000-plus-volume library was a real support to the Home Reading program. Because of it, parents and students who may have appreciated the Home Reading program in theory but would not have had the time or initiative to make weekly visits to a public library, had a vast array of wonderful children's literature available to them at a place they came to each and every day—the Everett School.

The Many Tongues of Parental Engagement

"Every Everett parent knows: Tuesday is the night that you better check the backpack," Kathleen laughed. "If you aren't going into those backpacks every night, you have to at least go in on Tuesday. Everything for the week comes home that day in the purple 'Parent Communication' folder." One side of the folder contained papers and notices that went home on Tuesday and stayed home. The other side contained papers that went home on Tuesday but needed to be signed and returned the next day.

In addition to the weekly Home Reading contracts, the purple folder contained the weekly newsletter to parents, *The Home-School Connection*. *Home-School* was a summary of everything happening at the Everett, within the BPS, or in the community that Kathleen felt might be interesting or useful to Everett parents. Similar to her reasoning behind the Morning Memo, *Home-School* was meant to empower the parents by keeping them informed. The day of the select group of involved, "in-the-know" parents was a thing of the past. Through *Home-School*, all parents had access to the same information; all Everett parents were now "in-the-know."

Despite the best of intentions, there was one crippling problem with the contents of the purple folders: 30 percent of Everett parents could not read them. These parents, primarily of Vietnamese and Cape Verdean heritage, were dependent on their children to translate the material sent home and keep them informed about what needed to be sent back. To provide something of a "safety net" for parents who could not read the English on their own, Kathleen asked teachers to go over the contents of the newsletter with their students each Tuesday afternoon, trying to ensure that if the students at least understood the topics covered in the newsletter, they could pass some of the information on to their parents

An examination by Kathleen and the ILT of the year-by-year progress of students described by the system as English Language Learners (ELLs) delivered a startling piece of news: The ELLs were losing ground academically relative to their peers who came from homes where English was the primary language. Kathleen assembled a multiconstituent committee charged with recommending how the school might improve services to ELLs and reach-out to non-English-speaking parents.

The committee was short lived, but one of its recommendations was a series of parent meetings conducted in the native languages of Kathleen's most dominant non-English-speaking groups: Vietnamese and Cape Verdean Creole. These family meetings were not merely translated into Vietnamese and Cape Verdean Creole; they were held in these languages and translated into English for Kathleen and any interested English-speaking teachers or parents who chose to attend. The language-based parent meetings provided a forum for parents to communicate and get to know one another. This built a connection between parents and the school their children attended, making it a place where they, too, were welcome. This forum enabled non-English-speaking parents to ask questions about policy and events going on within the school with translators present to ensure that they understood the replies. The meetings gave Kathleen an opportunity to build relationships with a group of parents with whom she'd always had a difficult time connecting ,the ones with whom she could not even exchange hellos.

The Everett ELL committee had decided to keep the meetings primarily social, celebrating cultural holidays, like the Asian New Year, so that parents would want to come and not feel any insecurity or pressure over a topic they were unfamiliar with. They wanted parents to feel that they could just *be* at their school, that the school wanted to reach out to them, to honor and respect their culture and traditions. But the staff did mention Home Reading and upcoming school events and ask parents if they had any questions.

Unlike at other meetings, non-English-speaking parents often vocalized their questions. It made sense; at meetings geared toward an English-speaking audience, even with translators present, revealing that you did not understand was embarrassing. At the language-based meetings, many parents admitted that they did not understand any of the parameters of the Home Reading program. They did not know how much they or their children were supposed to read; and because some of them could not read English themselves, they could not comprehend how they were expected to read to their children, or ascertain if and when their children were reading. Kathleen and her staff explained that parents could read to their children in any language and that if they came from an oral tradition, even telling their children a folktale would count toward the requirement.

One of the original goals of the meetings was to find leaders among parents in the Vietnamese and Cape Verdean communities who would be willing to join the schools' formal parent group, the School Parent Council, which had been all white and all English-speaking for as long as Kathleen had been at the Everett. She desperately wanted to bring some diversity to the group and make sure that all of her students were represented. She was having trouble finding willing leaders to bring aboard, however, so she hoped that leaders who had a strong interest in the school would naturally emerge at the language-based meetings. With some English language skills, these leaders could report back on the council's activities to the parent group whose language they shared.

Unfortunately, it was not that simple. Neither the Vietnamese nor the Cape Verdean sessions seemed to be yield a volunteer to join the School Parent Council. In addition, as the meetings carried on for two years, Kathleen began to sense some hostility on the part of the involved white parents on whom she had always relied for fundraising and other school needs. Although she did not understand the cause, Kathleen, ever-patient, chose not to question the parents. She instead waited until they were ready to approach her.

Finally, one parent with whom Kathleen had a good relationship broached the reason for the dissent in the council. It turned out that the time and energy put into the language-based meetings made them feel as though they were being discriminated against. Why was it that Vietnamese parents could have a new year celebration and Cape Verdean families could hold a "family night" and they—the parents who had always been there for the Everett, raising money, volunteering at festivals, and organizing the Halloween party—were not being invited to bring their children to school one evening for a celebration of any kind?

Kathleen understood that the events created to include parents who did not have a strong relationship with the school were, in effect, excluding parents who did. Although flyers for the meetings always cheerfully announced that all were welcome, she knew that the average English-speaking parent would not feel comfortable attending a gathering called "Vietnamese Parent Meeting"—especially if it was conducted in Vietnamese. She decided that parents and families who wanted to continue the language-based meetings would be welcome to do so, but the meetings could no longer be advertised as school-sponsored events.

Her goal had been inclusion and representation, and although she had succeeded in reaching out to non-English-speaking families, she felt that the project ultimately failed. Not only were there no Cape Verdean or Vietnamese parents on the School Parent Council, but the council itself had been virtually abandoned, even by its core members.

The language-based meetings had accomplished quite a bit, however. In addition to building community and strengthening Kathleen's relationships with many of her parents, there were also interesting data results regarding the Home Reading program: The contracts from Vietnamese and Cape Verdean children were coming back with far greater regularity than they had in the past.

Hard Work Pays Off: Others Invest in the Everett

Since Kathleen's arrival, the school community had changed drastically. After piloting and adopting the Open Circle Social Competency Curriculum to teach students necessary social and behavioral expectations and norms, Everett students had come together to create a schoolwide code of conduct that aligned rules and expectations across classrooms and grade levels. Students were unequivocally clear about what it meant to be an "Everett student" at an "Open Circle School" and used that knowledge to self-monitor and promote a positive atmosphere. It was obvious that students were taking more ownership of their school and were now the centerpiece of their learning community. Teachers at the Everett were still working hard, as they always had, but now they were working together to plan their lessons, analyze data, and motivate their students to achieve success. Parents were partners in education, too, as they joined with teachers and students to fulfill the requirements of the Home Reading program and become a more visible presence in the school.

The Everett was really moving forward, and outsiders were beginning to take note and get in on the action. Kathleen had successfully recruited three university partners, all of whom provided the Everett with student teachers and other resources. She brought on a social services partner to provide on-site counseling and a community outreach organization to provide translation services for non-English-speaking parents. She also enlisted the help of what she described as "the best business partner in the Boston school system," one who would make possible many things that the Everett would have never thought available before—an after-school program for low-performing students, a full-scale music program, and a beautiful award-winning school yard.

The school yard had been achieved in collaboration with the Boston Schoolyard Initiative, a public/private partnership launched in 1995 by Boston mayor Thomas Menino to fund and build school yards in Boston's public schools. The Everett community, with nothing but a parking lot and a muddy, eroding, unkempt hill in back, was ecstatic about building a real school yard for its students. Kathleen formed a committee, submitted a compelling grant, and won acceptance into the program. The Everett's vision far exceeded the modest funds allocated by the grant, but the school's business partner came to the rescue, providing a $100,000 supplement for the dream school yard, complete with an outdoor classroom, raised garden beds, and playground equipment.

In 1999, the Everett School was selected as one of twenty-six Effective Practice (EP) schools out of the 126 in the district at that time. The designation was not only an honor, but also gave the Everett additional implementation latitude. The Everett was chosen because the district believed that the Everett's practices would lead to long-term and sustainable improvement in student learning. But the selection was not without drawbacks. Agreeing to be an EP school meant that the Everett would forfeit some elements of privacy and be asked to take on extra work. The school would be on public display, a living model for others in the system to come visit.

CCL as Infrastructure for Continuous Improvement

When Kathleen first arrived at the Everett, professional development was scattered. Select self-motivated teachers were out there all the time, attending a variety of workshops, and others were not participating in any professional development at all. Under Kathleen's leadership, that quickly changed. Professional development became a schoolwide activity. When she felt something was important to learn, it was important for everybody to learn, not just the workshop-loving few.

By the late 1990s, Kathleen was trying to figure out how to implement a system of targeted professional development that would help individual teachers develop the skills they needed to deliver Readers and Writers workshops. Kathleen also wanted her teachers to feel some control over their own professional development. Knowing that the literacy coaching Everett teachers had been getting was not working, she wondered if there was some way that teachers could have a voice in their professional development without Kathleen losing the authority that allowed her to regulate coursework and ensure that it was headed in the right direction.

When the Everett, as a condition of membership in the Effective Practice School Network, was asked to pilot and adopt a new district-based professional development model, Collaborative Coaching and Learning (CCL), Kathleen cautiously hoped that it might be just what the Everett needed. Though she could not be sure that it would definitely work, she had heard good things about the model and thought it was worth trying. For teachers, CCL presented as an extra burden that would take time from their dedication to teaching. For Kathleen, CCL would provide a rare opportunity for teachers to regularly observe each other's practice—something she felt was key to sustaining continuous instructional improvement and something that had never been done at the Everett before.

A type of professional development occurring during the school day, CCL encouraged small groups of teachers under the guidance of a coach to identify problem areas in their current teaching and their curriculum; discuss why these areas are problematic; brainstorm and research "best practices" with the coach, often in conjunction with professional reading on the topic; and then individually practice the lesson themselves, observed by the rest of the group. After the lesson, the demonstrating teacher received feedback from the coach and the other teachers in the group. In between whole-group meetings, individual teachers were visited in their classrooms by their coach, who provided them with powerful feedback about their teaching.

Demonstrating their practice in front of their peers was the part that was hardest for Everett teachers. They were asked to expose themselves in a way they never had before. CCL called on teachers to subordinate their personal pride in the interest of trying to find the very best way to teach children. They had to reconfigure their relationships with each other and open themselves up to an increased level of vulnerability. It was something that teachers had to do themselves; they had to coach each other. Teachers were required to be in each other's classrooms, observing, suggesting, critiquing, praising—both inviting and giving advice, professional-to-professional, something professionals in any field are rarely asked to do. It was one thing to discuss cases in the neutrality of a conference room, but how often would a lawyer or doctor sit in on a colleague's visit with a client or patient? This was exactly what teachers were being asked to do.

Kathleen decided that she wanted to go into it full force. Some principals allowed coaches to lead many of the classroom demonstrations, but Kathleen told the coach to make two demonstrations only and then dive right in with the teachers. "The teachers need to demonstrate," Kathleen insisted, "not the coach. I am not worried about the coach's competence."

Initially the teachers hated it. "Making your practice public is hard," Kathleen readily admitted. "I don't care who you are. Demonstrating quality and competence in front of colleagues is not easy." CCL was about the teacher, not the students; that's what made it so difficult. It took teaching to the next level, making the conversation about student outcomes. Teachers were problem-solving together.

CCL seemed to be the model that Kathleen had been looking for. Though teachers found it stressful to have classroom time taken away, the bottom line for Kathleen was that she had never seen a form of coaching or professional development that worked so well. "I think it's really powerful," she said shaking her head slowly, as if in awe. "It changes instruction and supports that change."

Teachers would now be in a situation where they were learning new strategies and implementing new methodology. She felt that teachers were not generally allowed to experience the natural implementation curve that took into account how difficult it could be to try something out for the first time. As a principal, Kathleen felt that she needed to give her teachers time and space to fail before they ultimately achieved success.

CCL began informing Kathleen's criteria for hiring new teachers. She looked for people who understood that their practice would be public, that having someone come in and give them feedback would be a valuable resource, not an imposition. She discovered that often it was the younger, newer teachers who were okay with this. Instead of being thrown by someone coming in their room, they were actually eager to get feedback that would help them improve.

This model of professional development allowed teaches to try new, deep, and sophisticated strategies without the expectation that they would be "experts" at it. Their peers and coach would observe their "first go" at a new strategy and provide them with feedback about how it went and what they could do differently next time to implement it more successfully. Teachers, despite their resistance, sensed that the demonstrations they were giving were not meant to be perfect. "I felt at ease after a while," one teacher confided, "that it was OK if I make a mistake—I could still get through it. Watching the other teachers helps me learn how to teach my students better, and I guess I can do that for them, too."

By the second cycle of CCL, this new model had become the means for improving Readers Workshop. As one fifth grade teacher described the experience, "I was skeptical at first, thinking 'no way is this going to work.' But [CCL] gave me an opportunity to really see what was going on in my own classroom. People used to come in and tell us what they did in their classrooms, but their classrooms seemed a lot different from ours. . . . I had to see it work with our population of students—right here. When I saw it with my own kids, it just blew me away."

Markers of School Performance

In 1998, the first year of the MCAS, the Everett scored eleventh in the school system. Although Kathleen felt that it was phenomenal that they did that well, she thought of it as beginner's luck. Sure enough, the next year the Everett's scores went down and everyone else's went way up.

Though the MCAS was not necessarily representative of the Everett as a whole, the data did reflect the focus of fourth grade instruction in any particular year. After a year of poor performance on the MCAS long composition, Everett teachers spent what Kathleen later considered "an inordinate amount of time" preparing them for the long composition. That year the Everett had the highest long composition scores in Boston. But that was only one component. Because of the time teachers had devoted to issues of the long composition, Everett students did not do well in other areas.

The Everett teachers needed to better prepare their students for answering open-ended questions. They had to make sure students knew they should answer *every* question, even if they had to make an educated guess. They looked at their science scores on the MCAS, their highest MCAS scores, and thought about how the science specialist taught. It was about discovery, not about reading a story and writing out the answers to a bunch of questions. It valued big ideas; there were connections between the instruction and the world that made the subject powerful and helped kids understand it. Kathleen pushed her teachers to see the connection between the high-level constructivist teaching and the high MCAS scores. She reiterated that this kind of conceptual learning was what would help their students improve.

The Irony of Success

MCAS raised the bar for urban schools. The conversation about improvement suddenly had more urgency and there was no getting away from the consequences. Even so, as an urban educator Kathleen felt it was unfair. The No Child Left Behind Act required not only a minimum level of school performance but also a high yearly rate of improvement. Starting off at a higher level actually put a school at a disadvantage, making it unlikely that they would be able to continue to improve at a rate comparable to that of a lower-performing school. Because of these unrealistic guidelines, it was possible that some of the best urban schools in America, like the Everett, could eventually end up reconstituted by the state.

Having started off at a relatively high level of achievement in language arts, the Everett had still managed to improve steadily over the first several years. "I think if you look at our data," Kathleen reflected, "we were steadily improving like the stock market: sometimes there was a little bit of a dip, but we were generally going up." Then, as expected, the Everett reached a plateau. By 2004, the Everett was considered a "high-performing, low-improvement" school. Students were still scoring well for an urban elementary school, but the school's scores were no longer improving as rapidly as they had in the past. The Everett was in danger of becoming a victim of its own success.

If they maintained the plateau for two years in a row, the school would be added to a list of schools that were unable to reach Adequate Yearly Progress (AYP), a measure of success in achieving the annual goals of NCLB. Placement on the list of schools who did not make their AYP, "underperforming" schools, was a slap in the face to hard-working, high-achieving schools like the Everett, and with it came a whole slew of complications that would primarily serve to further impede their progress—such as being required to send out letters to all of their families stating that their child's school was now considered an underperforming school and that they could transfer out at the expense of the district, should they choose to.

The Continuing Struggle

By 2004, Kathleen was still fighting to improve instruction and achievement at the Everett. Despite the great strides she had made in winning the trust and confidence of her staff, she continued to push them and they continued to resist. (See Tables 5.2 and 5.3.)

Many years after common planning had become a regular part of life at the Everett, it suddenly became a hot topic once again. Kathleen realized that she could absolutely not build a sustainable, professional learning community without more discussion between teachers about their goals for the work. She felt it essential that grade-level teams meet for planning not just once per week, with only one planning period per month devoted to math, but twice each week—once for math and once for literacy.

This was not meant to make their lives harder, Kathleen insisted. In fact, it should make things easier. Ideally, they would be getting a good portion of their respective math and literacy planning for the week done inside these meetings. The meetings would be opportunities for staff to make sure they were on the same page all of the time, not just checking in with each other weekly or, in the case of math, monthly. They would no longer have to set aside important topics that came up in these meetings and be unable to continue them in the next because they could not remember where they'd left off, or because the students had moved on in the classroom and the ideas were already past relevance.

Table 5.2 Grade 4 Everett ELA MCAS Scores Compared to Boston Schools

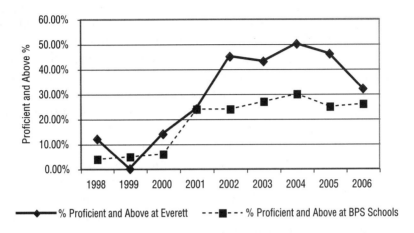

Source: www.doe.mass.edu

Table 5.3 Grade 4 Everett Math MCAS Scores Compared to Boston Schools

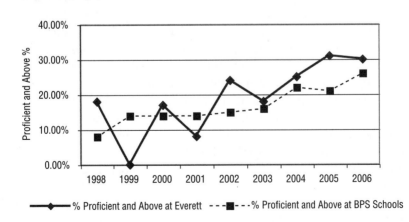

Source: www.doe.mass.edu

The idea was beyond unpopular. Teachers at the Everett, much to Kathleen's dismay, pointed to the Boston Teachers' Union contract and said that Kathleen owned only one hour per week of their planning time—and they weren't going to give her any more than that. Kathleen was crushed. She knew that the contract did not require teachers to plan together for two hours each week, but she was asking them to consider her plan in the interest of pursuing better practice. She appealed to their pride, to the quality of work that she knew they strove to achieve, but they would not back down. They did not want to "give up" two of their professional development points for common planning.

Typical of her usual tactics, Kathleen did not go so far as to insist that teachers engage in the twice-weekly planning. She knew, in this case, that she couldn't. She did, however, rearrange teachers' schedules so that grade-level pairs were available to meet twice a week. She dedicated an entire room in a school desperate for space (where counselors met with students in the book room in the basement and the nurse worked out of a walk-in closet off the computer room) as a teacher resource center, whose primary function was to provide a reliable meeting space for common planning. She also hung the schedule of each grade level's weekly meetings on the door and modified the ILT's "Teacher Expectations" document to reflect the expectation that teachers would be attending common planning twice each week.

Kathleen made twice-weekly common planning a condition of hire, and when she brought on four new classroom teachers that fall, she hired only those who would agree to her conditions. That made four willing teachers out of fourteen total, just under one-third of the staff. Slowly but surely she began engaging in one-on-one conversations with the returning Everett staff, carefully outlining the educational soundness of the twice-weekly plan, referencing the research that supported it, and emphasizing her strong feelings that this was the responsible thing to do. Two or three teachers agreed; she was gathering a critical mass. Yet without the participation of their grade-level colleagues, even willing teachers were unable to plan together. Kathleen temporarily set that problem aside, concentrating instead on getting at least verbal agreement from as many staff members as she could.

She knew that this battle was too important to let go. She intended to hold out and wait for the teachers to come around. She intended to apply pressure, reminding them that this would benefit their students, improve their school, and elevate their relationships with each other to a level of professionalism that could not be matched by professionals in other fields.

In a way, Kathleen's hands were tied. But she wasn't discouraged yet—far from it. "Even if there's something that we don't really want to do," an Everett teacher said, "if Kathleen can show us the real benefit of it, I think we usually come around because we all have the same thing in mind: getting the students to be better readers, better workers, helping them to become better citizens, to eventually go on to college. When she comes to us with something, we can rest assured that it's not fly-by-night—she's already researched it and she brings articles and backup because she knows we are going to question it."

The teachers had never been pushovers, and they weren't easily persuaded, but Kathleen was confident that they wanted to do the right thing. She knew how badly they wanted their practice to be effective and how much they wanted their students to benefit from their instructional success. Everett teachers cared about children, and, in the end, Kathleen knew she'd get them to come around. Until then, she would apply pressure, appeal to their conscience, stuff their mailboxes with articles supporting frequent common planning, and wait.

Always thinking one step ahead, Kathleen was concerned about the sustainability of the Everett's success. She knew that the road to sustainability was built on teacher leadership, and as she planned for her retirement in 2006, she wanted to be sure that systems and people would be in place to continue to drive improvement and support positive change.

Chapter 6

Leadership Lessons

This chapter reflects on the leadership practices demonstrated by the principals as they transformed their schools. Similarities among principals, as well as their unique contributions, are highlighted and supported with research evidence where appropriate.

Leveraging Leadership Strengths

These five principals were selected for study because, against all odds, they turned their schools around and placed them on a new trajectory that better served their students and greatly improved student achievement. All of them built on the talents they brought with them and leveraged these capabilities to transform their schools.

Casel Walker was a passionate crusader for the excluded even before her tenure at the Manning Elementary School. As an African American, her own background served as a contributing factor in her courageous approach to fixing Manning's skewed racial balance by bringing more black students to the school. If Walker's responses had been limited simply to moral outrage, imposing the LAB cluster on the cozy Manning could easily have resulted in disaster. Her deep compassion for others, her ability to speak to her staff in a direct fashion, and her determination not to micromanage were skill platforms she used to confront the ensuing turmoil and lead the school in a new direction.

Kim Marshall entered the Mather Elementary School with a first-rate intellect and the education to match. He brought a wealth of knowledge on school reform to the Mather and never stopped updating his knowledge base. Marshall's real talent for applying what he learned turned the Mather into a laboratory to create a more effective school that could raise student achievement. In a previous assignment, he wrote Boston's complete K–12 curriculum, making him uniquely qualified to align and integrate Mather's curriculum during his principalship.

Coming to the Shaw Middle School from the Trotter, where she had honed a unique, "tough love" interpersonal competency, **Muriel Leonard** immediately began coaching, appraising, and sometimes dismissing the disillusioned teaching staff, paving the way for the wholesale transformation of the Shaw. Her unique capacity to be compassionately tough served her well in promulgating high academic standards while still being supportive of those who had previously failed but now wanted to reach the high bar.

Michael Fung spurned the traditional managerial methodologies of supervision and performance appraisal, choosing instead to rely on his analytic and entrepreneurial abilities to reconfigure Charlestown High School's educational landscape. Who else would have thought to sidestep a whole cadre of veteran teachers and find a loophole to hire a new corps of energetic and socially inspired teachers loyal to him? Fung was clever in setting the terms for measuring success; he used only the tenth grade MCAS scores, for which his new hires were being held accountable, to mark progress, not the twelfth grade graduation rate, which remained depressingly low thanks to his "shelved" senior faculty.

Kathleen Flannery made a virtue of her willingness to be "converted." Ready to listen and be convinced by results, she was able to break into the tight community of the Everett Elementary School. She established new terms of engagement; data and evidence became the foundation on which they would collectively build a more educationally responsible school. Her own personal work ethic, energy, determination, and optimism served to inspire the same in her staff.

Achievement for All Students

At the time that they assumed their principalships, all five leaders were distinguished by their passionate belief that schools could make an unequivocal difference in every student's achievement. Complementary to this belief, the principals asserted that intelligence was not fixed at birth but could actually be a product of purposeful effort. With hard work, intellectual potential could be actualized to yield higher academic performance. While this position was not a part of conventional wisdom at the time, it is now commonly understood that intelligence is environmentally influenced. The remaining debate is over the degree of variability in intelligence, as measured by IQ tests. Bracey, drawing on several contemporary research studies, including a paper by Jeff Howard identified in Kim Marshall's chapter, asserts that there is a "correlation between IQ and years of schooling, even when potentially confounding variables are controlled or parceled out."[1]

The principals were particularly alert to subpopulations that were getting educationally short-changed. Students who had special needs, who did not speak English as their first language, or who belonged to different racial groups than their teachers' (who were predominantly white) were at increased risk of being held to lower standards by their educational community.

Academic achievement gaps among student subpopulations have bedeviled public schools from the start. By requiring schools to hold their subpopulations to the same performance goals as the overall population, NCLB has shone a bright spotlight on discrepancies that have long existed. Now, subpopulations of students are identified by the DOE and their scores are placed in the public record.[2] This quantitative evidence was not readily available to the five principals early in their tenures, so instead they focused primarily on improving the overall quality of instruction in their schools.

There is evidence that their efforts to close achievement gaps were ahead of their times. Mano Singham, in a paradigm-challenging article in the April 2003 issue of *Phi Delta Kappan*, "The Achievement Gap: Myths and Reality," argues with supporting data "that the achievement gap is a symptom of a more widespread educational problem. We should not treat it as a black problem, with white levels of achievement as the norm."[3] Singham asserts that such deficiencies are a product of a school's whole instructional system, and it is this system that needs improvement.

Each principal employed different tactics to identify and close achievement gaps. Improving their schools' instruction was a major component of each of their plans. Walker, Leonard, and Flannery used a hands-on approach, while Fung and Marshall depended on a more analytic strategy. The question, however, was the same: Who is being left out, a specific subpopulation or the school as a whole, and what can we do about it?

Prior to **Casel Walker's** principalship, the Manning was a two-class society; the first group was comprised primarily of white students who were expected to achieve and did, and the second was primarily black students who were not expected to achieve to the same degree and did not. Walker's leadership changed this practice by institutionalizing the ethic that all Manning students could and would reach a high standard of proficiency. Difficult students demanding more attention were no longer to be "cored out" and relegated to special education classrooms.

Kim Marshall almost lost his principalship when the Efficacy Institute workshop the school hosted produced results quite the opposite of his intention. He wanted to bring a positive message about "work hard, get smart" and unify the staff around a mission of high achievement. Yet, a small faculty cohort, the "Gang of Six," misinterpreted the workshop as a game of "gotcha" and, as a consequence, soured the day for many of the staff. This temporary setback did not thwart Marshall's continuous challenging of his teachers' assumptions that students graduated at the same level of intelligence they came in with on the first day of school. Conversely, Marshall believed that "smarts" could be achieved through effort; they were not exclusively a product of family history. Bringing in the Efficacy Institute reflected his commitment to breathing life into this philosophy at the Mather. Every day, the public address system reminded students and staff of the Mather pledge: "I must work hard today, get smarter in every way, helped by my teachers, my family and my friends. If I make some mistakes, I have what it takes to keep trying 'til I really succeed."

Marshall was not to be denied his mission: all students would be expected to perform to high standards and he would have measured proof of it. Indeed, Marshall's genius was inviting teachers to erect and operate an instructional system to prepare all students to meet high-achieving SMART goals. Student performance measurements locked Mather's teachers into closing the school's achievement gap.

Muriel Leonard witnessed in her initial classroom visits, the complete failure of Shaw staff to provide quality instruction to *any* students. Leonard carried a message of hope and inspiration to both students and teachers who were operating below standards: "You are capable of doing better, if you try and make good effort. We will be there to help you." She believed that through focused effort, not only students but teachers, too, could change and improve. She believed that most students could perform at grade level if they worked to do so, just as she believed that teachers were capable of instructing students to perform at this level if they worked to do so. This effort-based philosophy allowed her to set high expectations for everyone. Those who failed were challenged to try harder, and Leonard provided them with considerable support.

As a first step to teaching staff and students, Leonard coached them to value opportunities and reflect on their efforts. She advocated a crucial mind shift: Think of feedback not as summative judgment but as information on how to improve. On her first day, when she stepped into a mutinous classroom, Leonard promised Fs to those who deserved them and remedial help for those who wanted to work. No grade in the new Shaw was a final sentence; each was its own challenge to continue improving. Her early classroom visits planted the first seeds of change. She broke the spell of self-deprecating beliefs, telling teachers, "I believe you are capable of much more than you have previously exhibited; try something new and more challenging. I will support you in your first awkward steps, at least until you believe enough in yourself to make it a self-fulfilling prophecy."

She hired teachers with whom this message resonated; indeed, it was one of the most significant criteria for their selection. Her self-redemptive philosophy of effort-based improvement was tested and reached its apogee when the Milestone Products and Eligibility Lists were rolled out. The system demanded high standards from students, and the majority of students came to believe that they were capable of proficient performance as demonstrated by their completion of the Milestone Products.

Michael Fung believed his inherited faculty was incapable of demanding academic stretch from any student, much less a student of color. His strategy to close the achievement gap by transforming unprepared freshmen into students capable of proficient academic performance depended on the hiring of smart, well-educated, responsible women who wanted to be challenged and whom he could hold accountable for performance, as measured by annual MCAS scores. This plan was not as successful in all of Charlestown's units as it was with Unit III.

The Unit III team demanded standards of behavioral conduct, academic performance, and self-discipline that were so high that they would be judged ludicrous by any conventional wisdom. Yet, students were able to achieve them. Out of naivete, or perhaps in reaction to a chaotic beginning, the teachers set a high bar and stubbornly refused to compromise. Attendance and punctuality were mandatory. Every student would master algebra. This "unrealistic" expectation was just a part of the equation; backing them up was critical. Consequences for absences and lateness were severe. Math instruction was doubled if students were not succeeding. Unit III, with an extraordinary amount of brain power and tenacious effort, took the old paradigm of what could be expected from deprived urban students and turned it on its head. Unit III students performed at an academic level comparable to that of their suburban counterparts.

The inequalities confronting **Kathleen Flannery** at the Everett were more subtle. Early on, she sensed that race (veiled as "IQ") rather than performance level seemed to be dictating decisions regarding, for example, which students were selected to participate in the Reading Recovery Program. Rather than confronting this issue head-on, Flannery chose to temporarily discontinue the program. She then pursued a long-term plan to change the racial composition of the staff, hiring competent teachers who also represented the student populations they served, including teachers who were Cape Verdean, Vietnamese, and African American.

Data Makes a Difference

The five principals were at the vanguard of using data as integral to their reform. Presently, it is unthinkable to prosecute standards-based reform without analyzing student performance assessment data. Educational journals and newspapers regularly report the necessity of data management in pursuing standards-based reform. For example, in her 2006 *Education Week* article, "Data-wise School Systems Seen as Sharing Key Traits," Lynn Olsen highlights the centrality of data as an essential tool in the successful reform efforts of two school districts and two charter school management organizations.[4]

Essential to focusing a school on student achievement was the concomitant capacity to recognize the value and make meaning from data and evidence, both quantitative and qualitative. The five principals saw few results from their reform efforts until they led their faculty to use data and evidence to calibrate results and outcomes, inform dialogue, and influence decision making. For many in the schools, this was a hard sell. Longtime educators were not used to looking at results. They had been trained to look at process; the *way* in which you did it was all-important.

When the Massachusetts Educational Reform Act of 1993 gave birth to the MCAS in 1998, and was followed by the 2002 NCLB's Adequate Yearly Progress requirements, the pendulum swung in the other direction. Measured student performance was now the "it" outcome. Achieving proficient performance would become a product of interpreting the MCAS data to improve the quality of teaching and learning. For many teachers, processing feedback data to improve instruction was surprisingly difficult. They had tracked student progress for years with homework, quizzes, and student responses to classroom questions, yet crunching quantitative data baffled them. Interpreted data now held considerably more weight than the "gut feelings" teachers were used to relying on. Changing the minds and skill sets of their faculty became a daily challenge for the principals.

From the day she arrived at the Manning, **Casel Walker** insisted that all Manning teachers and students would be held to high standards. Faded color charts and teachers who "knew" a student was incapable would no longer be tolerated. Accurate monitoring demands hard evidence, and data interpretation became a regular part of the Manning's dialogue. One person's opinion was no better than another's—unless someone could point to commonly agreed-on evidence. The Manning was not going to get better unless there was consensus about what "better" would be. "Better" would not be based on individual gut feelings any longer but on solid, objective evidence.

Kim Marshall championed the cause of quantitative data. He brought to new heights the practice of recasting ambiguous concepts in a new, quantitative light. The Mather, like many schools, had a vision that was comprehensive and eloquent but difficult to recall and, therefore, difficult to live by. Marshall, with the help of his teachers, applied the SMART goals formula to a mission and vision that staff could use as a guide in decision making and Marshall could use to measure yearly progress.

While his colleagues in other schools and his classroom teachers were damning the advent of the MCAS as a misguided ploy to usurp valuable teaching time, Marshall immediately recognized how the rich database that MCAS test scores provided could be leveraged to improve instruction. The MCAS was a window into the state's curriculum standards and a tool for aligning Mather's curriculum. His call to arms was using data from the MCAS to "work backward."

Marshall's partially realized dream was to create a set of SMART goals for every course, provide every teacher with interim student performance feedback, and endow every teacher team with the skills to reach their end-of-year targets. He intended the system to be fool-proof, with tight quantitative measures preventing slippage. It did work, despite the fact that some teacher teams did not give their expected share to the effort. His basic model is now standard practice in many schools aspiring to improve student performance.

Muriel Leonard used data as a powerful instructional tool and as a means of coalescing staff to reach common objectives. Inspecting the early scores from the Turning Points survey and the Stanford 9 could have resulted in disaster, as the early Shaw marks were the lowest of the low. Instead, she orchestrated public, community events with the enlarged data posted on butcher paper around her office. She made learning a game: Who could spot patterns in the data that suggested areas for improvement? It was a way for the staff to come together and confront Shaw's problems and, with the help of the ad hoc committees, to do something about them. Consultancy protocols used peer feedback to critique and provide suggestions for improvement on teacher lesson plans. Students were also engaged in a feedback learning loop. The sought-after goal of making the Eligibility List stimulated a fervor of student motivation to complete satisfactory Milestone Products.

Data master **Michael Fung** made it clear in the first month of his administration that quantitative measurement would be a primary medium of exchange. His vision for Charlestown High was framed in an aspiration for increasing student achievement as measured by the Stanford 9 test scores. The faculty, unacquainted with this framing, was completely bewildered. In his new teacher recruits, however, he found a willing and capable audience who could, for example, disaggregate MCAS data and make instructional meaning.

Kathleen Flannery used data and evidence to preclude hasty decision making and establish ground rules by which decisions would be made. She established the precedent not only for staff but for herself as well. She felt incredibly uncomfortable with the grouped-by-ability tracking system, which played into unspoken racial biases. However, she did not feel that she had sufficient evidence to prove to her teachers and parents that integrated classrooms were as academically satisfying for higher-achieving students. The third grade teacher's naturally occurring experiment proved that an integrated classroom produced students with skills equal to those in a high-level tracked classroom. Having this teacher, a credible and unbiased source, informally "leak" the results though the teacher network provided evidence-based justification for the new system.

Another example of how Flannery waited for evidence occurred when she insisted on a full-scale critique of any reading program the Everett was planning to adopt. Despite her strong intuitive beliefs about the power of whole language, she refused to mandate the pedagogy at the Everett. Instead, she devoted an enormous amount of teacher time and energy to researching literacy programs, even challenging her own credibility as the school's leader on this one curriculum matter. When Won Way Phonics, Flannery's nemesis from her days in Lynn, was selected as the phonics program of choice, Flannery swallowed hard and allowed the teachers to bring it to the Everett. She did not have any evidence against Won Way Phonics and so felt she had no legitimate reason to turn it down.

Leveraging the MCAS

The principals found the yearly administration of Massachusetts' high-stakes student performance test to be a salient tool in raising academic standards and advancing student achievement. However, using the MCAS as a guide and standard would be appropriate only if the test was a credible reflection of Massachusetts' state standards. A 2001 study by Achieve, Inc., determined that this was, in fact, the case. But how did the MCAS compare with other states' assessments? The 2001 Achieve study confirmed the comparative rigor and quality of the MCAS, noting that it was actually the most challenging of all the state exit tests they assessed.[5] In October 2007, John Cronin, Michael Dahlin, Deborah Adkins, and G. Gage Kingsbury, in their study *The Proficiency Illusion*, found that twenty-six states' high-stakes tests varied greatly in their difficulty, but, once again, the MCAS was one of the most rigorous and challenging. The fourth grade mathematics MCAS standard ranked at the highest percentile, and the reading MCAS, along with reading tests in three other states, had the highest proficiency standard.[6]

How unique were the five principals in finding value in the MCAS? David Gordon, summarizing a nationwide survey of state high-stakes testing, found mixed reactions from students, principals, parents, and counselors. In his research, only teachers were found to have consistently negative reactions to standardized testing.[7]

The first administration of the MCAS, in 1998, came with a promise that the passing of the tenth grade assessment would become a mandatory requirement for graduation by 2001. The new guidelines obliged Massachusetts educators to suffer a tectonic shift in their thinking. Schools would now need to concentrate on measured student performance results. No Child Left Behind legislation, which followed in 2002, and reinforced Massachusetts' graduation requirements, also placed accountability with the schools. Student performance was the new gold standard.

However, the issue was not so clear-cut when the five principals started their reform efforts. The very mission of a school was in question, as **Casel Walker** realized when she started to peel back the cultural layers at the Manning; she found the school more focused on adults than on students.

Kim Marshall's story at the Mather makes clear how significant high-stakes tests can be. The MCAS proved essential for Marshall in galvanizing the faculty to unify its efforts. In order to integrate Mather's curriculum across grades and have it follow from district and state standards, he exhorted his staff to "work backward." As he subsequently learned, one had to work backward from a particular type of assessment: a high-stakes student performance test that truly measured curriculum knowledge. Repeatedly, but to no avail, he tried to mobilize his faculty to team their efforts, but he couldn't—until one fourth grade teacher, seeing how ill-prepared her students were for the first administration of the MCAS in 1998, pleaded with her colleagues to shed their lone ranger postures. Finally, staff became invested in coordinating their efforts. Her advocacy as a peer mobilized her fellow teachers in the process of curriculum alignment, a goal that had thwarted Marshall for years.

Neither was academic achievement part of the Shaw's vocabulary. Students intimidated teachers, and teachers found themselves striving to please rather than educate their charges. In her early years, **Muriel Leonard** did not have the backdrop of the all-powerful MCAS scores to demonstrate how the Shaw was failing its mission. Because the Stanford 9 provided the only data, she was forced to use this imperfect, norm-referenced test to prompt her teams to improve their instruction. It was a step-by-step inculcation process. Leonard started by inviting teachers to make meaning of the raw Stanford 9 student performance data displayed on newsprint tacked to her office walls. From there, she asked teachers to determine instructional interventions to remediate the gaps. Raising student achievement would be their collective goal.

If it were not for a high-stakes test demanding proficient, grade-level, academic performance, Leonard and her teacher team may never have questioned the fact that the system was set up to encourage students "to just get-by." There were no incentives for students to strive for excellence. However, Leonard and her staff addressed the problem with the Milestone Products and the Eligibility List. The goal of completing a Milestone Product was a real stretch for most Shaw students, but a highly worthy one; it benchmarked a proficient, grade-level standard of performance. She and her teacher teams cunningly positioned the carrot for this effort as one of the students' most-prized rewards: participation in extracurricular activities. In most cases, students had to make several tries to achieve a satisfactory Milestone Product, necessitating teacher feedback on each attempt. The contingency system worked; the Shaw succeeded in engineering a system for promoting high-level learning. Milestone Products and the Eligibility List were creative solutions to the vexing problem of student academic motivation. But this system was not a long-term panacea, because it made learning the means to the end (participation in extracurricular activities, especially sports) and did nothing to deepen students' interest in learning for its own sake.

Michael Fung exploited the publicity given to the yearly publication of school MCAS results by defining an artificial competition between Charlestown and the other regional Boston high schools. Although Charlestown was able to excel in this contest, the goal of raising student achievement was sometimes undermined in favor of test-taking strategies designed to achieve the immediate goal of optimizing test scores.

The team of Unit III teachers at Charlestown did not fall victim to the means-ends reversal and instead used the MCAS to truly focus their students' efforts, as well as their own. Unit III's high expectations for student achievement, academic support, and personal attention made the goals attainable. The NCLB standards, as measured by the MCAS performance, would be a meaningless, unattainable target had it not been translated by the team into challenging, but achievable, objectives for the students. The team teachers welcomed the data provided by the MCAS, as improving MCAS scores provided explicit measurable feedback on both their students' performance and their own. The Unit III teachers, anxious to use every piece of feedback, both quantitative and qualitative, to test the efficacy of their ongoing experimentation, had few, if any, exemplars to follow. They had to rely on their own ingenuity to serve their students. They were operating what has been referred to as a "learning organization"—consisting of experimenting, checking results, reflecting on what might work better, and trying again. With the goal of enabling all their students to achieve to their highest potential, the MCAS served as an excellent objective measure with which to evaluate progress and move forward.

Starting Smart

When taking over leadership of a school, a new principal must decide how much effort to invest in evaluating the school's cultural practices and how these practices may facilitate or inhibit student achievement. Prescribed entry plans for new leaders has been a topic in the education and business management literature for some time, but Jentz and Murphy's "Starting Confused: How Leaders Start When They Don't Know Where to Start" reflects lessons born of observing and coaching principals who were just beginning their tenures.[8]

Casel Walker and **Kathleen Flannery** were not aware of the authors' model, but their sensitivity to their schools' preexisting cultures echoes the spirit of the Jentz and Murphy piece. Rather than "hitting the ground running," as Jentz and Murphy questioned, they "hit the ground learning." Listening and reflecting was their primary entry strategy. Both consciously recognized the multiple tugs from students, parents, and their own moral compasses pulling them in different directions. They chose to process the various inputs first, waiting to act until they felt fully informed. Walker and Flannery did their investigative work well, and their reform strategies reflected the insights they had gained about the cultures of their schools.

Casel Walker's reform agenda was a product of careful investigative work that allowed her to affirm the Manning's strengths while simultaneously exposing negative cultural elements that prevented it from serving all students equitably. Not easily seduced by the school's "everything is okay" facade, Walker visited classrooms, inspected honor rolls, looked at the data, and listened to teachers and parents. Her inquiry led her to a disturbing conclusion: The Manning was unintentionally denying African American students the high expectations afforded white students. The pronounced advocacy that white parents exercised on behalf of their own children unintentionally caused inequitable treatment of blacks.

Teachers, by Walker's assessment, were not racist but had lost touch with the true mission of the school—the education of *all* students. On the basis of this assessment, Walker was prompted to bring in a LAB cluster.

Kim Marshall had a disastrous beginning, in part because he meted out "satisfactory" performance assessments instead of the automatic "excellent" that teachers had come to expect. Also damaging was the Efficacy workshop, intended to demonstrate that there was an achievement gap at the Mather, particularly among blacks, but instead received negatively by the high-status, white "Gang of Six" teachers. Black teachers, who initially saw promise in Marshall's administration, also began to question his leadership, further diluting his ability to lead. Realizing his rocky start, Marshall began to more closely align his reform strategy with the existing attitudes of his staff.

He swallowed his intellectual pride to sponsor the Myers-Briggs workshop, immersing himself in it as an equal participant. He knew, perhaps intuitively, that something had to be done to bridge the gap between him and the faculty, something that would allow him the leeway to lead the school with his agenda. The power of the Myers-Briggs workshop was that the facilitator illustrated how Marshall and the staff, while very different, needed and complemented each other in the service of educating their students. His choosing to rally the staff around what subsequently proved to be a highly successful 350th school anniversary celebration demonstrated a new acuity in acting respectfully toward his Mather constituency. He succeeded in accumulating enough respect to move forward with his agenda to reshape the Mather into an educationally sound school.

Muriel Leonard, with the Trotter change effort already under her belt, knew right where to start: the classroom. The success of her entry and subsequent reform strategy speaks to an apparently instantaneous assessment of the broken Shaw and the translation of her perceptions into a change agenda with effective results.

Michael Fung's entry into Charlestown High was impeded by his own limited interpersonal repertoire. By his own admission, he was not skilled at, and thus avoided, giving performance evaluations, a helpful tool in properly evaluating his veteran teachers. He failed to acknowledge the potential talent of his inherited faculty. Instead, he judged the school's merits on the basis of its disastrous scores on the Stanford 9 test and equating that with the considerable seniority of the teachers. He imposed his own agenda, alienating the veteran faculty along the way and making no headway in lowering the high drop-out rate, a congenital problem in Boston regional high schools. It was only after he had accrued a critical mass of new teachers that the previously distant and judgmental Fung turned a new face to his young hires. For Unit III, he demonstrated responsiveness to their needs, even going so far as to shower them with extra perks and gifts. He personally made special efforts to prepare these new hires for the rigors of an urban classroom.

Even at entry, **Kathleen Flannery** did not allow instincts to interfere with her leadership. She resisted making any critical decisions without the consensus of her hardworking, competent teachers. She was not above being proven wrong if the evidence wasn't on her side. Balancing her dedication to teacher self-determination and her uncompromising drive for excellence, she respected her teachers and listened to them—even allowing an underperforming teacher to assess his own capabilities and come to his own decision regarding his readiness to retire. By sitting back and listening to what her teachers had to say, Flannery allowed them the opportunity to explore their own strengths and weaknesses while at the same time giving herself a chance to really get to know them as professionals. A good example of the rewards of this approach occurred early in her tenure. At a faculty meeting on reading (to which she had not been invited), she began to understand why phonics was not being taught alongside the literature-based program. The teachers were inexperienced in teaching phonics without a text and afraid to admit it. Had she merely forbid them from dragging the basal readers off the shelf and bringing them back into the classrooms, this critical, pedagogical gap might never have come to the fore.

Creating a Sense of Urgency for Standards-Based Reform

There is sufficient written history of organizational transformations in education and business circles to substantiate the wisdom of preparing institutions for change rather than just charging forward. Explaining why the effort is being undertaken and creating urgency for this effort has proven to be a prudent first step. Disturbing habitual school practices and advocating new ones usually meets with resistance unless staff has been properly primed to understand the motivation behind the changes.

"Leading Change: Why Transformation Efforts Fail," an influential article by John Kotter, uses anecdotal evidence to argue that a successful "change process goes through a series of phases that in total usually require a considerable length of time. Skipping steps creates only the illusion of speed and never produces a satisfying result." He believes that "critical mistakes in any one of the phases can have a devastating impact, slowing momentum and negating hard-won gains." The first of these eight errors, "Not establishing a great enough sense of urgency," speaks directly to the importance of providing a dramatic reason for enduring the pain and upheaval that inevitably accompanies change.[9]

Currently in Massachusetts, the Department of Education has statewide school-level data available on its website. A principal of a faltering school could find a considerable amount of damning evidence on this website—perhaps enough to convince the faculty of the need to change their ways. According to NCLB, every school must have 100 percent of its student body achieve proficiency in math and English language arts by 2014.

Most urban schools have difficulty staying on target. Even if a school's aggregate student population meets performance, attendance, and graduation goals, subpopulations (comprised of groups of at least forty students) are often particularly vulnerable. Using the data from the DOE website to illustrate concern, a principal can demonstrate how students—particularly limited English proficient, special education, low income, black, Hispanic, and Native American—are bearing an enormous cost because of their school's failure to educate to high standards. Of course, it would take much more than a website for a school to undertake sustained remedial efforts. Nevertheless, a school's DOE statistics could initiate a compelling case for change.[10]

Yet dramatizing urgency for standards-based change was not always so clear-cut.

Self-satisfaction is a formidable force resisting a new principal's change efforts. When **Casel Walker** arrived at the Manning, the school community did not see its practice as problematic. Walker felt that some students were being deprived of a quality education, and she was prepared to act. She began the slow and deliberate process of working with the teachers she had inherited, adding new talent only when seniors retired. She was unprepared take the five or more years she realized it would take to transform the school.

When the opportunity presented itself, Walker jumped at the chance to create a greater sense of urgency by taking a calculated and risky course of action. There was a real possibility that the turmoil unleashed by her decision would be too much for her and her staff to manage. The LAB cluster was an innovative and gutsy way for Walker to recruit a new, critical mass of teachers—teachers who could elevate the Manning's academic culture. This caused a crisis, forcing the staff to come together to work it out. Without a skilled leader, the school might have found itself in a disastrous situation.

Students in the LAB cluster benefited greatly from an educational environment that put their learning first. The Manning changed dramatically because Walker introduced the cluster as a strategic opportunity for instructional improvement, shaking up the school and creating a sense of urgency for change where there had been none. She had created a hole for the staff to climb out of. She sorted out those teachers who wanted to grow and those who didn't want to or couldn't handle a new teacher challenge. Because so many teachers left of their own accord, the LAB cluster helped Walker avoid unnecessary negative teacher evaluations while providing a new generation of teachers the opportunity to work with the supposedly "uninstructable." The Manning became a school in which every student could achieve, not just the privileged. The veteran faculty members who chose to stay on were energized; they learned new skills to teach a new population of students. The remaining school community joined together to move forward.

Kim Marshall's frequently thwarted attempts to have his faculty embrace his standards-based reform agenda made for a long and problematic journey. Not having the well-publicized MCAS scores at his disposal until the middle of his tenure inhibited his change agenda. He did finally succeed, but it took years of softening teachers' resistance and introducing them to reform practices. The grade-by-grade objectives proved their value, even improving scores on the Metropolitan Achievement Test. Writing rubrics, another Marshall initiative, sharpened the staff's capacity to write crisp summative assessments, but the exercise had little sustaining draw for teachers.

Muriel Leonard wasted no time in confronting her faculty; one by one, each had to change her teaching to bring them up to Leonard's standards of excellence. Her personal authority, paired with the know-how behind her message, left little doubt in the minds of staff about Leonard's goals for improvement. Most Shaw teachers knew that they were letting their students down, particularly when Leonard confronted them with the bottom-line questions: "Would [you] send your child to your class?" and "Are you preparing the night before the way you would want to be prepared if your child were there?" She used guilt, as well as the threat of staff turnover, to create a sense of urgency for change. In her first two years, through a combination of retirements, resignations, and lay-offs, six underperforming teachers left the faculty of thirty-five.

Rather than energizing his inherited faculty to embrace standards-based reform, **Michael Fung**, coerced them into bending to his authority. In the end, practice did not improve schoolwide. Fung was successful in creating a sense of urgency for educating students to high-standards only among the well-educated, socially minded young women whom he had hired. They alone responded passionately to his challenge to make a difference for a population of students who had been severely neglected.

Kathleen Flannery walked into a school where teachers were quite self-satisfied and saw few reasons to alter their ways. The school had a record of moderate student achievement; parents who took an interest in the school were pleased, and the faculty's cohesiveness ensured a smooth, conflict-free work environment. With no credible evidence of student mediocrity to challenge the status quo, Flannery instead managed an incremental change process that was highly dependent on her own growing credibility with her faculty. No one event compelled the faculty to attempt new reforms or implement new ways of teaching and assessing students. Flannery relied on her faith that, when presented with the evidence, her faculty would make the right decisions, persuaded by their own sense of urgency (perhaps born from hers) that present student achievement was not good enough.

Selective Hiring, Frequent Classroom Observations, and Principal Feedback

Not surprisingly, teacher-student classroom interactions became the primary target of reform led by principals. What teachers knew and were capable of, as well as how much effort they were willing to put into improving their practice, were high-priority objectives for improvement. The principals made major changes to improve the quality of instruction, which ultimately raised the student learning.

All principals wanted, and to varying degrees accrued, a group of highly competent teachers who could challenge urban youth to higher levels
of academic performance. According to the research, their instincts were
correct. Robert Marzano's multistudy synthesis of research prioritizes effective teaching as having the most profound effect on student achievement. He notes, "On the average, the most effective teachers produced
gains of about 53 percentage points in student achievement over one year,
whereas the least effective teachers produced achievement gains of about
14 percentage points over one year. To understand these results, consider the fact that researchers estimate that students typically gain about 34
percentile points in an average year."[11]

All five principals used or created opportunities to hire new teachers
whose characteristics were consistent with the creation of a culture focused on student achievement.

Casel Walker quickly defined her teacher profile by radically altering
the Manning's student demographics, exposing pedagogical challenges
which teachers, old and new, were forced to confront.

Kim Marshall frequently stood up at Boston's annual teacher excess
pools (in which teachers without specific job assignments bid on vacancies in seniority order after principals described their schools' major features) and painted a vivid picture of the extraordinary work ethic
required at the Mather, trying to scare off teachers who did not fit his
profile. In these forums, Boston Teachers Union officials tried to coun-
teract his speech by saying that teachers had a right to choose any school
they wanted, to which Marshall would reply with great ferocity, "That's
true. But just remember, if you come to the Mather, you won't be reporting to them; you'll be reporting to ME!"

Muriel Leonard was compassionate but voracious in her appetite for
selecting teachers who could meet her high standards and work long
hours to build a high-performing school. In two years, six teachers left,
and she took the opportunity to replace them. Many of these new hires
were drawn to the Shaw because of Leonard's reputation; they were eager to take on the exacting and exciting challenges she would present.
During her tenure, Leonard made feedback a given at the Shaw. Mirrors
on performance were constantly held up to both teachers and students.
The culture of frequent feedback attracted those who thrived on learning and developing their skills and hungered for performance feedback.

Others, who found the abundance of feedback overwhelming, chose to exit.

Michael Fung, having dismissed the capacity of his veteran faculty to make a dent in MCAS results, recruited young, almost exclusively female candidates with superior intellect and academic pedigrees. Gewertz and Rhee and Levin, summarizing evidence from the New Teacher Project Study on urban district's recruiting of top-notch teachers, pointed to the layers of bureaucracy that have precluded the best qualified teachers from being hired.[12] Fung anticipated this problem, stepped over what he assumed would be an institutional maze, and discovered loopholes in the union contract that allowed him to bring new energetic talent to Charlestown—a credit to his ingenuity and innovation. If he had chosen to include actual teaching experience in his list of criteria, as he did with Karen Loughran, and provided more on-the-job professional development for all new teachers, Charlestown might have experienced less teacher turnover.

Kathleen Flannery's hiring practices were essential to her reform strategy. She hired highly competent teachers whom she believed would be able to live up to her expectations. "This is a school of teachers who work hard," she would say during interviews. "If you don't want to work hard, this isn't the right job for you." Believing that school culture was an essential component of student success, Flannery also evaluated potentials hires on their capacity to contribute to and enhance the values the school held dear. When she began to realize that the school, which her staff proudly referred to as a "community school," did not reflect the community it served, she made conscious efforts to begin to change that. Still subscribing staunchly to the belief that it was her responsibility to hire the "best person for the job," she also began to take cultural background into account, searching for candidates who had all of the qualities she had always looked for with the additional bonus of sharing a language or a culture with Everett students.

Just hiring high-quality teachers was not sufficient for any of the principals. Classroom observation and teacher feedback were essential to shaping instruction for improved student achievement. All five principals knew that if students were to achieve proficiency, the classroom was where it would happen. All five made visits, giving feedback they hoped would kindle instructional reform. Exactly how to make this difference was more problematic, and each principal developed his or her own style of classroom visits.

Michael Fung's visits were more infrequent and less formal than the others. **Casel Walker** and **Muriel Leonard** made use of early, intensive visits that were essential to remedying dysfunctional teaching habits and igniting their own reform agendas. As Leonard's reforms took on a life of their own, she increasingly relied on staff to raise each others' instructional standards. Inspired by her experienced principal mentor, Kim Marshall, **Kathleen Flannery** kept to a rigorous schedule of classroom visits, all the while making certain that she never exited a classroom without leaving her feedback on the teacher's desk. After constructivism became the doctrine of consensus at the Everett, she used its five points as prompts for her feedback to teachers.

Kim Marshall took on frequent, short observations accompanied by face-to-face feedback as his cause célèbres. He believed that "the dirty little secret of American schools is that principals rarely get into classrooms."[13] Marshall acquired a national reputation for putting the acute need for classroom observations on center stage, naming the forces inhibiting these observations and suggesting a way out of the dilemma. Built on his own practice, he made a strong case for five minutes in the classroom being a sufficient amount of time in which to make meaningful observations that could provide teachers with powerful feedback. The brevity of the visits made it possible for Marshall to visit forty-five teachers in a two-week period, verbally "sharing one interesting insight with the teacher" afterward. Though Marshall does not have research to back up the efficacy of his innovation to increase student achievement, his rationale has appealing face validity. Not only did the practice make him feel more like an instructional leader, but he also attributed the subsequent positive outcomes to the five-minute visits and feedback:

- "The feedback conversations played an important ethical role in this system: They gave teachers a chance to clue me in on the broader context of a particular teaching moment, to correct me if I misheard or got the wrong idea, and to push back if they disagreed with a criticism."
- "My visits also kept me in touch with the curriculum and made me a more effective participant in grade-level and school-site council meetings."

- Frequent visits gave Marshall more latitude in giving negative feedback. "[When] the principal [is] making a dozen visits a year and most of them are followed by genuinely positive comments, it's a lot easier for a teacher to hear criticism after the other three."
- "After a year, the staff got to like the system so much that virtually all the teachers were comfortable having me use my brief observations to write their official performance evaluations. We got away from the dog-and-pony shows of contrived, unrepresentative lessons designed solely for my benefit."
- I believe the time I took observing classrooms and giving detailed, clinical feedback created a more positive staff culture, which in turn made our school more attractive for good teachers looking for jobs."[14]

Professional Learning Communities

A cursory review of the contemporary literature on best practices in education would reveal that teacher teams are de rigueur for schools aspiring to increase student achievement. Actual practice, however, has trouble keeping pace with best practice. As the five principals would testify, on entry into their schools, they found teachers who taught in isolation, determined their own curriculum and pedagogy, measured student progress idiosyncratically and unconnectedly, and were the sole arbiters of who passed and progressed to the next grade level and who did not. The principals encouraged teacher teaming to break up isolation and promote collaboration. Several went even further to create powerful school-wide networks.

Over the last decade, a model has evolved outlining how school personnel should work together to continuously improve teacher instruction and student performance. The model is a product of identifying similarities among the practices of school communities that have successfully sustained increases in student achievement. These schools are often described as Professional Learning Communities (PLCs). There is no universally agreed-on definition, but based on the evidence presented, the clarity of presentations, and their reputations, Richard DuFour, Rebecca DuFour, Robert Eaker, and Thomas Many created the most compelling standard for defining PLCs.[15]

Collaborative teacher teams were at the center of all five principals' reform efforts, but none of them aspired to accomplish the full menu of

DuFour et. al. Indeed, at the time of these reform efforts, the best practice literature, which gave rise to such PLC agendas, had not been suffi-
ciently synthesized to guide practice, and findings were considerably less
publicized than they are today. It is both a confirmation of the PLC literature and a credit to the five principals, however, that their change trajectories moved their schools toward becoming full-fledged PLCs.

Excerpts from *Learning by Doing: A Handbook for Professional Learning Communities at Work*

Professional Learning Communities

- **Focus on student learning:** "The very essence of a *learning* community is a focus on and a commitment to the learning of each student."
- **Clarifying roles:** "[Members] make collective commitments to clarify what each member will do to create a [PLC]."
- **Results-oriented goals:** "...they use results-oriented goals to mark progress."
- **Adults as learners:** "...adults in the organization must also be continually learning."
- **Students learn essentials:** "[PLCs] exist to ensure that all students learn essential knowledge, skills, and dispositions."
- **PLCs composed of collaborative teams:** "Collaborative teams whose members work *interdependently* to achieve *common goals* linked to the purpose of learning for all. The team is the engine that drives the PLC effort and the fundamental building block of the organization."
- **Interdependent collaboration:** "...*collaboration* represents a systematic process in which teachers work together interdependently in order to *impact* their classroom practice in ways that will lead to better results for their students, for the team, and for the school."
- **Collective inquiry:** "...engage in collective inquiry into both best practice in teaching and best practice in learning."
- **Learning by doing:** "Members of PLC are action-oriented: They move quickly to turn aspirations into actions and visions into reality....Most powerful learning always occurs in a context of taking action."
- **Continuous Improvement:** "...constant search for a better way to achieve goals..."
  - "Gathering evidence of current levels of student learning"
  - "Developing strategies and ideas to build on strengths and address weaknesses in that learning"
  - "Implementing those strategies and ideas"

(continued)

Excerpts from *Learning by Doing: A Handbook for Professional Learning Communities at Work* (continued)

- "Analyzing the impact of the changes to discover what was effective and what was not."
- "Applying new knowledge in the next cycle of continuous improvement."

- **Results orientation:** "[Efforts] must be assessed on the basis of results rather than intentions."
    - "...each team develops and pursues measurable improvement goals that are aligned to school and district goals for learning,"
    - "...teams to create a series of common formative assessments that are administered to students multiple times throughout the year to gather ongoing evidence of student learning."
    - "Team members review the results from these assessments in an effort to identify and address program concerns..."
    - "[Teams] examine the results to discover strengths and weaknesses in their individual teaching in order to learn from one another."
    - "...assessments are used to identify students who need additional time and support for learning."

Although **Casel Walker**'s narrative does not provide a complete record of how she was able to transform the Manning into a high-performing school with many PLC characteristics, the outcomes she achieved speak to the efficacy of her efforts. She designed and monitored the change efforts that were propelling the Manning forward, but it was the staff who actually made the changes that led to their success. Shaken by the adverse consequences of holding the reigns of authority too tightly at her previous school, Walker deliberately demanded participation from the school-wide team at the Manning. The dramatic change from a focus on teacher accommodation to one of student learning was a product of Walker's efforts. By asking incisive and purposeful questions such as "Why is the library so small and hidden?" and, at a more penetrating level, "Why are white students receiving better marks than blacks?" she modeled a practice of collective inquiry that became a norm at the Manning.

Her personal crisis forced her teachers to take the helm for three and a half months and not only maintain but improve on the progress they had made up until that point. That the staff could organize and successfully lead the school during Walker's convalescence speaks to how well

they had learned and practiced their leadership roles. Winning an Annenberg Foundation grant and successfully negotiating BPS's schoolwide
audit was a testament to the competence of her teachers as well as to how
well Walker had prepared them to be a self-sustaining community accountable for student learning.

Kim Marshall independently developed many of the practices now
associated with PLCs. Early in his principalship, he realized that measured results of student academic efforts would be the axis around which
every other educational activity would revolve. This prescient assump-
tion was the catalyst for Marshall to cajole his grade-level teacher teams
to engage in a series of experiments designed to optimize student performance results.

He saw enormous potential in aligning Mather's curriculum and instruction with state standards. He cringed at the wasted effort of teachers who closed classroom doors and taught only their "interpretation" of
the district's curriculum standards without consultation with their peers.
With each succeeding grade level's failure to build on the previous year,
teachers were out of step with one another. Staff had difficulty embracing Marshall's vision for grade-by-grade objectives that took the whole
school into account, because teachers could not or did not want to see
beyond their own classroom walls.

Marshall demonstrated a methodology for teachers to tackle the seemingly Herculean task of coordinating their efforts with district and state
standards. He said, "Work backward," as he realized that a particular
assessment, the high-stakes MCAS, did actually align nicely with state
standards, as it had been designed to do. Because the MCAS had real
teeth, passing the tenth grade assessment was a graduation requirement,
and each school's scores were publicized in the local media, Marshall succeeded in motivating teachers to unify their curriculum and make the
MCAS scores the object of their efforts.

He knew the instructional infrastructure that he and his teachers had
created was vacuous unless teacher teams periodically took the pulse of
student learning and revised their instruction to better meet targeted se-
mester-end goals. This meant that teams at each grade level had to define
their contribution to students' eventual graduation by determining what
students should know and be able to do on successfully completing that
grade level. Grade-level teams were responsible for setting end-of-unit
SMART goals to measure completion and assist in measuring progress

during the semester. They developed and administered interim assessments, and the data they generated was analyzed by grade-level teams to measure interim student progress.

Mather's student performance improvement plan did work, and it worked well, even if it did not perform up to Marshall's high standards. Marshall's methodology, initiated in 1997, has a remarkable similarity to DuFour et al.'s 2006 PLC description of a "Results Orientation." Mather's teacher teams worked backward to align curriculum, develop SMART goals measured by summative and interim assessments, and analyze student performance data generated by the interim assessments to better focus instruction for all students. He framed an ambitious four-year educational experiment. Under his tutelage, Mather teachers committed themselves to measurable levels of student performance, eventually striving for 85 percent of third graders who had been at the Mather throughout their elementary careers to reach Level 3 (Proficiency) or 4 in each of the three major academic subjects and social competency. That was their goal, and they came very close to achieving it. In 2001, four years after the start of the experiment, 80 percent made the reading and writing targets, and 67 percent made the math and social competency goals.

Marshall had trouble generating sufficient staff commitment to maintain the momentum necessary to engender larger gains. Though grade-level teams designed the interim assessments, it was Marshall who processed the data from them. Teams took only a perfunctory interest. Yet it was the teachers, not Marshall, who were in a position to make a difference in student outcomes. By his own admission, this was one of the missing pieces that prevented the Mather from fully leveraging its potential.

There is one possible explanation for the Mather teams' lackadaisical attitude. Marshall's talent with words was a double-edged sword. He could clarify, amplify, and codify with great agility, but he could also get himself into trouble. Staff teams could rarely produce written products that met Marshall's demanding standards, which prevented them from embracing their own contributions to the final results. Staff-generated rubrics and grade-level student standards could never be compact, organized, or precise enough, unless they were edited by Marshall. The "word merchant" could not resist putting his mark on all school documents. He persistently maintained high standards, but he inadvertently took ownership away from the teams.

Binding the Mather community together into a cohesive whole was problematic for Marshall. Teachers came together more successfully as a community only during periods when Marshall was fortunate enough to employ assistant principals who could maintain student discipline. When he could not, as in the last two years of his tenure, suspensions escalated, and the resulting atmosphere infected teacher attitudes, distracting them from the cause that Marshall had hoped would drive them.

Muriel Leonard's change effort succeeded in getting her staff to take ownership of the Shaw and preparing them to be competent stewards of that responsibility, thus building what would now be labeled a PLC. The arc of that effort started with Leonard's classroom demonstrations and was followed by one-on-one coaching and the solicitation of staff volunteers. The next step was the formation of teams, which, in turn, became the building blocks on which self-governance and professional development materialized. Grade-level clusters, ad hoc school improvement committees, the Leadership Team, the professional consultants, and roundtables were components of the fluid infrastructure that provided the context for teachers to grow and develop as professionals and assume responsibility for building the Shaw and educating students to high standards.

Leonard used the teams as the school's primary instrument of teacher professional development. They shaped the staff's skill set, belief structure, and relationships with one another. Cluster teams had to work together to develop common rubrics, learn to negotiate with each other, come to consensus, and forge a spirit of collaboration. The staff's need to see each other's classroom innovations prompted the roundtable presentations. Leonard transformed every change problem into an opportunity for professional development and molded a community not only skilled at but also committed to student learning.

The Unit III team at Charlestown High, internally led by Karen Loughran, provides a model of how urban youth can be taught to meet ninth and tenth grade educational standards. Remarkably, they had no particular theory to guide them, certainly no literature on PLCs. The Unit III team organically generated a collaborative practice exhibiting many of DuFour et al.'s definitions of a PLC. **Michael Fung** provided the opportunity, set the stage, and coached the fledglings to create Unit III's success. Hiring young, well-educated teachers with deep social missions who were unencumbered by family responsibilities provided the necessary firepower to ignite a wholly new paradigm of educating urban youth at Charlestown.

Fung's efforts, however, did not guarantee results; many units at Charlestown, even those populated by teachers demographically similar to Unit III's, floundered. The yawning gap between unprepared, undisciplined, and unwilling entering freshmen and their potential for grade nine proficiency was too much for many of the neophyte teachers also teaching ninth and tenth graders. There was not enough support and supervision, and they left. Unit III teachers were an exception, in some measure due to Fung's coaching and close attention, as well as the leadership of Karen Loughran and the persevering talents of her four teammates. They treated the gap as a challenge to be surmounted, making continuous, incremental improvements. If students were consistently absent or tardy, and the disciplinary code corrections were insufficient, phone calls home and network connections with truancy officers were the next steps. As it became clear, the majority of students were not achieving in math. Lobbying for more math instruction time was the next step; and if that wasn't enough, they would develop another solution.

Loughran brought unique skills to her team that were critical to its success. A seasoned teacher, she was familiar with the urban population that characterized Charlestown. She focused on team building and collaborative decision making and problem solving and was more than willing to subject herself to critique when evaluating new instructional practices. She was particularly adept at recognizing and capitalizing on the unique talents of her fellow team members. Loughran did not allow pride to interfere with her efforts; she considered herself just another team member, allowing the effectiveness of her contributions to determine the impact of her influence.

The collective problem-solving spirit that Unit III developed as they confronted and eventually solved the problem of discipline served as a model that ultimately pervaded all aspects of their educational efforts. Collaborative interdependency was a necessity; they had to leverage their individual talents for the collective good. Seeing their work as highly interdependent enabled them to take this approach in tackling issues of curriculum, instruction, assessment, guidance, and, eventually, whole-student success.

A significant portion of Unit III's success can be attributed to their vision of educating the whole student. Their objective was not merely getting students to earn proficient scores on the MCAS, nor was it even limited to academics itself. The student's moral, social, civic, behavioral, and overall well-being were at stake. Each student was a personality to be supported, heard, challenged, disciplined, and positioned to take on their next challenge in life. When home issues interfered, they were there. When personal crisis interfered, they were there. When more schooling was needed, they were there. When achievement begged recognition, they were there. And when the students' futures looked uncertain and bleak, they were there.

Kathleen Flannery had the advantage of entering a school where staff respected each other and had a genuine, shared interest in curriculum and learning. They did not, however, have any experience with formal teacher leadership, a unified school vision, or team-based collaboration. Flannery recognized the value of the staff cohesiveness that existed at the Everett, but she also knew that their pedagogy was out of date and that their expectations were not always uniformly high. Flannery exploited the expertise and strengths of her new staff while simultaneously nudging and prodding them into becoming a team-based, collaborative, more effective educational learning community with student achievement at the center of their efforts.

Flannery worked hard to unite the Everett community around the goal of raising student achievement and devoted herself to becoming the champion of that cause. The lengthy reading wars were, in part, a product of her insisting that preferences for a particular teaching pedagogy did not take precedence over the real question: What was optimal for student learning? This was Flannery's "bottom line." She also desperately wanted the Everett to rally around a common vision that would guide their instruction. In constructivism she found a methodology that staff would eventually agree to work toward implementing. To get to that decision, Flannery introduced new research literature on constructivism to her staff and engaged in an inquiry-based discussion of its merits at instructional leadership team meetings. This approach, while new to the Everett, fits neatly into the context of an effective PLC.

Flannery, never content with any one achievement, was constantly pushing her teachers to improve student achievement. Preempting a subsequent district directive, Flannery encouraged teacher teams to craft or adopt formative assessments that would provide snapshot portraits of student performance in each subject area and grade level. Though utilizing the interim assessments effectively and drawing instructional implications from the data was problematic, Flannery closely monitored and coached teachers to keep teaching aligned with student learning needs and to meet end-of-semester targets.

Aware that to help students learn more and better teachers had learning to do so as well, Flannery eagerly embraced the Collaborative Coaching and Learning (CCL) model, which encouraged her teachers to engage in powerful job-embedded learning that incorporated current research, team inquiry sessions, lesson planning, and demonstration lessons that took place in teachers' own classrooms. Greater than the sum of any of its individual parts, CLL enabled teachers to work together, taking real action steps toward improving their own instruction.

Under Flannery's guidance, the Everett became a robust and high-functioning community of educational practice. Testament to the efficacy of their enterprise was the substantial number of innovations the school launched and the number of times these innovations were either adopted by the district or anticipated the district's own initiatives. The development and use of formative assessments was a clear example of the latter. Everett's Home Reading program, an example of the former, became a model for other BPS schools as the subject of a how-to video distributed within the district. The selection of the Everett as one of the district's twenty-six Effective Practice schools speaks to the success of the collective synergy Flannery was able to generate.

Winning Trust and Buy-in

Garnering trust and earning buy-in from staff are critical components for any leader attempting to sustain a change agenda. **Casel Walker** created a cultural crisis with the introduction of the LAB cluster. Those who chose to stay pledged an initial loyalty to Walker that she subsequently solidified by virtue of her inclusive leadership.

It was never easy for **Kim Marshall** to capture the heart of the Mather staff. He began well behind the starting line, burdened with obstacles in winning the teachers trust before he even reached the Mather's door. Marshall began his principalship with a credibility gap: his nine-year urban teaching credential at a middle school did not register with an influential segment of the Mather's elementary school staff. They saw a fast-thinking, prep school and Harvard-educated white guy, who had come down from district headquarters to "save" the Mather. His aggressive pursuit of increased student achievement meant that he was constantly pushing staff to alter their habits, learn new skills, and change their beliefs, particularly about the educability of all students. This was a tall order for a staff unfamiliar with radical change. Ultimately, staff came to endorse Marshall's leadership once they recognized his enormous knowledge base, his expertise, his consistent communications as exemplified by the daily *Mather Memo,* his commitment to the education of all students, his attention to detail, his capacity to get up and try again after a false start or mistake, and his work to make the Mather a school of which they could all be proud.

Marshall attained and sustained credibility with the faculty because they respected him. It was not necessarily important to him that they like him, though many of them did. But the very nearly unanimous vote of confidence he received from them, when his word was pitted against that of a fellow faculty member and he chose to put his own principalship on the line, was a testament to the credibility Marshall had earned with his staff six years into his principalship.

Muriel Leonard built a following by practicing what she preached and subtly influencing the staff to take small steps before embracing her change agenda. Leonard was not above modeling for her staff. If managing a class of unruly youths seemed impossible, Leonard took a shot at it herself. If she asked teachers to devote time to developing student products, she devoted the time as well. If the task was disaggregating quantitative data from tests or attitude surveys, Leonard was there pitching in. Modeling served several purposes. First, it demonstrated to the cautious the positive outcomes of the effort. Second, practicing what she preached, Leonard had an immediacy and credibility that was difficult to deny. Modeling had the effect of shrinking the hierarchical distance between Principal Leonard and her staff.

A master at giving direction, Leonard enticed others to take the first steps and then cognitively and emotionally commit themselves to take successive steps on their own volition. It was a fine line: If the direction was perceived as a command, with potential repercussions for noncompliance, Leonard had the locus of control, and the recipient took little personal responsibility for subsequent actions. If the direction was perceived as optional and teachers had no accountability, they were far less likely to comply.

Early in her tenure, she encouraged teachers to be available to students after school by offering extracurricular activities in accordance with their own interests. The majority of staff found this easy enough, even attractive. What they might not have realized was that this "baby step" was the first in a march toward what would eventually become a silent agreement to volunteer large amounts of time for "Striving for Excellence Tuesdays." It didn't stop there. Leonard made it a habit to display the results of the Turning Points Surveys and the Stanford 9 student performance tests on poster-sized displays, encouraging teachers to make meaning of the feedback data. It was not Leonard's acts of interpretation and suggestions for improvement that enticed teachers to feel responsibility for closing academic gaps and solving problems revealed by the data; instead, it was their own efforts and investment in the process.

Michael Fung, at least as a start, "bought" allegiance. He hired new teachers who, as a condition of their employment, owed their loyalty to him. He went further, however, establishing a reciprocal rapport with them not found in his other relationships at Charlestown. They asked for and listened to his advice, and he was consistently responsive to their requests, giving them the freedom to create an original community of high educational performance.

Kathleen Flannery recognized and valued teachers' professional judgment, practiced what she preached, and made the effort to win staff's commitment to decisions rather than settling for their compliance. She was willing to take into account her faculty's professional expertise, even when the message was contrary to her own beliefs. The idea of Won Way Phonics at the Everett was abhorrent to Flannery, but her respect for and commitment to listening to her teachers' points of view paved the way for the Everett's successful home-grown literacy program. And when structured phonics proved to be an important element in a balanced literacy program, she never hesitated to credit her teachers with noticing what she (and the district) had not.

Flannery was fortunate to assume leadership of a school that had already internalized many of the values she held dear: hard work, teacher leadership, and dedication to student learning. However, there was still much to improve. Flannery wanted to build a culture of evidence-based decision making, fair and consistent instructional practices, high expectations for all students, and inclusive, consensual decision making among the staff.

She always practiced what she preached. She worked as hard, or harder, than any teacher in the school, kept the longest hours, addressed every concern (student, teacher, or parent), and shied away from no challenge. She did not mandate whole-language reading instruction because the evidence wasn't there. She pointedly embraced anything that appeared to enhance student learning and promoted equity and fairness. And she treated with reverence and sanctity the deliberations of the Instructional Leadership Team (ILT), proving just how much she herself valued teacher input and inspiring teachers to challenge themselves to come forward and assume leadership and responsibility within the school.

The resolution to the "reading wars" was a product of her resolve: The faculty must choose its own literacy program. The faculty had to make the choice, and without any prompting, to apply for acceptance into Boston's Plan for Excellence's Cohort 1. The fourth grade teacher had to choose to retire. The ILT had to choose to embrace constructivism and forge the Everett's five principles. The faculty's indignation when Flannery chose not to involve them in the decision to go forward with common planning time is evidence that she had, as far as the faculty was concerned, institutionalized their right to have input on any decision that would affect their professional lives.

Parents as Instructional Partners

Every principal chronicled here went beyond the ritualistic and perfunctory parent-teacher nights and actively engaged parents in their children's education. Marzano, representing a number of researchers, names "parental and community involvement" as a distinct and major contributor to student achievement, ranking it third in order of impact among five school-level factors.[16]

Four principals extended their community practice beyond the school building walls, because they needed parents as educators. With an exacting focus on student learning, parents become ripe targets for inclusion as partners. Research confirms this and goes further, detailing specifically how parents can be most efficacious in their children's learning. Jeremy Finn, in his careful appraisal of the literature, dismisses parental engagement at school as being far less efficacious at elevating student achievement than parent engagement at home. Involvement has traditionally meant parental visits to school, volunteer work, attendance at school events, and, for a few, participation in school site councils. While these may have symbolic value in yielding closer relationships between school and parents, Finn's research finds few, if any, academic performance pay-offs from school visits and the like. Finn identified "three types of paren-tal engagement at home" consistently associated with students' school performance: "actively organizing and monitoring the child's time; help-ing with homework; and discussing school matters with the child." He found that a fourth set of activities, "parents reading to and being read to by children," was also associated with student achievement, particularly for younger children.[17]

Kim Marshall, never taking his eye off the prize of higher student achievement, relentlessly blanketed parents with invitations to partici-pate in their children's learning. He ensured that curriculum summaries for each grade level were sent home each year, detailing curriculum goals and exemplars of student writing (e.g., what proficient third grade writ-ing looks like at the end of the year) and reading passages representing the level each grade should attain. At the suggestion of a Mather teacher, roughly half of the teachers sent home "Ask Me" curriculum scripts on a weekly basis. These gave parents a customized list of questions to ask their children in order to allow them to verbalize their learning. Accord-ing to Marshall, it was a way to "get parents involved and knowledgeable about the curriculum, making them an additional teacher of each child and reviewing important [curriculum] for the children. . . . [They] loved showing off what they had learned to their parents." Marshall, harnessing his word-smithing skills, produced a weekly, one-page parent letter with "nitty-gritty information and preaching about limiting TV, kids getting enough sleep, etc. The back side [had] clippings or articles . . . on key parenting issues (e.g., bullying, TV, nutrition, etc.).

With the implementation of the home-school compact, **Muriel Leon-ard** and her staff procured a promise from Shaw families that they would become actively involved in their children's education. Realizing that ac-cess was often a barrier to participation, Leonard took exceptional mea-sures to make it easier for parents to attend the Shaw's many new cur-riculum-related events, training her own students to serve as babysitters during events and even holding events off-site at locations easier for par-ents to travel to.

In **Kathleen Flannery**'s school, parents were essential instructional partners in the education of their children and had a direct impact on their academic performance. With the weekly Home Reading contract, Flannery engaged parents as partners in the education of their children. It was but one of her methods to extend the Everett, opening up the previously insular school to the community. The ambitious library and schoolyard projects would be two other prominent examples. The Home Reading contract, born of a genuine educational need (reading scores at the Everett, after a steady increase, would plateau unless, as the research literature argued, students read and were read to for longer periods of time) proved that the parental role need not exclude educational contributions; parents could be disciplined educators who could hold their children to a regular schedule of reading, whether in English or their native language. The Everett reading scores climbed after the introduction of the Home Reading program.

Principal Behaviors Correlated with Student Academic Achievement

Each of these five principals demonstrated the behaviors that other research studies suggest are associated with student achievement, namely the large-sample meta-analysis by Robert J. Marzano, Timothy Waters, and Brian A McNulty, *School Leadership That Works: From Research to Results,* which identifies twenty-one school leader behaviors correlated with student academic achievement.[18] (See Table 6.1)

There are a number of striking parallels between the behaviors of the five principals studied and those found in the Marzano et al. study. Student achievement was the dependent variable and school leader behavior the independent in both research efforts. With its considerable sample size and statistical techniques, Marzano et al.'s research provides a useful context for assessing the actions of the five principals; their behaviors can be statistically associated with student academic achievement.

There is overwhelming evidence that all five principals more than qualify as "change agents" (2) using Marzano et al.'s terms. In actively and successfully challenging their school's status quo, they set themselves apart from the majority of Boston principals in the late 1990s and thereby won a place in this book. They went further, inspiring and leading new innovations. Each was an "optimizer" (15): Walker leveraged the LAB cluster for Manning's makeover; Marshall designed a perpetuating instructional improvement system; Leonard instituted Milestone Products; Fung recruited a whole new cadre of teachers; and Flannery institutionalized constructivism as the Everett's exclusive pedagogy.

Table 6.1 School Principal Behaviors Correlated with Student Academic Achievement

	Behavior	The Extent to Which the Principal...
1	AFFIRMATION	Recognizes and celebrates accomplishments and acknowledges failures
2	CHANGE AGENT	Is willing to challenge and actively change the status quo
3	CONTINGENT REWARDS	Recognizes and rewards individual accomplishments
4	COMMUNICATION	Establishes strong lines of communication with and among teachers and students
5	CULTURE	Fosters shared beliefs and a sense of community and cooperation
6	DISCIPLINE	Protects teachers from issues and influences that would detract from their teaching time or focus
7	FLEXIBILITY	Adapts his or her leadership behavior to the needs of the current situation and is comfortable with dissent
8	FOCUS	Establishes clear goals and keeps those goals in the forefront of the school's attention
9	IDEALS/BELIEFS	Communicates and operates from strong ideals and beliefs about schooling
10	INPUT	Involves teachers in the design and implementation of important decisions and policies
11	INTELLECTUAL STIMULATION	Ensures faculty and staff are aware of the most current theories and practices and makes the discussion of these a regular aspect of the school's culture
12	INVOLVEMENT IN CURRICULUM, INSTRUCTION, AND ASSESSMENT	Is directly involved in the design and implementation of curriculum, instruction, and assessment practices

(continued)

Table 6.1 School Principal Behaviors Correlated with Student Academic Achievement *(continued)*

	Behavior	The Extent to Which the Principal...
13	KNOWLEDGE OF CURRICULUM, INSTRUCTION, AND ASSESSMENT	Is knowledgeable about current curriculum, instruction, and assessment practices
14	MONITORING/ EVALUATING	Monitors the effectiveness of school practices and their impact on student learning
15	OPTIMIZER	Inspires and leads new and challenging innovations
16	ORDER	Establishes a set of standard operating procedures and routines
17	OUTREACH	Is an advocate and spokesperson for the school to all stakeholders
18	RELATIONSHIPS	Demonstrates an awareness of the personal aspects of teachers and staff
19	RESOURCES	Provides teachers with materials and professional development necessary for the successful execution of their jobs
20	SITUATIONAL AWARENESS	Is aware of the details and undercurrents in the running of the school and uses this information to address current and potential problems
21	VISIBILITY	Has quality contact and interactions with teachers and students

Source: School Leadership That Works, by Robert J. Marzano, Timothy Waters, and Brian A. McNulty.

When Marzano et al.'s twenty-one school leader behaviors are listed in order of correlation with student achievement, "situational awareness" (20) is the highest, followed by "flexibility" (7). These behaviors speak to a leader's awareness of and sensitivity to their inherited school culture and their ability to adopt reform strategies to incorporate this information. Walker, Leonard, Flannery, and Loughran of Charlestown's Unit III successfully walked a delicate line; they found and honored the best of what they discovered in their teacher populations, neutralized the adverse, and simultaneously laced cultural intelligence into their reform strategies. Marshall took some hard falls before he realized he would be the only one who embraced his optimizing-student-achievement agenda unless he adapted it to the eccentricities of the Mather culture. And so he did. Fung, after his teachers rebuked his unilaterally initiated project-based learning pedagogy, relinquished any interest in finding potential value in Charlestown's veteran teachers. Only his young teacher hires were the recipients of his concerns and solicitations.

All five principals, with varying degrees of success, aspired to transform their schools into professional learning communities. In building their communities, Walker, Leonard, Flannery, and Loughran can certainly be given credit for stimulating student achievement by fostering "culture" (5), "input" (10), "relationships" (18), "communication" (4), "resources" (19), and "visibility" (21).

Although Marshall fell short in orchestrating a vibrant school community, he compensated with a barrage of systemic instructional innovations, products of his deep familiarity with curricular, instructional, and assessment issues. Marzano et al. found a leader's "knowledge of [13] and involvement in [12] curriculum, instruction and assessment" confidently predicted student achievement. Other correlatives that Marshall's leadership evidenced were "focus" (8) and "monitoring/evaluating" (14). Without doubt, Marshall's preeminent skill was "intellectual stimulation" (11).

There is no better final comment on reviewing the parallels between the five principals' leadership and student achievement than to note that they embraced, communicated, and operated from strong beliefs about schooling—"ideals/beliefs" (9). Indeed, the courage of these five principals in taking enormous risks to promulgate their schools' reform sprang from their strong convictions: Every student could reach Proficient performance or better, and their schools would be the enabling force for this transformation.

Glossary of Terms

Adequate Yearly Progress (AYP)

A measure of the extent to which a district, school, or subgroup within a school demonstrates progress toward the goal of reaching 100 percent proficiency in a given content area by the year 2014 as prescribed by NCLB legislation.

Assessments:

Formative
Interim
Summative

Formative assessments are frequently made on a systematic basis during the semester to inform teachers and sometimes students of the degree of progress students are making in reaching end-of-unit goals. The information gathered by teacher teams is used to modify instruction as well as identify and assist students not making adequate progress. Kim Marshall and others refer to these as "Interim Assessments." Summative assessments are end-of course/year assessments that evaluate students' learning and are used for grading and accountability purposes (e.g., MCAS).

best practices

Effective or promising methods of teaching, leadership, and school practices that maximize student learning.

Boston Plan for Excellence (BPE)

The primary partner of the BPS in designing, piloting, refining, implementing, and institutionalizing elements of the district's reform initiative.

constructivism

Constructivist teachers 1) seek and value students' point of view; 2) structure lessons to challenge students' suppositions; 3) recognize that students attach relevance to the curriculum; 4) structure lessons around big ideas not small bits of information; 5) assess student learning in the context of daily classroom investigations, not as separate events.[1]

Collaborative Coaching and Learning (CCL)	A collegial form of professional development that takes place during the school day and asks teachers to demonstrate and observe lessons in each others' classrooms, discuss and critique the work of their colleagues, and reflect on their professional practice through inquiry sessions facilitated by a coach. BPE introduced CCL to Effective Practice Schools in 2001–2002, and the method was adopted by the district in 2002–2003.
Developmental Reading Assessment (DRA)	A test published by Pearson Learning Group "to help educators identify a student's reading ability and level, document progress, and tailor teaching to drive effective reading instruction."[2]
Education Reform Restructuring Network (ERRN)	A Massachusetts network of middle and high schools committed to undertaking multiyear, whole-school reform in order to successfully assist all students in meeting high standards of education reform.
Efficacy Practice Schools	A small number of Boston public schools selected by the school committee and superintendent for their capacity to sustain long-term improvement in student achievement and used by the district as lab sites to test and refine reform efforts before they are mandated districtwide.
Efficacy Institute, Inc.	A national, not-for-profit agency for education reform founded in 1985 by Dr. Jeff Howard that is committed to developing *all* children to high standards. Its central objectives are to build belief that virtually *all* children can "get smart" and to build the capacity of adults to set the terms to help them do so.
English Language Learner (ELL)	Child whose first or home language is something other than English.

Focus on Children	A five-year education reform plan initiated in 1996 by BPS superintendent Thomas Payzant to focus on whole-school change. Rather than improving a few "elite" schools, the objective was to raise all district students and schools to a high standard. The focus was on the following elements:

- Setting clear expectations for what students should learn in all major subjects (i.e., citywide learning standards)
- Establishing a rigorous, more uniform curriculum to give all students and teachers access to the same high-level content
- Creating expectations about instructional practices by asking all teachers and schools to use the same literacy pedagogy (i.e., Readers and Writers Workshop)
- Providing extensive support for teachers through coherent professional development designed to help them improve their instructional practices (e.g., CCL)
- Developing and using formative and summative assessments.

Focus on Children II, an extension of the original plan, was adopted in 2001 and included development of the Six Essentials for Whole-School Improvement.[3]

Individualized Education Plan (IEP)	Individualized legal document describing the educational needs of a special education student (i.e., one who cannot progress effectively in a regular education program). The IEP defines the specific services a given student needs and why, as well behavioral and academic goals for that student.
Instructional Leadership Team (ILT)	A team required in all Boston public schools to promote teacher leadership by bringing teachers from representative grade levels and content areas together with the principal and coaches to lead and monitor reform efforts in the school.

John Saphier's *The Skillful Teacher*	A course (and book) designed and delivered by Research for Better Teaching, Inc., that examines the knowledge base on teaching and cultivates collegiality and experimentation among participants. Participants in the course expand their repertoire of instructional strategies and learn skills for effective peer support and observation.
Learning Adaptive Behavior (LAB)	A special education placement offered to BPS students with moderate behavioral problems who require a program with an integral behavior management component. Classes are considerably smaller than regular education classes.
Learning Disabilities (LD) Program	A special education placement offered to BPS students with a diagnosed learning disability, but average cognitive ability, who perform significantly below grade level academically. Classes are considerably smaller than regular education classes.
Looking at Student Work (LASW)	A collaborative process that helps educators improve teaching and learning by examining student products as a means of refining instruction.
Massachusetts Comprehensive Assessment System (MCAS)	MCAS is the statewide standards-based assessment program developed in response to the Massachusetts Education Reform Act of 1993. The MCAS, a criterion-referenced student performance test, has three primary purposes: 1) to inform and improve curriculum and instruction; 2) to evaluate student, school, and district performance according to the Massachusetts Curriculum Framework content and performance standards; and 3) to determine student eligibility for the Competency Determination requirement in order to award high school diplomas.
Massachusetts Education Reform Act of 1993	The Massachusetts Education Reform Act of 1993 was legislation mandating several reforms over a seven-year period. The reforms included the introduction of charter schools and the MCAS standardized test.

Math Leadership Team (MLT)	A team required in BPS elementary schools to promote teacher leadership by bringing teachers from representative grade levels together with the principal and coaches to lead and monitor mathematics reform efforts in the school.
Metropolitan Achievement Test (MAT)	A norm-referenced student performance test administered to BPS students annually prior to 1996.
Metropolitan Council for Educational Opportunity (METCO)	A program started in 1966 to offer inner-city families of color the opportunity to send their children to school in the suburbs. METCO is designed to provide students with educational opportunities to enrich their academic, personal, and interpersonal experiences through a strong academic foundation in an academic environment rich in cultural, educational, ethnic, and racial diversity.
Myers-Briggs Type Indicator (MBTI)	A personality questionnaire first published in 1921 designed to identify certain psychological differences according to the typological theories of Carl Gustav Jung.
No Child Left Behind (NCLB)	A 2002 federal law reauthorizing a number of federal programs and aiming to improve the performance of U.S. primary and secondary schools by increasing the standards of accountability for states, school districts, and schools as well as providing parents more flexibility in choosing which schools their children will attend. NCLB enacts the theories of standards-based education reform, formerly known as "outcome-based education," which is based on the belief that high expectations and setting of goals will result in success for all students. NCLB requires states to develop assessments in basic skills to be given to all students in certain grades in order for those states to receive federal funding for schools. (The MCAS is the state-authorized test for Massachusetts.)
project-based learning	Students work (usually in teams) to explore real-world problems and create presentations to share what they have learned.

School Site Council	A school-based council legally chartered in Massachusetts as an advisory agency to the principal on school policies. Headed by the principal, this team is comprised of parents, teachers, and community members.
Six Essentials for Whole-School Improvement	Key components of Payzant's 2001 education reform plan, *Focus on Children II*. The essentials identified six areas of practice for schools to focus on in their improvement efforts:

1. Use effective instructional practices and create a collaborative school climate to improve student learning
2. Examine student work and data to drive instruction and professional development
3. Invest in professional development to improve instruction
4. Share leadership to sustain instructional improvement
5. Focus resources to support instructional improvement and improved student learning
6. Partner with families and community to support student learning

Special Education (SPED) Instruction	Instruction that provides the accommodations and modifications outlined in the IEP of a student with special needs (such as learning differences, mental health problems, or physical or developmental disabilities) to ensure that student the free and appropriate public education to which he or she is entitled.
Stanford 9	A nationally norm-referenced achievement test that compares students' knowledge in math and reading to a national norm group. This test was first administered to BPS students in 1996.
Supportive Academic Remediation (SAR)	A special education placement offered to BPS students with moderate cognitive delays who require educational support in all academic areas. Classes are considerably smaller than regular education classes.

Turning Points	A reform and research effort sponsored by the Carnegie Corporation and used as a catalyst for middle school reform that called for, among other specifications:

- Rigorous curriculum
- Instructional methods that would prepare all students to achieve higher standards
- Targeted professional development opportunities for teachers
- Involved parents and communities.

21st Century Schools	A collaborative, multiyear venture initiated by the Boston Plan for Excellence that was designed to enable Boston's schools to move forward with standards-based reform to increase student learning and achievement. A competitive solicitation for participation in Cohort 1 (1996–1997) offered professional development, financial support, and whole-school change coaches to implement Boston's "Six Essentials of Whole-School Improvement." To be considered, 75 percent of the faculty had to vote affirmatively for the school's application. Twenty-seven early learning centers and schools were selected for the first cohort, including Flannery's Everett, Walker's Manning, and Leonard's Shaw.

Notes

Introduction

1. James S. Coleman, Ernest Q. Campbell, Carol J. Hobson, James McPartland, Alexander M. Mood, Frederic D. Weinfield, and Robert L. York, *Equality of Educational Opportunity* (Washington, DC: Government Printing Office, 1966).
2. George Madaus, Peter Airasian, and Thomas Kellaghan, *School Effectiveness: A Reassessment of the Evidence* (New York: McGraw-Hill, 1980).
3. Ronald R. Edmonds, "Making Public Schools Effective," *Social Policy* 12, no. 2 (September/October 1981): 15–27.
4. Robert J. Marzano, *What Works in Schools: Translating Research into Action* (Alexandria, VA: Association for Supervision and Curriculum Development, 2003), 72.
5. For a multiperspective account of Dr. Thomas Payzant's Boston superintendency, see S. Paul Reville and Celine Coggins, eds., *A Decade of Urban School Reform: Persistence and Progress in the Boston Public Schools* (Cambridge, MA: Harvard Education Press, 2007).

Chapter 2: Kim Marshall and Mather Elementary School

1. Excerpted from a teaching case study written by Kim Marshall for *New Leaders for New Schools* (2004).
2. Marshall case study, 2004.
3. Marshall case study, 2004.
4. Kim Marshall, "How I Confronted HSPS (Hyperactive Superficial Principal Syndrome) and Began to Deal with the Heart of the Matter," *Phi Delta Kappan* 77, no. 5 (January 1996): 338.
5. Marshall, "How I Confronted HSPS," 339.
6. Kim Marshall, "Recovering from HSPS (Hyperactive Superficial Principal Syndrome): A Progress Report," *Phi Delta Kappan* 84, no. 9 (May 2003).
7. Marshall, "Recovering from HSPS."
8. Marshall case study, 2004.

Chapter 5: Kathleen Flannery and Edward Everett Elementary School

1. Martin G. Brooks and Jacqueline Grennon Brooks, "The Courage to Be Constructivist," *Educational Leadership* 57, no. 3 (November 1999).

Chapter 6: Leadership Lessons

1. Gerald W. Bracey, "Getting Smarter in School," *Phi Delta Kappan* 73, no. 5 (January 1992): 414–16.
2. Massachusetts' DOE identified subpopulations: Limited English Proficiency, Special Education, Low Income, African-American/Black, Asian or Pacific Islander, Hispanic, Native American, and White (accessed April 18, 2008, from http://profiles.doe.mass.edu/mcas.aspx).
3. Mano Singham, "The Achievement Gap: Myths and Reality," *Phi Delta Kappan* 84, no. 8 (April 2003): 586–91.
4. Lynn Olsen, "Data-wise School Systems Seen as Sharing Key Traits," *Education Week*, February 14, 2006, 5.
5. Achieve, Inc., *Measuring Up: A Report on Education Standards and Assessments for Massachusetts* (Washington, DC: Achieve, 2001), 5–7.
6. John Cronin, Michael Dahlin, Deborah Adkins, and G. Gage Kingsbury, *The Proficiency Illusion* (Washington, DC: Fordham Institute and NWEA, 2007), 6–7.
7. David Gordon, "Teaching and Learning in a High-Stakes Environment," *Harvard Education Letter*, July/August 2003.
8. Barry C. Jentz and Jerome T. Murphy, "Starting Confused: How Leaders Start When They Don't Know Where to Start," *Phi Delta Kappan* 86, no. 10 (June 2005): 736–44.
9. John P. Kotter, "Why Transformation Efforts Fail," *Harvard Business Review*, March/April 1995, 59–67
10. Accessed April 18, 2008, from http://profiles.doe.mass.edu/mcas.aspx..
11. Marzano, *What Works in Schools*, 72.
12. Catherine Gewertz, "Urban Hiring Rules Faulted for Driving Away Best Teachers," *Education Week*, September 24, 2003, 1, 20; Michelle Rhee and Jessica Levin, "Hiring Too Late . . . and Other Mistakes That Keep High-Quality Teachers out of Urban Classrooms," *Education Week*, October 15, 2003, 48, 37.
13. Marshall, "Recovering from HSPS," 701. This was the second of two articles. The first was Marshall, "How I Confronted HSPS," 336.
14. Marshall, "Recovering from HSPS," 701.

15. Richard DuFour, Rebecca DuFour, Robert Eaker, and Thomas Many, *Learning By Doing: A Handbook for Professional Learning Communities at Work* (Bloomington, IN: Solution Tree, 2006), 2–5.

16. Marzano, *What Works in Schools,* 15–21.

17. Jeremy D. Finn, "Parental Engagement That Makes a Difference," *Educational Leadership* 55, no. 8 (May 1998): 20–24.

18. Robert J. Marzano, Timothy Waters, and Brian A. McNulty, *School Leadership That Works: From Research to Results* (Alexandria, VA: Association for Supervision and Curriculum Development, 2005), 42–43.

Glossary of Terms

1. From Brooks and Brooks, "The Courage to Be Constructivist."

2. Accessed April 25, 2008, from http://www.pearsonlearning.com/index.cfm?a=37.

3. From Reville and Coggins, *A Decade of Urban School Reform.*

About the Authors

Gerald C. Leader is Professor Emeritus at Boston University. He has researched and taught leadership for more than thirty years in educational, nonprofit, and private-sector organizations. After earning an undergraduate degree in engineering, he completed his MBA and doctorate at the Harvard Graduate School of Business. He has been on the graduate business faculties of Harvard University, Tulane University, Boston University, and Stanford University, where he also served on the faculty of the Graduate School of Education.

Currently, Professor Leader directs and teaches in the Educator Leadership Institute, which he founded in 2002 to prepare educational leaders for public and charter schools in the metropolitan Boston area. The Institute, a program within the Educational Collaborative of Greater Boston, is a self-sustaining, nonprofit organization preparing teacher candidates through graduate coursework and an intensive internship for principal and director licensure. Contact Professor Leader at gleader@bu.edu.

Amy F. Stern has been on staff at the Edward Everett Elementary School in Boston from 2002 to the present. She served for four years as special assistant to Principal Kathleen Flannery (Chapter 5) and is currently the director of school programs. Prior to working in the Boston Public Schools, Ms. Stern was a research assistant at Education Development Center, Inc., in Newton, Massachusetts. She earned her BA in psychology from Vassar College and her EdM in school leadership from the Harvard Graduate School of Education.

Index